Romantik
Journal for the Study of Romanticisms

Editors
Cian Duffy (Lund University), Karina Lykke Grand (Aarhus University), Thor J. Mednick (University of Toledo), Lis Møller (Aarhus University), Elisabeth Oxfeldt (University of Oslo), Ilona Pikkanen (Tampere University and the Finnish Literature Society), Robert W. Rix (University of Copenhagen), and Anna Lena Sandberg (University of Copenhagen)

Advisory Board
Charles Armstrong (University of Bergen), Jacob Bøggild (University of Southern Denmark, Odense), David Fairer (University of Leeds), Karin Hoff (Georg-August-Universität Göttingen), Stephan Michael Schröder (University of Cologne), David Jackson (University of Leeds), Christoph Bode (LMU München), Carmen Casaliggi (Cardiff Metropolitan University), Gunilla Hermansson (University of Gothernburg), Knut Ljøgodt (Nordic Institute of Art, Oslo), and Paula Henrikson (Uppsala University)

Romantik
Journal for the Study of Romanticisms

Volume 08|2019

V&R unipress

Contents

Foreword 7

Articles

Andreas Hjort Møller (Aarhus University)
Bards, Ballads, and Barbarians in Jena. Germanic Medievalism in the
Early Works of Friedrich Schlegel 13

Kang-Po Chen (University of Edinburgh)
'Sick within the rose's just domain': the 'Material Sublime' and
Pathological Poetics in Keats's *Isabella; or, the Pot of Basil* 35

D. Gareth Walters (Swansea University)
Espronceda's *The Student of Salamanca* and Chopin: Poetry and
Musical Structures 59

Marie-Louise Svane (University of Copenhagen)
Tragedy or Melodrama? The Greek War of Independence in European
Theatre 77

Natalya Khokholova (North Eastern Federal University, RF)
Gossiping and Ageing Princesses in Odoevsky's Societal Tales 111

Troy Wellington Smith (University of California, Berkeley)
Romantic Latecomers: P. L. Møller on Pushkin, Kierkegaard, and
Flaubert 131

Reviews

Gunilla Hermansson
C. J. L. Almqvist, Murnis: Idyllion. Ed. by Petra Söderlund 155

John Öwre
The Reception of William Blake in Europe. Ed. by Morton Paley and
Sibylle Erle 159

Mattias Pirholt
Fantasiens morgonrodnad. By Ljubica Miocevic 163

About the Authors 167

Foreword

Romantik: Journal for the Study of Romanticisms started out as a print publication but has for a number of years been a periodical with open access. All articles published during the lifetime of the journal are now available in various digital formats. The development of the journal reflects how the reading, viewing, and conceptualization of romanticism is changing. As students and researchers, we find ourselves in the fortunate situation that a number of digital projects related to the texts and art of the romantic period have received funding, and more such projects will undoubtedly emerge in the years to come. There is a certain comfort and convenience in handling print material, but the new digital platforms bring several advantages: they are searchable in terms of content, and it is often possible to zoom in to study artworks or facsimiles of book pages close up. The photomechanical reproductions that are confined to the printed book remain inflexible in this regard.

One of the romantic-period artists who has benefitted greatly from the new technology is William Blake (1757–1827). His composite art, combining both illustration and text (what he himself referred to as 'illuminated printing' in his 1793 prospectus), can now be accessed as high-resolution images on *The William Blake Archive* (http://www.blakearchive.org/). Launched in 1996, this archive was one of the earliest free websites focusing on romantic texts with a visual component. The scope, content, and features of the platform have expanded exponentially over the years. As all areas of individual plates or pictures have been tagged with detailed descriptions, it is now possible to explore a large body of Blake's pictorial art by using the image-searching tool. Users are able to scrutinise the minute particulars of an image in high resolution without the need to touch the often fragile original, and the *Archive* affords users the possibility of comparing different versions of plates from several copies. For example, one may study the widely diverse colourings of Blake's illustration to his famous poem 'The Tyger' and ponder how each version may convey a different idea of the animal, which come across as either ferocious or (most often) a little tame. Such a comparative study would have been well-nigh impossible for researchers in pre-*Archive* days, as copies of Blake's works are scattered at research libraries, rare books reading rooms, as well as private collections across the UK and North America. A large number of those who have bought Blake's works have given the *Archive* permission to include thousands of images and texts on the website.

The reason why we have singled out *The Blake Archive* as an example of technological innovation is not only because it remains at the forefront of development, but because 2019 is also a particular interesting year for scholars and admirers of Blake's work. This year will see a special exhibition of Blake's works at Tate Britain, London (*William Blake: The Artist*, from 11 September 2019 to 2 February 2020). Tate Britain has for long time had a permanent Blake room in the museum, but the new exhibition will be the largest display of Blake's paintings since 2000, with over 300 original works on show. The sheer scale of the exhibition contrasts with the more modest display Blake himself organised in 1809, above his brother's humble hosiery shop in Broad Street, London. At that time, only sixteen works were shown. Nonetheless, Blake thought this number sufficient to promote himself as a painter worthy of public attention. This was his attempt to avoid being pigeonholed as merely an engraver and sometime illustrator. The exhibition in 1809 was a disaster, with only a few visitors, and it became a public humiliation for Blake. (Accounts of and reactions to the exhibition can be found in G. E. Bentley's *Blake Records*, new ed. [London and New Haven, Yale University Press, 2004], pp. 281–295).

Visitors to the 2019 Tate Britain exhibition will be able to experience the small domestic room in which Blake showed his art. Perhaps a re-evaluation of what was on offer 210 years ago is now in order? The press release also promises that one of Blake's dreams may be fulfilled. Blake had grand ambitions as a visual artist and wanted to show his works as 'frescoes' on a huge scale. However, his commercial failure as an artist made this unrealisable in his own time. This aspiration is brought to fruition through the use of digital technology, which will enable the immersive experience that Blake intended his art to provide. The two paintings *The Spiritual Form of Nelson Guiding Leviathan* (c. 1805–1809) and *The Spiritual Form of Pitt Guiding Behemoth* (c. 1805) will be digitally enlarged and projected onto the gallery wall. So, in the museum world, too, advances in technology are opening up avenues for the new ways of consuming and exploring romantic art.

This issue of *Romantik* features a review of the recently published *The Reception of William Blake in Europe* (edited by Morton Paley and Sibylle Erle). This is the first comprehensive guide to the extensive influence that Blake had across Europe. Chapters on individual countries or regions examine Blake's phenomenal impact on literary production, art, music, and culture, but also his status as a political and countercultural icon throughout the twentieth and twenty-first centuries.

But the contents of the 2019 number of *Romantik* also range well beyond the work of William Blake. We have six articles that cover a variety of romantic-period works from various parts of Europe. Gareth Walters' article 'Espronceda's *The Student of Salamanca* and Chopin: Poetry and Musical Structures' focuses on José de Espronceda, who is considered to be one of the most representative Spanish romantic poets, and his narrative poem *El estudiante de Salamanca*. Through an analysis of formal characteristics, Walters proposes that structural details and devices in Espronceda's poem align with Chopin's second piano sonata, the 'Funeral March' sonata, as well as other contemporary musical works.

Kang-Po Chen's essay '"Sick within the rose's just domain": the "Material Sublime" and Pathological Poetics in Keats's *Isabella; or, the Pot of Basil*' provides a new analysis of John Keats' reflection upon the inherent danger of erotic love. The contemplation on the destructiveness of love is identified as a form of pathological poetics that manifest itself in the poem as a 'material sublime'. Kang-Po Chen argues that the poetics of suffering correlates in certain respects with Keats' understanding of poetic creation.

In 'Bards, Ballads, and Barbarians in Jena: Germanic Medievalism in the Early Works of Fr. Schlegel', Andreas Hjort Møller re-evaluates the reception of the Nordic medieval literature in German works. The emphasis is on Friedrich Schlegel's early texts and how these texts connect with his poetics and politics. This is a critical departure from previous research into Schlegel's medievalism, in which the focus has primarily been on Schlegel's later writings. In his article, Møller explores a dynamic milieu of exchange between the Jena Romantics and the Copenhagen circle of German writers.

In 'Gossiping and Ageing Princesses in Odoevsky's Societal Tales', Natalya Khokholova takes up the term 'gossip' in relation to nineteenth-century Russian literature and not least how it plays a unique role in Vladimir Odoevsky's so-called 'society tales'. Odoevsky was a fascinating figure in Russian culture, often mentioned alongside Pushkin and Gogol in his own day. The article shows how 'gossip' assumes a central role as a defence mechanism for Odoevsky's fictional characters. Khokholova also looks at how ideas in Odoevsky's fiction helped develop the realist tradition in Russian literature.

Marie-Louise Svane is widely known for her many contributions to our understanding of Nordic and international romanticism. In her new article, 'Greek Tragedy or Melodrama: Staging the Greek War of Independence on the European Theatre Stage', she looks at how the Greek War of Independence resonated in the world of theatre. The Greek struggle for independence from the Ottoman Empire was supported by liberal minds throughout Europe, prompting celebrated literary responses by, for example, Percy Shelley and Lord Byron, and was frequently represented on the stage in London and Paris during the 1820s. Svane draws attention to a number of philhellenic plays that, in one way or another, reflect a process of European self-identification by recasting the battle lines between East and West as popular drama. The article discusses how individual characters in the plays are often ambiguous and challenge the idea of an absolute divide.

The Danish author, critic, and publisher Peder Ludvig Møller is an important figure in Scandinavian culture. Troy Wellington Smith's article 'Romantic Latecomers: P. L. Møller on Pushkin, Kierkegaard, and Flaubert' is an analysis of how Møller appraised three significant authors at the time. Pushkin, Kierkegaard, and Flaubert had all achieved international fame. Møller was sceptical of the move towards realism he detected in the writings of Kierkegaard and even more so in Flaubert's novels, while he commended Pushkin for following the lead of Lord Byron, the towering figure of European romanticism. Smith's article provides a fascinating insight into the uncertainties surrounding romanticism in Scandinavia at a time when the continued existence of this movement was threatened by the onward march of realism.

Welcome to *Romantik!*

The Editorial Board

Articles

Andreas Hjort Møller
(Aarhus University)

Bards, Ballads, and Barbarians in Jena. Germanic Medievalism in the Early Works of Friedrich Schlegel

Abstract
The early German romantics were highly interested in medieval literature, primarily poetry written in romance vernaculars such as Dante's *Inferno*. Only later did the German romantics turn to northern medieval literature for inspiration. In the case of German romantic Friedrich Schlegel (1772–1829), the usual opinion is that he would not have cared for northern (primarily Scandinavian) medieval literature and art before his late phase, beginning around 1802. In this phase, his literary criticism stood under the sway of his conservative politics. This article examines the reception of Germanic medieval literature in Schlegel's early essays, reviews and fragments, in order to discuss the role of Germanic medieval literature in his work and the extent to which it is connected with his poetics and politics.

Keywords
Friedrich Schlegel, Medievalism, romanticism, Germanic and romance medieval literature, Antiquarianism.

Traditional histories of literary criticism inform us that Friedrich Schlegel began his literary career as a classicist historian of Greek and Roman Literature (1794–1796), then went on to study romance literature (1797–1801) and only later, during his time in Paris around 1802, gained an interest in Germanic medieval literature that would persist for the remainder of his life.[1] Schlegel's interest in the medieval is commonly taken to have emerged from his so-called conservative or nationalist turn that culminated in Schlegel's conversion to Catholicism in the Cologne Cathedral in 1808 and his participation in the Congress of Vienna as a

---

1 For instance, Kozielek dates the beginning of the interest of the early German romantics to Ludwig Tieck and the year 1801, even though he notes that Tieck and Wilhelm Heinrich Wackenroder payed attention to Old German literature in the 1790s, *Gerard Kozielek: Mittelalterrezeption. Texte zur Aufnahme altdeutscher Literatur in der Romantik* (Tübingen: Max Niemeyer Verlag, 1977), 13. This anthology of medievalist romantic critical texts spans the years 1803 to 1831. Not to be forgotten: The novel fragment *Heinrich von Ofterdingen*, written by Novalis (Friedrich von Hardenberg, 1772–1801) has a Germanic medieval setting.

Metternichian agent.² It is interesting to note, however, that the romantic poetics of Schlegel seems to recall that of the earlier generation of Sturm und Drang poets and critics Gottfried August Bürger (1747–1794), Johann Wolfgang von Goethe (1749–1832), and Johann Gottfried von Herder (1744–1803), as well as the British mid-eighteenth-century antiquarians who inspired them. Some of the central ideas of the Jena romantics are very much like those of the earlier generations of critics, who were mainly interested in Germanic literature. Indeed among these earlier critics were several members of Schlegel's immediate family. In what way did Germanic medievalism, i.e. reinventions of a Germanic past and the development of medieval scholarship, contribute to the genesis of romantic literary criticism?

I will start answering these questions by 1) laying out the influence of literary historian and translator Herder and the writer of popular ballads Bürger, the two most important medievalist members of the Sturm und Drang movement. 2) I will move on to the members of the Copenhagen German Circle. 3) I will then examine the young Schlegel's occupation with early eighteenth-century English antiquarianism. This approach is in reverse chronological order, in that Herder constitutes the link between Jena and Copenhagen, and in that the chief inspirational source for the 'Nordic Renaissance' in Copenhagen 1750–1770 was British antiquarianism. 4) Based on these influences, I will argue for the fact that Schlegel's northern medievalism was to some extent present in his early work and that his interest in the Germanic past was not solely political. 5) I will give a conclusion.

1. Connections between Early Jena Romanticism and Sturm und Drang

In his position as a shaper of Jena romanticism, Herder was significantly influenced by the British antiquarians Richard Hurd (1720–1808), Bishop Thomas Percy (1729–1811) and Thomas Warton the younger (1728–1790) and the critical epistles of the German-born Danish citizen and critic Heinrich Wilhelm von Gerstenberg (1737–1823).³ Hans Eichner (1921–2009) revealed the profound-

---

2 Manuel Bauer discusses Schlegel's late Germanic-oriented criticism as a conversion to themes 'die nationalideologisch fruchtbar gemacht werden können' [that could be turned into a national ideology], Manuel Bauer, 'Konversionen in Friedrich Schlegels später Literaturkritik, Philologie und Hermeneutik', in *Figuren der Konversion. Friedrich Schlegels Übertritt zum Katholizismus im Kontext*, ed. Winfried Eckel and Nikolaus Wegmann, (Paderborn: Ferdinand Schöningh, 2014): 160–179, quotation on p. 167.

3 A. Gillies: 'Herder's Preparation of Romantic Theory', *The Modern Language Review* 39.3 (1944): 252–261, quotation on p. 252. doi: 10.2307/3717862.

ness of this influence in a reading of Schlegel's review of Herder's *Briefe zur Beförderung der Humanität* [Letters for the advancement of humanity] (1793).[4] Schlegel published this review in the journal *Deutschland* in 1796, well before the famous fragments. There are striking similarities between Herder's poetics of the novel and Schlegel's theory of romantic poetry:

> Die ... *Fragmente über den Geist und Wert der modernen Poesie* sind nicht etwa vollendete Bruchstücke eines unvollendeten Ganzen: sie sind auch im einzelnen *fragmentarisch*, wie die nachlässiger geschriebenen Briefe auch des geistvollsten Schriftstellers wohl sein können, und sein dürfen.
>
> [The ... *Fragments on the Spirit and Worth of Modern Poetry* are not just complete shards of an uncompleted whole: They are also each one of them *fragmentary*, in the same way that the more carelessly written letters of a most brilliant writer can sometimes be and indeed may be].[5]

Schlegel's review consists of a series of such Herderian quotes followed by short questions or remarks. After this sentence, the young reviewer ponders the value of German medieval poetry as compared to that of the Greeks:

> Alle deutsche Nationen, die das Römische Reich unter sich teilten, kamen mit Heldenliedern von Taten ihrer Vorfahren in die ihnen neue Welt....
>
> [All German nations won over by the Roman Empire came into a world new to them with heroic songs about the deeds of their ancestors....][6]

Schlegel then asks the question:

> Hat aber die Abenteurlichkeit des Mittelalters nicht einen ganz eignen, von der Lebensart und Denkart der Griechen im heroischen Zeitalter durchaus verschiednen Charakter?
>
> [Does the chivalry of the Middle Ages not possess its very own quality, completely different from the lifestyle and thought of the Greeks of the Heroic Age?][7]

Schlegel does not go beyond reiterating the main points of Herder's book, focusing on his positive view on the Middle Ages. One example is his defence of the Middle Ages when compared to the Renaissance: '[i]n jenen Zeiten, welche wir *barbarische* nennen, *vor* der sogenannten Erweckung der Alten, gab es einen

---

4 Hans Eichner, 'Friedrich Schlegel's Theory of Romantic Poetry', *PMLA*, 71.5 (December 1956): 1018–1041, quotation on p. 1019. doi: 10.2307/460525.
5 I refer to the unfinished multivolume edition Friedrich Schlegel, *Kritische Friedrich-Schlegel-Ausgabe*, ed. Ernst Behler (Paderborn: Ferdinand Schöningh, 1958-), henceforth abbreviated as KFSA, followed by a volume number. Unless otherwise noted, all translations are my own. For the quote, see KFSA 2, 47.
6 KFSA 2, 50.
7 Ibid.

Dante', [in yonder times, which we call *barbaric*, *before* the so-called awakening of the Greeks and Romans, there was *Dante*].⁸

Fig. 1: Andrea del Castagno, Dante, c.1450, Fresco, Ufizzi, Florence.

Herder remains an idol for Friedrich Schlegel, who also mentions him favourably in *Über das Studium der Griechischen Poesie* [On the study of Greek poetry] from 1797.⁹ In 1807, he had reviewed Johann Gustav Gottlieb Büsching and Friedrich Heinrich von der Hagen's newly published anthology, *Sammlung Deutscher Volkslieder mit einem Anhange Flammländischer u. Französischer, nebst Melodien* [Collection of German folk songs with an appendix in Flemish

---

8 Ibid., 52.
9 See KFSA 1, 364.

and French, along with melodies]. In this review, he paid homage to Herder's translation of European ballads, which he thought 'aus den mit Schmück und Zierat überladenen Kunstgärten der gelehrten oder vornehmen modischen Dichtkunst in das Freie zurückführte' [brought back the fashionable poetry of the learned or posh into freedom, out of the artificial gardens cluttered with dazzling ornament].[10] The ballad was the core genre for Herder and Goethe's generation, and a particularly famous practitioner was Bürger. From early on, Schlegel took a critical stance towards Bürger's reinvention of the *Volkslied* [ballad]. He would never really deviate from this stance, even though he softened his view on the ballads so popular in his time. We find his first classicist attack on the ballad in his agreement with Friedrich Schiller (1759–1805), who published an attack on Bürger, in four parts, in the January 1791 editions of the *Jena Allgemeine Literatur-Zeitung* [Jena general literary review]. Schiller condemned Bürger's remark about a poem's popularity being a sure sign of its perfection:

> Dieser Satz ['Popularität eines poetischen Werkes ist das Siegel seiner Vollkommenheit', AHM] ist durchaus Eins mit diesem: Was den Vortrefflichen gefällt, ist gut; was allen ohne Unterschied gefällt, ist es noch mehr.
>
> [This sentence ['The popularity of a poetic work is the seal of its perfection', AHM] is very much the same as this: What pleases the admirable, is good, what pleases everyone with no exception is even better.][11]

In a letter to his brother, dated 11 December 1793, Schlegel asserts that Bürger's style belongs to the simple middle, 'gemein' [crude], yet admits that 'B.[ürger] in einigen seiner Romanzen Originale-Höchstes erreicht habe, aber nicht daß ihm dieß auf den Namen eines großen Dichters gültigen Anspruch giebt' ['B.[ürger] had achieved the sublime in some of his ballads, but not that this lends credence to his claiming to be a great poet'].[12] He echoes Schiller's opinion: 'ich begreife nicht, was Du Schönes oder Großes in seinen Werken findest' [I cannot fathom what you find so beautiful or great in his works].[13] This statement stands in stark contrast to the position of his elder brother, who had a deep veneration for Bürger, whom he once in a letter called 'des heiligen deutschen Reichs erwählten

---

10 KFSA 3, 103.
11 For the first quote see Gottfried August Bürger, 'Gedichte. Erster Theil. Vorrede', *Dr. Rudolf Brandmeyer, Universität Duisburg-Essen Fakultät für Geisteswissenschaften / Germanistik; Projekt Lyriktheorie*, https://www.uni-due.de/lyriktheorie/texte/1789_buerger.html#popula (retrieved on 4 August 2019). For the second quote see Friedrich Schiller, '[Rezension] Göttingen, b. Dieterich: Gedichte von G. A. Bürger. Mit Kupfern. 1789. Erster Theil. 272 S. Zweyter Theil. 296 S. 8. (1 Rthlr. 16 gr.)', *Dr. Rudolf Brandmeyer, Universität Duisburg-Essen Fakultät für Geisteswissenschaften / Germanistik; Projekt Lyriktheorie*, https://www.uni-due. de/lyriktheorie/texte/1791_schiller.html (retrieved on 4 August 2019).
12 KFSA 23, 165 (letter no. 82, 11 December 1793).
13 KFSA 21, 155 (letter no. 77, 13 November 1793).

Volkspoëten, allzeit Mehrer des guten Geschmacks etc. etc.' [the favourite people's poet of the Holy German Empire, perennial augmenter of good taste etc. etc.][14] Friedrich then turns to the subject of the English antiquarian Bishop Thomas Percy (1729–1811):

> Ich gestehe Dir, daß die Griechen und Göthe mir volksmäßig genug sind, und daß die *Volkspoesie* des Percy u.s.w. für mich – zur gelehrten Litteratur gehört, bis auf äusserst wenige Ausnahmen.
>
> [I admit that the Greeks and Goethe are folkish enough for me and that Percy's folk poetry etc. – for me at least – falls into the category of academic literature, with very few exceptions].[15]

This is a reference to Percy's ballad collection *Reliques of Ancient English Poetry* (1765), which inspired the romantics' obsession with folk ballads. Schlegel utters a critique very similar indeed in a review of a selection of lyrical ballads in Schillers journal *Musenalmanach für das Jahr 1796* [Almanack of the muses for the year 1796]. He finds some of Herder's romance-inspired ballads worth reading, but notes their overall imperfection. Ludwig Gotthard Kosegarten's (1758–1818) ballad *Schön Sidselil und Ritter Ingild. Nach dem Altdänischen* [Beautiful Sidselil and the knight Ingild. From old-Danish] displays the same flaw: '*Sidselil* von Kosegarten könnte rührend sein, wenn es von einigen widerlichen Zügen gereinigt, und weicher gehalten wäre', [*Sidselil* by Kosegarten could be moving, if it were cleansed of some abhorrent characteristics and kept in a softer tone].[16]

We find Schlegel's lengthiest pondering on the ballad in his 1808 review of Johann Friedrich Cotta's Goethe edition *Goethes Werke* of 1806. In this case, he seems to be fond of the genre, as he writes: 'Lieder wie diese sind es vorzüglich, die … im lebendigen Munde des Gesanges als ein Eigentum des gesamten Volks die Jahrhunderte überdauern mögen' [it is primarily ballads such as these … that endure for centuries in the vibrant oral song, as a relic of the whole people].[17] The doubts he had concerning Bürger are still present, yet he praises him 'trotz der Einseitigkeit seines Geschmacks, und der Übertriebenheit seiner Behandlungsart' [despite the bias of his taste and the exaggeration of his style], for his 'große unleugbare Verdienste um das Volkslied, dessen Tiefe zu erforschen er redlich bestrebt war' [great indisputable merits concerning the ballad, the depths of which he rightly strove to scrutinise].[18] In the review of Büsching and

---

14 August Wilhelm Schlegel, 'August Wilhelm Schlegel *an* Gottfried August Bürger', *Digitale Edition der Korrespondenz August Wilhelm Schlegels [Version-07-19]*, http://august-wilhelm-schlegel.de/briefedigital/letters/view/494?left=text&right=druck (retrieved on 4 August 2019).
15 KFSA 23, 165 (letter no. 82, 11 December 1793).
16 KFSA 2, 4.
17 KFSA 3, 115.
18 Ibid., 116.

Hagen's collection of ballads from 1807, he repeats the critique, stating the plea: 'wenn nur nicht so manches Schlechte mit aufgenommen, so manches Eigne und Fremdartige eingemischt wäre' [would that not so much bad poetry be incorporated, so much peculiar and alien intertwined].[19] The primary error of the collected ballads is 'gesuchte ... Seltsamkeit' [artificial oddity] and that 'man das Rohe und Gemeine ... mit dem Volksmäßigen verwechselt' [one mistakes the crude and ordinary ... for the folkish].[20] Having said that, Schlegel proceeds to lampoon the popularity of the bad ballads:

> ... es vergeht wohl kein blauer Montag, an dem nicht in größern und kleinern Städten des ehemaligen heil. römischen Reichs zusammengerechnet einige hundert solche Lieder gedichtet werden. Und sollte dies alles noch nicht zureichen, so könnten wir einen leichten und unfehlbaren Handgriff angeben, wo es an Volksliedern, die man sammeln könnte, gebrechen sollte, dergleichen selbst in beliebiger Mengen *zu machen:* Man nehme das erste beste Gedicht von *Gellert* oder *Hagedorn*, und lasse es von einem Kinde von vier oder fünf Jahren auswendig lernen; es wird gewiß an romantischen Verwechslungen und Verstümmlungen nicht fehlen, und man darf dieses Verfahren nur etwa drei- bis viermal wiederholen, so wird man zu seinem Erstaunen statt des ehrlichen alten Gedichts, aus dem goldenen Zeitalter, ein vortreffliches Volkslied nach dem neuesten Geschmack vor sich sehen.
>
> [... there does not pass a single Monday, on which in total some hundred such ballads would be written, in the big and small towns of the former Holy Roman Empire. As if this was not enough, we could show you an easy and infallible means of *making* as many as you like, if collecting them should fail: One takes any poem of *Gellert* or *Hagedorn* and gives it to a child of four or five years to memorise. Surely, there will be no lack of romantic confusions and mutilations, and one need only repeat this three or four times, and you will to your surprise see before you a perfect ballad, in the newest fashion, instead of the honest old poem from the Golden Age.][21]

In this passage, the first and foremost proponent of romantic fragmentation and irony criticises 'romantic confusion' and the simplicity and popularity of the ballads. In Schlegel's theory of universal romantic poetry, 'Verwechslung' [confusion] and 'Verstümmlung' [mutilation] exemplify a negative chaos, in which the romantic confusion is not intellectually pleasing. In the classicist text *Über das Studium der Griechischen Poesie*, he compared the well-liked chivalric romances of the medieval and baroque periods, i.e. 'die geistlose Monotonie der barbarischen Chevalerie' [the trivial monotony of barbaric chivalry] with the truer heroism of Greek epic poetry, using such terms as whole, unity, and mass.[22] In

---

19 KFSA 3, 103.
20 Ibid.
21 Ibid, 107.
22 KFSA 1, 280. The passage on unity in chaos is extensive, see KFSA 1, 280–281.

the same text, we find a second instance, where Schlegel dismisses modern Gothic literature as tantamount to cheap consumer goods:

> Wie in einem ästhetischen Kramladen steht hier Volkspoesie und Bontonpoesie beisammen, und selbst der Metaphysiker sucht sein eignes Sortiment nicht vergebens; Nordische oder Christliche Epopöen für die Freunde des Nordens und des Christentums; Geistergeschichten für die Liebhaber mystischer Gräßlichkeiten, und Irokesische oder Kannibalische Oden für die Liebhaber der Menschenfresserei; Griechisches Kostüm für antike Seelen und Rittergedichte für heroische Zungen; ja sogar Nationalpoesie für die Dilettanten der Deutschheit!
>
> [Here one finds – as if one were in a general store of aesthetics – folk poetry and courtly poetry next to each other. Even the metaphysician can find there his own assortment. There are Nordic or Christian epopees for the admirers of the north and Christianity; ghost stories for the lovers of mystical horrors, Iroquoian or cannibalistic odes for the lovers of cannibalism; Greek costume for antique souls; knightly poems for heroic tongues; and even national poetry for the dilettantes of Germanness!][23]

The 'general store of aesthetics' is obviously not a place of true art, and the 'assortment' no list of great works. As Asko Nivala points out, the 'epopees' might refer to Ossian.[24] The 'ghost stories' might in the same manner be a reference to Bürger's ballads, which Schlegel associated with popular literature and mass entertainment. To Schlegel, Bürger's poetry is a paradox: On the one hand, it exemplifies popular mediocrity at its worst. On the other hand, it offers a return to simple, folkish literature. This paradox is a general characteristic of the romantic movement in Jena: the romantics were an elitist group of academics who, in academic aphorisms and essays written for the learned, praised romantic literature as 'kunstlos' [artless, naïve], i.e. not necessarily following classicist poetics.[25] In the *Athenaeum*, Schlegel characterises the ballad as a romantic genre par excellence. He muses on the 'Romanze' [ballad], acknowledging its nature as 'unendlich bizarr' [infinitely bizarre] as well as confusing in a positive way.[26] His prime example of such a ballad is Goethes *Braut von Korinth* [The bride of Corinth] published in Schiller's *Musenalmanach* in 1798. This is a ballad that depicts a female specimen of the vampiric undead and thereby epitomises the type of ghostly ballads that Schlegel denounced in the case of Bürger. He had read Bürger as early as 1793 as a young classicist, but reading Goethe's ballad in 1798 must have been a different experience, because Goethe, a supporter of the Jena romantics, was not in their eyes connected with vulgarity and entertainment

---

23 KFSA 1, 222–223. In the English translation, I quote Stuart Barnett's English translation from Asko Nivala, *The Romantic Idea of the Golden Age in Friedrich Schlegel's Philosophy of History* (New York: Routledge, 2017), 132, doi: 10.4324/9781315206523.
24 Ibid.
25 KFSA 2, 182, fragment 116.
26 KFSA 2, 250, fragment 429.

literature. Instead, Goethe represented the court at Weimar as well as the composition of certain classicist genres, such as tragedy.

2. Connections between Jena and Copenhagen: Friedrich Schlegel and the Copenhagen German Circle

Copenhagen was with its fellow academy town Sorø a literary centre in the years 1750 to 1770, not at all unlike Weimar and Jena, the seat of academia in the small duchy of Sachsen-Weimar. During these years, the German-born prime minister of Denmark, Count Johann Hartwig Ernst von Bernstorff (1712–1772) invited a number of prominent foreign academics and poets to entertain the Danish King Frederik V. Among these royal invitees were the German poet laureate Friedrich Gottlieb Klopstock, Gerstenberg, and Swiss historian and translator Paul Henri Mallet (1730–1807). On the periphery of this cultural hub were members of the Schlegel family, namely three brothers, the playwright Johann Elias Schlegel (1719–1749), the historian Johann Heinrich Schlegel (1726–1780) and Johann Adolf Schlegel (1721–1793), the father of Friedrich and August Wilhelm. This circle of friends and associates popularised medieval Germanic literature for a large European readership. Johann Elias Schlegel found inspiration in Germanic myth and the historiography of the North in tragic plays such as *Hermann* (1743) and *Canut* (1746), the latter of which was influential in German as well as Danish literature.[27] He thereby laid the foundation of the romantic preference for Northern mythology over Greco-Roman mythology. Mallet translated parts of the Icelandic *Poetic Edda* into French and gained huge success with his bestselling *Monuments de la mythologie et de la poesie des Celtes, et particulierement des anciens Scandinaves* [Monuments of the mythology and poetry of the Celts, and particularly of the ancient Scandinavians] (1756), which most people today know from Percy's translation *Northern Antiquities* (1770), into which it is incorporated. In addition, Gerstenberg, inspired by British antiquarians, wrote extensively about the Danish ballad tradition, thereby drawing Herder's attention to Nordic medieval poetry.

Strangely, Mallet seems not to appear anywhere in the critical edition of Schlegel's work. Schlegel also largely ignores his uncle Johann Elias Schlegel, who died as a relatively young man in 1749. In a letter dating from 10 March 1796 to Christoph Martin Wieland (1733–1813), a friend of his father's and a famous Shakespearian translator and poet in his own right, the young critic denounces

---

[27] See my article 'Gravhøjen åbnes. Fra rokoko-middelalderisme i Johann Elias Schlegels Canut til vikinge-romantik i Johannes Ewalds Rolf Krage', *Passage: tidsskrift for litteratur og kritik* 81 (2019): 121–135.

the works of his father and uncle as 'das Wenige, was er und sein Bruder Elias zur Zeit der Morgenröthe der Deutschen Kunst als *Schriftsteller* gethan hat' [the little which he and his brother Elias had accomplished as *writers* during the dawn of German art].[28] However, Schlegel praises his uncle in the 1811 review of literary historian Wilhelm Körte's (1766–1846) biography of Johann Wilhelm Ludwig Gleim (1719–1803). He mentions Johann Elias in connection with Herder, Lessing, Klopstock, and the rebirth of German literature during the Late Enlightenment, and does not forget to lament his premature death.[29]

Gerstenberg does not figure prominently in Schlegel's published fragments, notebooks, or critical essays either. Nonetheless, subtle signs do point to the fact that he was an influence on the young Schlegel. In 1798, Novalis wanted to invite not only Franz von Baader (1765–1841) but also the ageing Gerstenberg to contribute to the *Athenaeum*, but it remains unclear whether Schlegel knew of the plan to include him or not.[30] However, Schlegel had come across Gerstenberg's name in a newspaper article that inspired him to write one of his countless fragmentary notes.

The yet unpublished early notebook *Studien des Alterthums* [Studies of Antiquity] contains a parenthetical mention of the playwright William Mason (1724–1797): '(Mason's Versuche d[en] Chor wieder in die Engl.[ische] Tragödie einzuführen – in Elfriede und Caractacut)' [(Mason's attempts at reintroducing the choir into the English tragedy – in Elfriede and Caractacut)].[31] The first title mentioned is *Elfrida, A Dramatic Poem. Written on the Model of The Ancient Greek Tragedy* (1752). Schlegel or the transcriber of the manuscript misspells the second title, but it must be a reference to Mason's 1759 play *Caractacus. A Dramatic Poem: Written on the Model of The Ancient Greek Tragedy*. This paragraph, tucked away among hundreds of short quotations and philological musings, reveals that Schlegel had come across Mason's eulogy in the 1797 December edition of the *Intelligenzblatt der Allgemeinen Literaturzeitung* [News magazine of the general literary review]. The anonymous eulogist characterises two of Mason's plays about Anglo-Saxon history, druids, kings of old, and Roman Britain in the following manner:

> Die Elfride, die wir auch durch Hrn. *Bertuchs* deutsche Bearbeitung kennen, und der Caractacus, sind bekanntlich im Zuschnitt nach dem griechischen Trauerspiel, mit

---

28 KFSA 23, 288.
29 KFSA 3, 218.
30 See KFSA 24, 418.
31 Fragment 233 of the *Studien des Alterthums*, page 15ʳ. This collection of notes will be published in a future volume of the KFSA. See Christian Benne and Ulrich Breuer, 'Einleitung', in *Antike – Philologie – Romantik. Friedrich Schlegels altertumswissenschaftliche Manuskripte*, ed. Christian Benne and Ulrich Breuer (Paderborn: Ferdinand Schöningh, 2009), 7–14.

Chören, das glücklichste, was von solchen Nachahmungen in neuern Zeiten versucht worden ist.... Unsere Literatur kann ihnen nur Gerstenbergs Minona entgegenstellen.

[Elfride, also known to us in Mr. *Bertuch's* German translation, and Caractacus are, as is generally known, in their being modelled on the Greek tragedy, with their tragic choirs, among the most fortunate of such imitations that have been tried in recent times.... In our literature, only Gerstenberg's Minona rivals them.][32]

Hence, Schlegel knew the title of Gerstenberg's Ossianic drama *Minona oder die Angelsachsen. Ein tragisches Melodrama in vier Akten* [Minona or the Anglo-Saxons. A tragic melodrama in four acts], published in Hamburg in 1785. From early on, he wanted to reshape German theatre on the stylistic model of Greek tragedy, but with medieval themes. He framed his famously criticised *Alarcos. Ein Trauerspiel* [Alarcos. A tragedy] (1802) as a play 'im antikken Sinne des Worts, aber in romantischem Stoff und Costum' [in a classical sense, but in romantic fabric and costume].[33] The often-quoted footnote reads: 'Vorzüglich nach dem Ideale des Aischylus' [Preferably modelled after Aeschylus].[34] In the *Alarcos*, the interest in musicality and form (e.g. embedded sonnets and end rhymes by means of assonance) far outweigh any concerns Schlegel might have had with the plot or lack thereof. Debates on the reintroduction of the tragic choir constitute a central problem in the Quarrel of the Ancients and the Moderns. I have found only one mention of Gerstenberg in Schlegel's work. It occurs in a review article written for the *Österreichischer Beobachter* [Austrian spectator] in 1811 on stylistic decorum in contemporary German authors. He dedicates one short sentence to him: 'Gerstenberg ist späterhin in andere Gattungen übergegangen' [Gerstenberg has at a later time gone into other genres], revealing a knowledge of the romantic genres in which he wrote.[35]

Schlegel was thus aware of the labours of the German Circle in Copenhagen. He associated his famous uncle J. E. Schlegel and Gerstenberg with the romantic drama, which had very different genre characteristics as well as a medieval European setting when compared to the tragedies of Aeschylus, Sophocles and Euripides. William Mason's plays, which bore a similarity to Gerstenberg's *Minona,* and indeed to J. E. Schlegel's *Canut* and Schlegel's own *Alarcos*, were a strange mix of classicist and medievalist literature typical of eighteenth-century early romanticism.

---

32 *Intelligenzblatt der Allgemeinen Literaturzeitung*, Numero 170, 30 December 1797, 1411. Friedrich Justin Bertuch published his German version of the play in Weimar in 1775, entitled *Elfriede: ein Trauerspiel in drey Aufzügen*. The paragraph is clearly based on the eulogy and therefore dates the manuscript to a date not earlier than 30 December 1797.
33 KFSA 3, 14.
34 Ibid.
35 KFSA 3, 212.

3. Friedrich Schlegel and the English Antiquarians

Ernst Behler (1928–1997) characterised Schlegel's infatuation with English literature as 'schon sehr früh einsetzend …' [present from very early on].[36] From their very beginning, Schlegel's studies centred on Shakespeare. There is scattered evidence of Schlegel's studies of the English antiquarians, who in their turn influenced the German Circle in Copenhagen as well as Herder. The most influential are Bishop Thomas Percy, Richard Hurd and Thomas Warton the younger. As James Engell points out, the connections between early English and German romanticisms make up 'a larger comparative map of English criticism and German romanticism, a map whose intricate territories remain relatively uncharted by Germanists and virtual *terra incognita* for readers of English literature'.[37] Another recent study points to similarities between James Harris (1709–1780) and Schlegel, yet concludes that Harris might have influenced the German scholar Friedrich August Wolf (1759–1824), whose significance for the Jena romantics cannot be overstated. Dorit Messlin writes that 'vermutlich der klassische Philologe Friedrich August Wolf mit seiner Rezeption der Überlegungen von James Harris die Anregung gegeben hat' [probably the classical philologist Friedrich August Wolf had inspired him by means of his review of the thoughts of James Harris].[38] As seen in this article, Schlegel mentions Harris in several notes. The exact nature of the influence of the earlier generation of learned Englishmen eludes us. However, Engell finds that Schlegel's criticism at its earliest stage was under the sway of Hurd, from his borrowing of Hurd's concept of 'universal poetry' and 'romance', as well as the 'fantastic', 'sentimental' and 'mimetic'. He equally idolises Homer, Shakespeare, and Spenser.

Schlegel quoted Hurd's *Letters on Chivalry and Romance* (1762) as early as 1797, disagreeing wholeheartedly with Hurd's appreciation of criticism and literature from the Hellenistic and Roman eras.[39] Schlegel preferred the severe style of texts from the archaic and classical era. In 1797, he was still very much the radical neoclassicist and stern philologist, who thought that only he who 'sich die Objektivität der ganzen Masse, den schönen Geist der einzelnen Dichter, und

---

36 KFSA 11, 336.
37 James Engell: 'Romantische Poesie: Richard Hurd and Friedrich Schlegel', *Archiv für das Studium der neueren Sprachen und Literaturen* (1993), 6–17, quotation on p. 17. Engell concludes: 'Any grasp of Schlegel or of German Romanticism may reach out to include not only the role played by Herder and of course Schiller, but the role played by Hurd and the English Critics', ibid.
38 Dorit Messlin, 'Ordo inversus. James Harris und Friedrich Schlegel', in *Friedrich Schlegel und die Philologie*, ed. Ulrich Breuer, Remigius Bunia and Armin Erlinghagen, (Paderborn: Ferdinand Schöningh, 2013): 59–69, quotation on p. 69.
39 Engell quotes this place, see Engell, 16 (see footnote 37). For the quote showing Hurd's appreciation of Hellenistic and Roman literature, see KFSA 1, 350.

Fig. 2: Johann Peter Krafft, Ossian and Malvina, 1810. Private collection.

den vollkommnen Stil des goldnen Zeitalters zueignet' [acquires the objectivity of the whole mass, the beautiful soul of the individual poet, and the complete style of the golden age] would be able to produce a true work of art.[40] This was about to change. Schlegel did not forget about Hurd, as can be seen from one of his critical fragments written in 1810 on the subject of British scholarship:

---

40 KFSA 1, 331.

> Wie die Englische Litteratur unter *Beda* und *Alcuin* d[en] andern <Ländern> zuvorgeeilt, so auch in neuern Zeiten. *Locke* und die andern haben die *französische* φσ[Philosophie] veranlaßt; *Warton, Hurd, Harris,* <Blair> pp die deutsche Kritik ....
>
> [As English literature during the times of Bede and *Alcuin* rush ahead of other <countries>, in this manner also in recent times. *Locke* and others have laid the foundation for French φσ[philosophy]; *Warton, Hurd, Harris,* <Blair> pp German criticism....][41]

Schlegel praises the medieval scholars, the Venerable Bede (early eighth-century) and Alcuin (eighth-century) for being ideal philologists. Locke is a precursor to French philosophy, and the four British critics seem as forerunners of German literary criticism. Schlegel has not mentioned Blair before, but he must be thinking of James Macpherson's Scottish ally and author of the *A Critical Dissertation on the Poems of Ossian, the Son of Fingal* (1763) Hugo Blair (1718–1800). In the same fragment, he connects 'romantische Poesie' [romantic poetry] with Spenser, Shakespeare, and Milton. This is a reference to Hurd, who coined the phrase 'the romantic Spirit of his Age' in connection with Spenser.[42] Notwithstanding the fact that this fragment ends with the curious notion of English insularity ('Die Engl.[ische] φσ[Philosophie] bloß für ihre Insel brauchbar' [Engl.[ish] φσ[philosophy] only useful for its island]), he readily pledges his allegiance to English criticism in the second part of the 1812 Vienna lectures *Geschichte der alten und neuen Literatur* [A history of old and modern literature], published in 1815.[43] Schlegel in this case writes about classical philology:

> Die Kritik der Engländer und einige ihrer Schriften über Poesie, oder auch über bildende Kunst waren freier, eigentümlicher, und meistens auch gelehrter in der Kentnis des Altertums, als die französischen Schriftsteller dieser Gattung, entsprachen daher dem deutschen Geiste mehr. Doch hat die deutsche Kritik nur die erste Veranlassung von den Engländern Harris, Home, Hurd, Warton genommen, und sich bald durchaus selbstständig entwickelt, mehr vielleicht als irgend ein anderer Zweig unsrer Literatur.
>
> [The criticism of the English, as well as some of their writings on poetry, or perhaps also on painting, were more free, original and for the most part also more learned in their knowledge of Antiquity, than were the French writers of this genre, and they therefore better match the German spirit. However, the Englishmen Harris, Home, Hurd and Warton prompted German criticism, which has evolved into something much more independent, perhaps more so than any other branch of our literature.][44]

In this canon of English critics, Schlegel fails to mention Thomas Percy, to whom he had referred, two pages earlier in the context of Germanic medieval poetry:

---

41 KFSA 17, 191, fragment 82.
42 Richard Hurd, *Letters on Chivalry and Romance* (London: A. Millar & W. Thurlbourn and J. Woodyer, 1762), 116.
43 KFSA 17, 191, fragment 82.
44 KFSA 6, 336. See Engell, 16 (see footnote 37).

Früh schon erwachte durch Percy und mit der Liebe zum Shakespeare, zugleich auch die Liebe zu den alten Balladen und Volksliedern; je größer nun der Reichtum derselben ist, den man aufgefunden hat, besonders der schottischen, je mehr scheint das Gefallen daran jede andere Gattung von Poesie verdrängt zu haben, den alltäglichen Hausbedarf von Romanen und Schauspielen ausgenommen .... In England begann sie mit ersten Betrachtungen oder dichterischen Naturbeschreibungen, und endigte mit der allgemein verbreiteten Liebhaberei an den alten Volkslidedern, einzeilnen Anklängen von der verlornen Poesie einer noch ältern Zeit.

[From early on, at the behest of Percy and concurrent with the love for Shakespeare, awoke also the love for the old ballads and popular songs; the greater one found their richness, especially in the case of the Scottish ballads, the more seems their popularity to extrude that of other genres, apart from the household's everyday need of novels and plays .... In England, it [higher poetry] began with the first contemplations or poetic descriptions of nature, and ended with the common and widespread pastime pleasure of reading old ballads, solitary reminiscences of the lost poetry of an even older time.][45]

The Vienna lecturer apparently holds the English critics in high esteem, yet the description of the development of English romanticism turns out slightly, if not alarmingly, pejorative: it has become 'alltäglich' [pedestrian] and part of the cultural 'Hausbedarf' [household needs] along with novels and plays, probably of a certain popular kind. What took its beginning as high poetry, petered out as a 'widespread pastime' and 'solitary reminiscences'. Schlegel has a wide, positive vocabulary for expressing longing for the past, God, or hidden knowledge. Reminiscences, expressing the hollow echoes of something not quite as sturdy as the original, is not part of it. On a later page, he sarcastically welcomes contemporary English drama as successful 'poetische Manufaktureware' [poetic consumer goods], hardly a welcome praise for romantics of any nationality.[46]

The third important English critic is the literary historian Thomas Warton the younger, an important romantic predecessor according to Eichner.[47] He encouraged Gerstenberg and Herder's interest in Spenser, but only appears in Schlegel's notebooks as the author of the *Inscriptionum Romanarum Metricarum Delectus* (1758) a critical edition of Roman epigraphy.[48] Schlegel does, however, quote another critic named Warton: '*Sacchetti* published tales *before Boccacc[io]* in which are many anecdotes of *Dante* and his contemporaries'[49]

---

45 KFSA 6, 334.
46 KFSA 6, 336.
47 KFSA 2, p. LIV in the preface.
48 KFSA 16, 51, fragment 190, see also the commentary to the fragment, KFSA 16, 531.
49 KFSA 16, 125, fragment 485. The fragment is part of the *Fragmente zur Litteratur und Poesie* [Fragments on literature and poetry] (1797). The note is in English. Sacchetti is not earlier than Boccaccio is, as Eichner notes, ibid. 550. Schlegel quotes page 64 of the 1782 first edition of the second volume of Warton's book.

In this case, he cites Thomas Warton's brother, Joseph Warton's (1722-1800) *An Essay on the Genius and Writings of Pope* (1756). Other philologists mentioned are Richard Bentley (1662-1742), William Warburton (1698-1779), both of whom have 'φλ [philologische] Natur' [a philological nature], and Harris, the latter of whom Schlegel characterises as 'bedeutender φλ[Philolog] vielleicht nur durch sein bischen φσ[Philosophie]; desgleichen ein bedeutender Kritiker' [an important φλ[Philologist], perhaps only because of his traces of φσ[Philosophy], therefore also an important critic].[50]

In conclusion, Schlegel became an enthusiastic recipient of English philological treaties who preferred philosophical criticism, in which readings of Greek and Latin texts intertwined with cultural history and a proscriptive poetics of modern literature. Schlegel's own literary criticism was of this kind. He made the distinction between pedantic and philosophical criticism in the polemical *Athenaeum* fragment no. 389, that denounces the dull positivism of some English critics: 'Denn von Sinn für die Poesie findet sich in Harris, Home und Johnson, den Koryphäen der Gattung, auch nicht die schamhafteste Andeutung' [For there is not an ounce of sense for poetry in Harris, Home, and Johnson, the luminaries of the genre].[51] This fragment constitutes a blatant attack on the classicist opponents of Hurd and other preromantics and a staunch defence of what we could call philosophical literary scholarship.

4. The Re-Invention of the Wheel? Jena Romanticism and Eighteenth-Century Medievalism

A vast number of critical studies show us that Schlegel in his late phase politicises the medieval era. But what, in fact, *did* Schlegel write himself on Germanic medieval literature in his young years – when not quoting Herder or English critics? In a notorious fragment from the third volume of the journal *Athenaeum*, he rejects the heroes and heathen gods of old as ideals for the new age. Renaissance and Enlightenment artists and philosophers take their place:

> Nicht Hermann und Wodan sind die Nationalgötter der Deutschen, sondern die Kunst und die Wissenschaft. Gedenke noch einmal an Kepler, Dürer, Luther, Böhme; und dann an Lessing, Winckelmann, Goethe, Fichte.

---

50 For the first quotation consult KFSA 16, 76, fragment 165, for the second KFSA 16, 55, fragment 229.
51 KFSA 2, 238, fragment 389. Samuel Johnson (1709-1784 was an opponent of romanticism. See KFSA 2, p. LIV in the preface.

[Not Hermann and Odin, but art and science are the national deities of the Germans. Think only upon Kepler, Dürer, Luther, Böhme; and then on Lessing, Winckelmann, Goethe, Fichte].[52]

Was he truly disinterested in the Germanic past? In the *Epochen der Dichtkunst* [Epochs of poetry], part of the *Gespräch über die Poesie* [Dialogue on poetry] from 1800, we find an apparently roseate description of Germanic poetry: 'Mit den Germaniern strömte ein unverdorbener Felsenquell von neuem Heldengesang über Europa' [A pure fountainhead of new heroic poetry flowed across Europe with the appearance of the Teutons].[53] This paragraph on North-European literature is short when compared to what he writes about Greek, Roman and Romance poetry. On the following pages, he mentions Petrarch, Boccaccio, Ariost, Boiardo, Guarini, Cervantes, and Shakespeare as well as the genres romance, canzone terza rima, chivalric novel, pastoral novel, and the novella. At the end of the text, Goethe, Johann Joachim Winckelmann (1717-1768), Paul Flemming (1609-1640), Georg Rudolf Weckherlin (1584-1653), and the *Nibelungenlied* [The Song of the Nibelungs] are listed, but these latter German authors, as well as the national epic, are merely mentioned without any further characterisation. What matters is Italian and Spanish poetry, as well as Shakespeare. In *Über das Studium der Griechischen Poesie*, Schlegel notes the following:

> So wie viele Reisende in weiter Ferne suchen, was sie in ihrer Heimat ebenso gut und näher finden könnten: so bewundert man nicht selten im Homer allein das, worin der erste der beste Nordische oder Südliche Barbar, wofern er nur ein großer Dichter ist, ihm gleich kommt.
>
> [So many travellers sought in the remoteness what they could just as easily and at a shorter distance find in their home country: Therefore, one often praises in Homer only that with which any northern or southern barbarian, provided that he be a great poet, would bear comparison.][54]

Schlegel, who played a part in the discovery of the mutual root of most European languages, must be thinking of the fact that all Indo-European peoples share the same tradition of oral poetry, the tradition of storytelling by singing:

---

52 KFSA 2, 269-270, fragment 135. See also Gottfried Salomon's discussion of Schlegel's 'Europeanism' in *Das Mittelalter als Ideal der Romantik* (München: Drei Masken Verlag, 1922), 66.
53 For the German quote, see KFSA 2, 296. In the English translation, I quote Friedrich Schlegel's *Dialogue on Poetry and Literary Aphorisms*. Translated, introduced, and annotated by Ernst Behler & Roman Struc (University Park, PA; London: Pennsylvania State University Press, 1968), 67.
54 KFSA 1, 278.

> Der allgemeine Umriß eines Charakters, wie Achilles hätte vielleicht auch in der Fantasie eines Nord- oder Süd-Homerus entstehen können: diese feineren Züge der Ausbildung waren nur dem Griechen möglich.
>
> [The general outline of a character such as Achilles could also have originated from the imagination of a northern or southern Homer: These, the finer points of experience were only feasible for the Greek.][55]

Later, he connects this Homeric poetry with the concept of 'Wahrheit' [truth], 'Kraft', [power] 'Anmut' [grace] and 'Natürlichkeit' [naturalness], hallmarks of romanticism. The use of the word 'Barde' and not 'rhapsode' reveals an early Ossianic influence:[56]

> Die treue Wahrheit, die ursprüngliche Kraft, die einfache Anmut, die reizende Natürlichkeit sind Vorzüge, welche der Griechische Barde vielleicht mit einem oder dem andern seiner Indischen oder Keltischen Brüder teilt.
>
> [The loyal truth, the original vigour, the simple grace, the charming naturalness are advantages, which the Greek bard perhaps shares with one or other of his Indian or Celtic brothers.][57]

Nevertheless, something uniquely Greek does exist in the character Achilles, which no barbarian would be able to capture in a piece of poetry: 'Die Homerischen Helden, wie den Dichter selbst unterscheidet eine *freiere Menschlichkeit* von allen nicht-Griechischen Heroen und Barden' [A *freer humanity* differentiates the Homeric heroes as well as the poet himself from all non-Greek heroes and bards].[58] Another early example of Schlegel delving into Germanic literature is the one and a half page long lecture *Die nordische Literatur* [Nordic literature] dating from the Paris lectures of 1804. In this lecture, Schlegel writes: 'Die deutsche Poesie ... vereinigte schon frühe alle Eigenschaften der nordischen und romantischen' [Already at an early point in time, German poetry ... united all qualities of the Nordic and romantic].[59] The only Germanic texts mentioned are the *Prose Edda* and *Poetic Edda.* Schlegel lets Nordic poetry precede romance literature:

---

55 KFSA 1, 279.
56 Wolf Gerhard Schmidt notes the lack of an analysis of Schlegel's reception of Ossian, but lists numerous passages in which Schlegel mentions or paraphrases Ossian, at least dating back from the Jena years around 1799. Wolf Gerhard Schmidt, '4.2 Zwischen "alter" und "neuer" Mythologie. Zur Funktion der ossianischen "Wehmut" in Friedrich Schlegels transzendentalpoetischem Modell', in '*Homer des Nordens' und 'Mutter der Romantik'. James Macpherons Ossian und seine Rezeption in der deutschsprachigen Literatur*, Vol. 2, ed. Howard Gaskill et al. (Berlin: Walter de Gruyter, 2003), 952–969.
57 KFSA 1, 279.
58 Ibid., 280.
59 KFSA 11, 178.

Mit den deutschen ergoß sich der neue Strom dieser nordischen Dichtungen über alle eroberten Länder. Aus ihm schöpfte die romantische Poesie jene Sagen von Riesen, Zwergen, zauberischen Kräften, wunderbaren Tieren ....

[With the Teutons, this new wave of Nordic poetry flowed across all conquered countries. Out of this wave, romantic poetry created tales of far-off giants, dwarfs, magical powers, fantastical creatures ....[60]

This Paris lecture from 1804 formed the basis of the Vienna lectures *Geschichte der alten und neuen Literatur* [A history of classical and modern literature] (1812/13), in which medieval Germanic literature plays a much larger role.[61] The one and a half page on medieval Germanic literature from 1804 expands into four long lectures, nos. 6, 7, 8, and 10.

The most vibrant text by Schlegel concerning Germanic medieval literature is the essay *Über nordische Dichtkunst. Ossian. Die Edda, Sigurd und Shakespeare* [On Nordic poetry. Ossian. The Edda. Sigurd, and Shakespeare] (1812), a text known for its subtle apology of Ossian's songs, which Schlegel, in part, acknowledged as medieval, even though he would not date them to the earliest days of the post-Roman era of the British isle, but rather to the later Norman period.[62] In *Über nordische Dichtkunst*, Schlegel vehemently defends the concept of literature as a national phenomenon and the Middle Ages as suitable material for a poet. He rejects the common expression 'Finsternis des Mittelalters' [The Dark Ages], admitting that medieval man might have lived in a kind of cultural night, compared with the 'light' of the common man in early nineteenth-century Germany, but in that case, the medieval era was 'eine *sternenhelle Nacht*' [a *starry* night] in the history of humanity.[63] He indirectly refers to the antiquarian tradition in the remark that literary criticism 'fast durchaus *Geschichte* sein muß' [must almost entirely be *history*].[64] In a similarly indirect reference, he compares the romantic critic with the miner, who digs deep into the foundations of the land in order to excavate precious metals, 'alles zerstreut und begraben unter den Ruinen einer versunkenen Riesenwelt' [all of it displaced and buried under the ruins of a lost heroic world].[65] He gives thanks to the Copenhagen German Circle in his appraisal of the Danish romantic N. F. S. Grundtvig (1783–1827)

---

60 Ibid., 179. The quote is quite similar to the one from *Gespräch über die Poesie*, see footnote 53.
61 See Andrea Polaschegg, '52. "Geschichte der europäischen Literatur"', in *Friedrich Schlegel Handbuch. Leben – Werk – Wirkung*, ed. Johan Andres (Stuttgart: J. B. Metzler Verlag, 2017), 233–234, doi: 10.1007/978-3-476-05370-1_52.
62 Wolf Gerhard Schmidt, 'Zwischen "alter" und "neuer" Mythologie'. Zur poetologischen Funktion Ossians bei Friedrich Schlegel', *Athenäum – Jahrbuch der Friedrich Schlegel-Gesellschaft* 14 (2004), 129–150, quotation on p. 134.
63 KFSA 3, 234.
64 Ibid., 224.
65 Ibid.

who, as a medievalist poet, academic, and translator, was very much influenced by the Copenhagen German Circle: 'Ein sehr geistvoller dänischer Schriftsteller, Grundtvig, dessen Werk [NORDENS MYTOLOGI ELLER UDSIGT OVER EDDALAEREN, 1808] als die beste Einleitung dieses ganze Studium betrachtet werden kann', [a very talented Danish writer, Grundtvig, whose work [MYTHOLOGY OF THE NORTH, OR A SURVEY OF EDDA SCHOLARSHIP] can be seen as the best introduction to this field].[66] Schlegel even translates a couple of pages from Grundtvig's introduction to the book.[67] Interestingly, Schlegel translates the beginning chapter on Danish romantic literature, in which Grundtvig celebrates the earlier generation of Danish medievalist poets, namely Johannes Ewald (1743–1781), Christen Henriksen Pram (1756–1821) and Jens Baggesen (1764–1826) as well as Adam Oehlenschläger (1779–1850), whom Grundtvig in Schlegel's translation calls a 'Skalde' [skáld], using an Icelandic word that Gerstenberg had made famous.[68] Thereby, he continues an interest in contemporary Danish literature first seen in his 1811 review *Axel und Walburg. Eine Tragödie von Öhlenschläger* [Axel and Walburg. A tragedy by Öhlenschläger]. In the German romantic's opinion, Oehlenschläger's tragedy has the same flaw as the 'großen Hafen unsrer Ritterstücke' [abundance of our knightly plays], namely the caricatured depiction of the villain.[69] He finds that Oehlenschläger, whom he had met in Paris in 1807, should not have observed the classicist unity of place.[70] However, he concludes that the portrayal of the mutual roots of the Germans and Scandinavians are most pleasing, concluding, '[d]aß sich *Normannen* und *Germanen* lieben' ['that *Normans* and *Germans* love one another'].[71]

Friedrich Schlegel would not publish scholarly texts focused on Germanic medieval poetry during the famous two years in Jena. However, it is evident that

---

66 Ibid., 239.
67 Friedrich Schlegel translated this passage from Danish into German himself, as Grundtvig records in a letter from 28 April 1812. He also wrote to Grundtvig and invited him to write on a Nordic subject for the journal *Deutsches Museum* [German museum], to Grundtvig's surprise. See Breve til og fra Grundtvig. I (1807–1820), ed. Georg Christensen and Stener Grundtvig (Copenhagen: Gyldendal, 1924), 72. Schlegel's letter to Grundtvig, from 17 January 1812, is printed on p. 55–56 in this volume. On 10 November 1812, Danish historian Christian Molbech stated in a letter to his friend Rasmus Nyerup that August Wilhelm had shown him the translated passage in Stockholm and that his brother Friedrich was very fond of Grundtvig's northern mythology. For Molbech's letter, see S. Birket Smith, *Til Belysning af literære Personer og Forhold i Slutningen af det 18de og Begyndelsen af det 19de Århundrede. En Samling Breve* (Copenhagen: Andr. Fred. Høst & Søns Forlag, 1884), 307. I thank Flemming Lundgreen-Nielsen for these references.
68 KFSA 3, 240.
69 Ibid., 215.
70 See Adam Oehlenschläger, *Oehlenschlägers Erindringer. Første Bind* (Copenhagen: Andr. Fred. Høsts Forlag, 1850), 124.
71 KFSA 3, 216.

he leaned on the Germanic medievalist tradition that he primarily knew from Herder and Bürger, but also from his own comprehensive studies of European literary history. It still seems unclear why we find so few passages on Germanic Medieval literature in the published text. I can think of two explanations: He was tired of the vast popularity of knightly plays, novels, and ballads set in a northern medieval world, and, he wanted to distance himself from the generation of his father and uncles. In 1802, when his chivalric play *Alarcos* was staged in Weimar, he had thought to become a playwright, contemplating also on Nordic medievalist titles such as 'Robinhood' or 'Der Krieg auf d.[er] Wartburg' [The Wartburg Contest].[72] Schlegel never wrote these other plays, but he did publish a number of medievalist poems with a Germanic medieval setting, published in volume 5 of the critical edition under the title *Romanzen und Lieder* [Romances and Ballads], one of which carries the title *Bei der Wartburg,* [At the Wartburg] (1802), an homage to the medieval castle Wartburg as a symbol of chivalric culture and the minstrels' singing contest.

5. Conclusion

To conclude, it does not seem correct to attribute Schlegel's Germanic turn – on the whole – to the growing nationalism in the wake of the Napoleonic Wars. There are traces of a Germanic medievalism present in the earliest of his texts. We therefore cannot ridicule these post-1800 texts as purely 'nationalist', even though it seems clear that Schlegel in his later life understood the Middle Ages primarily as a political ideal in opposition to the French Revolution. The German-American sociologist Gottfried Salomon (1892–1964) discusses this in his 1922 book *Das Mittelalter als Ideal in der Romantik* [The Middle Ages as an ideal in romanticism] on the political romantics' vision of the Middle Ages. But he ignores the medievalist tendencies in the time of the journal *Athenaeum*, whose classicist aesthetics he calls 'das Objektive' [the objective]. He dates Schlegel's German medievalism, the 'Wiedergeburt altdeutscher Kunst und Religion' [Rebirth of ancient German art and religion] or 'ästhetischer Nationalismus' [aesthetic na-

---

72 The first title can be found in KFSA 16, 365, no. 15. The scond title can be found in KFSA 16, 368, no. 29. For a contribution to Schlegel's reception of medieval Latin literature see Mark-Georg Dehrmann, 'Eine "neue Epoche in der Geschichte der Poesie". Friedrich Schlegels philologische Poesie der Moderne am Beispiel des *Roland*-Epos', in *Friedrich Schlegel und die Philologie*, ed. Ulrich Breuer, Remigius Bunia and Armin Erlinghagen (Paderborn: Ferdinand Schöningh, 2013), 203–217, as well as Andreas Härter, 'The Ring of Longing: A View on Friedrich Schlegel's Medievalist Poetry', *Poetica. An International Journal of Linguistic-Literary Studies* 39–40 (1994), 207–223.

tionalism], to his 1808 review of Adam Müller's lectures on German literature.[73] This is one of the first of Schlegel's published texts dealing with the German medieval period, but, as we have seen, there are a number of earlier comments in the form of side remarks in published texts or unpublished notes. The rise of non-classicist literary forms, a most important element of romanticism, based itself on a true historical interest in the Middle Ages. Nationalism plays an increasingly large part in the history of romantic medievalism, but was not the sole force. We see this in Schlegel's affinity to Hurd, Herder, and other romantic predecessors, in his experiments with the Germanic medieval drama, in his reception of Ossian, as well as in his lifelong preoccupation with Bürger. Schlegel himself notices the nationalist turn in *Über nordische Dichtkunst*, commenting on the rise of the medieval in contemporary Germany:

> Besonders aber ist seit den letzten zehn oder zwölf Jahren, wie das Gefühl des Vaterlandes überhaupt von neuem erweckt und aufgeregt, so auch die Liebe zu unsern alten vaterländischen Dichtern sichtbar allgemeiner und lebhafter geworden ....
>
> [Especially in the last ten or twelve years, as the love for king and country has been awoken and stirred, so has also the love for our good old national poets become visibly more common and more vital ....][74]

I therefore concur with David E. Barclay who lists five different types of medievalism within German romanticism. He calls the beginning of the medievalist turn in the late eighteenth-century 'cosmopolitan medievalism' or the 'Gothic revival': the Medieval as a literary space yet open to interpretation and influenced by Northern vernacular literature, neither necessarily devoid of nationalist ideas nor driven solely by a wish to strengthen the nation.[75] From early on in his career, Schlegel had a poetological interest in medieval northern literature, but his fascination with Antiquity overshadowed it. The rise of 'national romanticism' spurred Schlegel to intensify his study of medieval literature, but this study was on its part overshadowed by his wish to find a historical model for his own political and religious ideas. Barclay even notes that 'scattered remarks and observations of Friedrich Schlegel' bear witness to 'a developing linkage between medievalism and nationalism before 1806'.[76] As we have seen, the earliest 'scattered remarks and observations' are in fact primarily poetological in nature.

---

73 Salomon, 64 (see footnote 52).
74 KFSA 3, 225.
75 David E. Barclay, 'Medievalism and Nationalism in Nineteenth-Century Germany', *Studies in Medievalism* 5 (1993), 5–22, quotation on p. 7.
76 Both quotations can be found in Barclay, 8 (see footnote 75).

Kang-Po Chen
(University of Edinburgh)

'Sick within the rose's just domain': the 'Material Sublime' and Pathological Poetics in Keats's *Isabella; or, the Pot of Basil*

Abstract

This essay examines Keats's unique pathological poetics in *Isabella*. It argues that the destructiveness of the love between Isabella and Lorenzo is not only brought forth by her brothers' violent interference but is already present in their relationship. Apart from the conflict between innocent love and cruel reality, Keats accentuates the innate danger of erotic love, whose power does not lie in the fulfilment of desire and its liberation from moral restraints and class barriers, but in the unhealthy and self-destructive aspects of the human body and psyche. Keats presents this unique phenomenon through a form of pathological poetics, which, at the end of the poem, actualises his concept of the 'material sublime' as pertaining to human suffering, especially in a somatic sense. Such a representation of erotic love corresponds to Keats's understanding of poetic creation. In *Isabella*, both erotic love and poetic creation are Keatsian experiences of self-annihilation.

Keywords
John Keats, *Isabella*, The material sublime, Eroticism, Self-annihilation

In 'Sleep and Poetry', the concluding poem of his 1817 collection *Poems*, Keats announces his farewell to the sensual delights of 'the breath / Of flowering bays, that I may die a death / Of luxury' and 'The o'erwhelming sweets, 'twill bring to me the fair / Visions of all places:' (ll. 57–59).[1] In his subsequent career, he is determined to 'pass them for a nobler life, / Where I may find the agonies, the strife / Of human hearts' (ll. 123-124). This announcement leads to Keats's 1820 volume *Lamia, Isabella, The Eve of St. Agnes, and Other Poems*, which explores the darker aspects of erotic love. As Jeffrey N. Cox comments, in the three narrative poems highlighted in the volume's title, despite their forms as romances, Keats 'created a kind of anti-romance capable of confronting the sor-

---

[1] All Keats's poetic texts are quoted from *The Poems of John Keats*, ed. Jack Stillinger (London: Heinemann Educational, 1978), except the 'Epistle to John Hamilton Reynolds', which is quoted from *The Letters of John Keats, 1814–1821*, ed. Hyder Edward Rollins, 2 vols. (Cambridge, MA: Harvard University Press, 1958), hereafter cited in the text as *Letters*.

rows of life beyond the wish-fulfilling enchantments offered by conventional romance'.[2] As one of the 'anti-romances', *Isabella; or, the Pot of Basil* is Keats's versified retelling of the fifth story of the fourth night from Boccaccio's *Decameron*, possibly inspired by William Hazlitt's lecture 'On Dryden and Pope' on 3 February 1818.[3] Following Boccaccio's story, Keats continues the theme of innocent love between two youths being ruined by capitalist calculation, which, along with an undertone of class struggle, forms the basis of mainstream critical discussion of the poem. Louise Z. Smith observes in the poem that 'the hearteasing love of Isabella and Lorenzo contends with the jostling world' and 'impassioned sensibility must yield to the damnation of the real world's fierce destruction'.[4] Evan Radcliffe also perceives that 'Isabella in particular lingers over the problems resulting from the entrance of harsh reality into the lives of "ideal" lovers'.[5] Diane Long Hoeveler deems the tragedy of Isabella and Lorenzo the embodiment of 'Keats's worst fears about his class origin … and his own anxieties about his identity and future as a poet'.[6] Jack Stillinger considers the plot of *Isabella* a degenerating process from romance to realism.[7] Michael LaGory regards the poems as Keats's 'awareness of the insufficiency of naïve sentiment'.[8] In addition, Cox reads it as Keats's attempt 'to explore the privatization of love in a world dominated by the money-getting private enterprise of Isabella's brothers'.[9] He later reaffirms that *Isabella* is about 'the "iron chains" that men with "hearts of stone" impose on those who dream of something beyond the commercial world'.[10] Nicholas Roe also suggests that in the poem, 'An obvious "reality" would be to recognize how the brothers' greedy, bourgeois principles are destructive of romance'.[11] Most recently, R. S. White approaches the poem from a Freudian perspective, analysing Isabella's 'loss, grief, mourning, and melan-

---

2 *Keats's Poetry and Prose*, ed. Jeffery N. Cox (New York: W. W. Norton & Company, 2009), 410.
3 See Cox's introduction to *Isabella* in *Poetry and Prose*, 429.
4 Louise Z. Smith, 'The Material Sublime: Keats and *Isabella*', *Studies in Romanticism* 13.4 (1974): 311, doi: 10.2307/25599944.
5 Evan Radcliffe, 'Keats, Ideals, and *Isabella*', *Modern Language Quarterly* 17.3 (1986): 261, doi: 10.1215/00267929-47-3-253.
6 Diana Long Hoeveler, 'Decapitating Romance: Class, Fetish, and Ideology in Keats's *Isabella*', *Nineteenth-Century Literature* 49.3 (1994), 322, doi: 10.1525/ncl.1994.49.3.99p00 93s.
7 See Jack Stillinger, 'Keats and Romance', *SEL* 8.4 (1968): 603–4, doi: 10.2307/449467.
8 Michael LaGory, 'Wormy Circumstance: Symbolism in Keats's *Isabella*', in *Studies in Romanticism* 34.3 (1995), 322, doi: 10.2307/25601124.
9 *Poetry and Prose*, 430.
10 Cox, 'John Keats, Medicine, and the Young Men on the Make', in *John Keats and the Medical Imagination*, ed. Nicholas Roe (London: Palgrave Macmillan, 2017), 121.
11 Nicholas Roe, *John Keats: A New Life* (London: Yale University Press, 2012), 226–227.

cholia' after Lorenzo's murder by the brothers.[12] It is observable that there is a dualism – between Isabella/Lorenzo and her brothers, love and commerce, naivety and calculation, passion and reality – in major criticism of this poem.[13]

From an alternative perspective, this essay examines Keats's unique pathological poetics in the poem and demonstrates how it embodies his concept of the 'material sublime'. In a departure from the aforementioned dualism, I propose that the destructiveness of the love between Isabella and Lorenzo is not only brought forth by her brothers' violent interference but is already present in their relationship. In other words, apart from the conflict between 'the heart-easing things' and 'the jostling world', Keats also accentuates the innate danger of the erotic love between Isabella and Lorenzo. In *Isabella*, the power of erotic love does not lie in the fulfilment of desire and its liberation from moral restraints and class barriers, nor does it reinforce human subjectivity and individuality. In contrast, it manifests its highest potency in the violent, unhealthy, abnormal, and self-destructive aspects of the human body and psyche. Keats presents this unique phenomenon through a form of pathological poetics. To better illustrate this unique poetics, I will first examine Keats's verse letter to John Hamilton Reynolds on 25 March 1818, which presents the idea of the 'material sublime', a term equally significant concerning Keats's poetic creation, but not receiving as much critical attention as 'Negative Capability'. In addition to preceding interpretations by scholars such as Stillinger, Stuart, Sperry, and Smith, I locate the 'material sublime' in the nineteenth-century medical context, in which case the word 'material' denotes a sense of corporeal pathology. The 'material sublime', therefore, also represents a form of aesthetics empowered by human suffering, especially in a somatic sense. The pathological poetics of erotic love in *Isabella* embodies the concept of the 'material sublime' and the dangerous aesthetics it represents. Isabella's final creation of the pot of basil that contains Lorenzo's head, as this essay concludes, actualises the 'material sublime' by indicating that both erotic love and poetic creation are Keatsian experiences of self-annihilation.

---

12 R. S. White, 'Keats, Mourning, and Melancholia', in *John Keats and the Medical Imagination*, ed. Nicholas Roe (London: Palgrave Macmillan, 2017), 139.
13 In another more recent study *Keats, Modesty, and Masturbation* (Surrey: Ashgate, 2014), Rachel Schulkins also discerns this dualism in existing criticism of *Isabella*. Her argument focuses more on the excessive desire and 'private fantasies of self-fulfilment' in Isabella's 'female masturbation' (p. 73), which will be discussed in later in this article.

The 'Material Sublime' in the 'Epistle' to John Hamilton Reynolds

The 'Epistle' to John Hamilton Reynolds, originally aiming to entertain the ill Reynolds, reveals Keats's concerns for artistic creation and the unique mental state it entails while encountering the 'material sublime'. Keats opens the poem with his half-slumberous experience, a 'disjoined' mental state that synthesises pain and pleasure. This state is reminiscent of his oversleeping indolence described in another letter to George, which is 'a rare instance of advantage in the body overpowering the Mind' (*Letters*, II, 79) pointing to the somatic emphasis in the term 'material sublime'.[14] In this trance-like vision, what emerge are illogical and unreasonable images: the grotesque fusion of 'Witch's eyes' and 'Cherub's mouth', the indecorous 'Voltaire with casque and shield and habergeon, / And Alexander with his nightcap on', and the anachronistic Socrates with 'his cravat' (*Letters*, I, 259). All these images convey the idea of breaching conventional relationships of association and identification. The second stanza presents a pagan sacrificial ritual of 'Some Titian colours' that predates Stanza 4 of the later 'Ode on a Grecian Urn'.[15] From classicism to medievalism, Keats, in the next stanza refers to another painting of Claude Lorrain, *The Enchanted Castle*, which is 'upon a rock, on the border of a Lake, / Nested in trees' (*Letters*, I, 260). The 'old magic-like Urganda's Sword' and the 'Merlin's Hall' evoke medieval romance and fantasy, engendering an unrealistic atmosphere much detached from the present and physical world where Keats and Reynolds dwell.

Both the classic and medieval scenes develop into the central idea of the 'material sublime' in the eighth stanza: 'O that our dreamings all, of sleep or wake, / Would all their colours from the sunset take: / From something of material sublime' (*Letters*, I, 261). By reading it as 'sublime (adjective) material (noun)', Stillinger gives the phrase a rather simple meaning: something 'elevated, uplifted from the world' and 'unearthly, like the fantastic dreams'.[16] Sperry interprets the phrase as 'the desire of the imagination to possess at once the best of both worlds, the ethereal and the concrete'.[17] Smith proposes that the 'material sublime' is both 'noun-adjective and as adjective-noun', arising from the external world rather than subjective feeling. She further argues that for Keats, dreaming 'is not an escape from the jostling world, but an intense perception of beauty and

---

14 This letter is also the pretext of 'Ode on Indolence'; both describe Keats's vision in languor of the three figures – Love, Ambition, and Poetry – on a Greek vase.
15 As Stuart Sperry and several other critics have noted, there is no such a painting by Titian that portrays this scene of sacrifice, and Keats probably was thinking of Claude Lorrain's *Sacrifice to Apollo*. See Sperry, 'The Epistle to John Hamilton Reynolds' in *Keats's Poetry and Prose*, 585.
16 Stillinger, 'Keats and Romance', 596.
17 Sperry, 'The Epistle', 589.

truth in that world'.[18] While both Sperry and Smith believe that through the 'material sublime' Keats is promoting an aesthetic ideal that counters the Platonic dichotomy of metaphysical ideas and physical matters, Betsy Winakur Tontiplaphol more recently stresses Keats's wish for 'sensory surfeit, not the grand immateriality' in *Romanticism and Pleasure*.[19]

Aside from the above interpretations, the meaning of 'material' can be situated in early modern medical contexts, defined by Samuel Johnson's *A Dictionary of the English Language* as 'corporeal', and by the *Oxford English Dictionary* as 'of a disease'. The correlation between Keats's medical background and his poetic creation has been addressed extensively in Keats studies, from Hermione de Almeida's 1991 monograph *Romantic Medicine and John Keats* to the 2017 essay collection *John Keats and the Medical Imagination* edited by Nicholas Roe. In these studies, though Keats's medical background and his life – oft-impacted by disease and death – are traced to offer new insights into his poetic works, the possible medical meaning of the 'material sublime' is not considered. Almeida does discuss the 'Epistle', arguing that the verse-letter represents 'the poet's attempt to use his imagination to soothe and comfort a sick friend and to counteract actual disease with images of health', but she pays no attention to the 'material sublime'.[20]

W. P. Albrecht notes that Keats's usage of the word 'sublime' reflects 'a state of mind remote from ordinary perception dulled, as it is, by self-centeredness, materialism, and the confusion of daily cares', adding that 'Keats does not separate the sublime from the beautiful except as "sublime" may mean the intensity of emotion necessary to beauty'.[21] However, in Keats's letters, the sublime also emerges alongside his heightened worries for Tom's illness, such as the 'sublime Misery' in the one to Benjamin Bailey in October 1818 (*Letters*, I, 173). During his stay in Dumfries, visiting Robert Burns's Cottage and Tomb, Keats encountered a vulgar man, 'a curious Bitch', 'a flat old dog', whose indecorous manner, in Keats's view, disgraced the solemn air of Burns's heritage and 'hindered my sublimity' (*Letters*, I, 324). Such 'sublimity' that Keats strongly perceived in the Cottage was engendered by the Scottish bard's suffering, as he laments that 'His Misery is a dead weight upon the nimbleness of one's quill', and, alluding to King Lear in prison, 'he was miserable – We can see horribly clear in

---

18 Smith, 'Material Sublime', 303.
19 Betsy Winakur Tontiplaphol, 'Pleasure in the Age of Talkers: Keats's Material Sublime', in *Romanticism and Pleasure*, ed. Thomas H. Schmid and Michelle Faubert (New York: Palgrave Macmillan, 2010), 46.
20 Hermione de Almeida, *Romantic Medicine and John Keats* (Oxford: Oxford University Press, 1991), 43.
21 W. P. Albrecht, 'The Tragic Sublime of Hazlitt and Keats', *Studies in Romanticism* 20.2 (1981): 196, doi: 10.2307/25600295.

the works of such a man his whole life, as if we were God's spies' (*Letters*, I, 325). That is, despite Keats's assertion that the sublime is an essential component of the 'eternal Being' of beauty, it intrinsically co-exists with human suffering, both physical and mental, signifying 'the power of otherness to bring desolation'.[22] Combining the word 'material', which indicates unhealthy corporeality in the medical context of Keats's time, the Keatsian 'material sublime' thus denotes a form of aesthetics that is empowered by the human body, particularly the abnormal and pathological body afflicted by disease or violence, such as Reynolds's current sick body and those victimised by 'an eternal fierce destruction', reified by Keats's description of 'The Shark at savage prey, the Hawk at pounce, – / The gentle Robin, like a Pard or Ounce, / Ravening a worm' (*Letters*, I, 262).

This interpretation of the 'material sublime' brings forth the crucial role of human suffering in Keats's idea of poetic creation. Following the 'material sublime', Keats discerns that 'For in the world / We jostle', a pessimistic line that echoes his reflection on *King Lear* about 'the fierce dispute / Betwixt damnation and impassion'd clay'. In the 'Epistle', Keats underscores the inability of knowledge and reason to redeem human beings from the destined suffering; he dares not 'philosophize' and he will never be awarded 'the prize of High reason' (*Letters*, I, 262). In the line 'Things cannot to the will / Be settled, but they tease us out of thought', the idea of 'Negative Capability' as 'uncertainties, Mysteries, doubts' (*Letters*, I, 193) re-emerges and Keats recapitulates the decentralisation of knowledge and the subversion of epistemological order. The 'Things' not only include objects and scenarios in the exterior world – natural grandeurs in the Burkean sublime – but also human feelings responsive to the exterior world and to human interactions, benign or malignant. The 'material sublime' complicates the nature of this verse letter, originally meant to entertain the sick Reynolds, with the transition from the fantastic and pleasant references and depictions of Lorrain's neoclassic art to a pessimistic evaluation of human subjectivity and selfhood that are based on knowledge and its will to truth. This pessimism over the deposition of epistemological order corresponds to the grotesque, indecorous, and anachronistic chains of association (or anti-association) in the first stanza.

While he recognises that scientific knowledge and philosophical reasoning cannot settle the negativity in the material world, 'Where but to think is to be full of sorrow', as he laments in 'Ode to a Nightingale' (l. 27), Keats does not deem poetry an ideal substitute for knowledge and reason to emancipate human beings from suffering. Conversely, poetic imagination is 'yet still confin'd, / Lost in a sort of Purgatory blind' (*Letters*, I, 262). In other words, the 'Epistle' indicates that

---

22 Stuart A. Ende, *Keats and the Sublime* (New Haven: Yale University Press, 1976), 90. Ende also contends that Keats believes in the positive aspect in the sublime, 'a capacity to humanize loss with love'.

poetry is not an instrument that can restore human subjectivity and re-establish a new epistemological order. A poet deepens the loss of human subjectivity through versification and offers an alternative perspective to survey suffering in the human world, instead of absolving them. As Tim Milnes insightfully observes, for Keats, when 'reason lurches into scepticism, and thence into alienation and indifference, the consolation of the aesthetic is increasingly imbued with power of alterity'.[23] But at the end of the 'Epistle' and later in *Isabella*, there seems to be no consolation at all, as Keats has moved away from his earlier optimism about poetry and love in, for example, *Endymion*, which possess the power to break the 'prison, / Of flesh and bone' that 'curbs, and confines, and frets / Our spirit's wing', and withstand the 'despondency' that 'besets / Our pillows', and redeem 'our dull, uninspired, snail-paced lives' (Book IV, ll. 20–23, 25).[24] Rather than providing comfort and hope as positive drives for human beings to sustain subjectivity in their agonising existence, *Isabella* generates a sort of negative pleasure by eroticising human suffering. The poem reveals Keats's understanding of poetic creation, not only as a state of anti-knowledge and anti-truth, 'uncertainties, Mysteries, and doubts', but it is also a process that is anti-living, unhealthy, pathological, self-corroding and self-destructive. That is, while writing poetic works such as *Isabella*, Keats is neither a man, nor a poet, as he postulates in the letter to Richard Woodhouse on 27 October 1818: 'As to the poetical Character itself ... it is not itself – it has no self' and 'A Poet is the most unpoetical of any thing in existence; because he has no Identity' (*Letters*, I, 386–387). Furthermore, Keats detaches his poetry from himself as a poet: 'not one word I ever utter can be taken for granted as an opinion growing out of my identical nature – how can it, when I have no nature?' (*Letters*, I, 387). Here we have a 'Keats's paradox'. Keats is the most poetical because he fulfils, to the greatest extent, the condition of self-annihilation; in other words, Keats is the most *poetical* because he is the most *unpoetical*.

While he acknowledges the unique state of writing poetry as anti-epistemological and self-annihilating, Keats as a poet still aspires to have positive contributions to the world, 'ambitious of doing the world some good' (*Letters*, I, 387). He is conscious of this destined contradiction between a poet's will to social contribution and his poetic creation that tends to overthrow such a will, as he deems himself 'the camelion Poet', who delights in 'conceiving an Iago as an Imogen', a sort of amoral, 'beyond good and evil' aesthetics that 'shocks the

---

23 Tim Milnes, 'The Truth about Romanticism: Pragmatism and Idealism' in *Keats, Shelley, Coleridge* (Cambridge: Cambridge University Press, 2010), 68.
24 Later in *The Fall of Hyperion*, Keats re-aspires to the redemptive quality of poetry, or what Hugh Roberts terms 'therapeutic drive' in English Romanticism, by declaring that 'sure a poet is a sage; / A humanist, physician to all men' who 'pours out a balm upon the world' (Canto I, ll. 189–190, 201).

virtuous philosopher' (*Letters*, I, 387). At the end of this crucial letter to Woodhouse, after confessing that what he has been saying about 'the poetical Character' is perhaps not 'from myself; but from some character in whose soul I now live' (*Letters*, I, 388), Keats assures his friend that his affections and regards for him are 'from myself'. In other words, Keats is unable to recognise his friendship with Woodhouse when he is in the mode of writing poetry. Once again, Keats intimates that 'the poetical Character' and the state of poetic creation are anti-social phenomena of self-annihilation and oblivion of all positive social connections. Based on the above formulation of 'material sublime' and Keats's idea of poetic creation, the following discussion will focus on the pathological poetics in *Isabella*, which, as I have proposed, epitomises Keats's concept of the 'material sublime' as a form of negative aesthetics empowered by human suffering, especially in a somatic sense. Furthermore, Isabella's creation of the 'Pot of Basil' that contains Lorenzo's severed head is the actualisation of Keats's poetic creation that borders on anti-social and self-annihilating oblivion, which also corresponds to the poet's oblivion of his social connection with his friend at the end of the letter to Woodhouse.

Pathological Poetics in *Isabella*

Keats's pathological poetics emerges in the very beginning of *Isabella*, which is better highlighted if juxtaposed with his source from *Decameron.* In Boccaccio's story, the initial relationship between Isabella and Lorenzo is simple and filled with sheer happiness:

> This Lorenzo being of comely personage, affable, and excellent in his behaviour, grew so gracious in the eyes of Isabella, that she affoorded him many very respective looks, yea, kindness of no common quality. Which Lorenzo taking notice of, and observing by degrees from time to time, gave over all other beauties in the City, which might allure any affection from him, and onely fixed his heart on her, so that their love grew to a mutuall embracing, both equally respecting one another, and entertaining kindnesses, as occasion gave leave.[25]

In this passage, from falling in love with each other to potential sexual contact, the couple does not encounter any obstruction. Their interaction is based on mutual affection, not very different from what Richard Sha calls 'idealized as a form of

---

25 Giovanni Boccaccio, *Decameron*, trans. John Florio (London: Isaac Iaggard, 1620), 159. The English translation of *Decameron* here is John Florio's 1620 version, the first English translation, whose 1680 edition was read by Keats in his time. See Cox's introduction in *Poetry and Prose*, 430.

consent and of liberation' in English romanticism.[26] In the first stanza of *Isabella*, however, we see a more complicated representation of this romantic relationship:

> FAIR Isabel, poor simple Isabel!
> Lorenzo, a young palmer in Love's eye!
> They could not in the self-same mansion dwell
> Without some stir of heart, some malady;
> They could not sit at meals but feel how well
> It soothed each to be the other by;
> They could not, sure, beneath the same roof sleep
> But to each other dream, and nightly weep. (ll. 1–8)

Different vastly from Boccaccio's positive and swift progression of love, Keats transforms love to a long process of lingering struggles. The word 'malady' establishes the idea of love as pathological and anti-living, echoing with the phrases of 'sick longing', 'sad plight', cheeks paler', 'sick' and 'Fever'd' in later stanzas. Here Keats inherits the theme of love as 'rig'rous torment' and the idea that 'Lovers should nobly suffer pain' in Petrarchan tradition, in which the language of love is replete with unfulfilled desire and the mental and bodily suffering it entails.[27] Critics have noted Petrarch's influence on Keats, in terms of both poetic forms and thematic ideas.[28] Petrarchan love, though starting from the poet's agonised longing for Laura's affection, will finally attain consolation by incorporating itself into religious devotion. This is illustrated in *I Trionfi*, which, as A. J. Smith observes, shows a progress from 'the miserable frailty and inevitable disillusionment of sexual love to eternal bliss', because for Petrarch, only 'love of God gives them a secure expectation of enduring beauty, lasting love and bliss'.[29] In *Isabella*, Keats adopts Petrarchan language of love as 'sweet burden, and sweet ill'.[30] However, he also exacerbates the physical illness, which does not lead to spiritual consolation at the end of the poem. Furthermore, unlike Petrarchan lovesickness, which is caused by Laura's unresponsiveness and lack of reciprocity, Keatsian pathology in *Isabella* retains its potency even in the couple's mutual affection. It then reminds us of Keats's avid reading of Robert Burton's

---

26 Richard Sha, *Perverse Romanticism: Aesthetics and Sexuality in Britain, 1750–1832* (Baltimore: Johns Hopkins University Press, 2005), 2. Sha's study evokes the contemporary scientific discourses, highlighting their influence on the Romantics, who, with such an influence, present sexuality as aesthetic representations of mutual love and liberation free from the purpose of reproduction.
27 Francesco Petrarch, *Petrarch Translated; in A Selection of His Sonnets, and Odes*, trans. John Nott (London: J. Miller, 1808), 12, 49.
28 See Mary Anne Myers, 'Keats and the Hands of Petrarch and Laura', *Keats-Shelley-Journal* 62 (2013): 100–101.
29 A. J. Smith, *The Metaphysics of Love: Studies, in Renaissance Love Poetry from Dante to Milton* (Cambridge: Cambridge University Press, 1985), 150.
30 Petrarch, *Petrarch Translated*, 125.

The Anatomy of Melancholy, which describes the bodily symptoms of love-melancholy: 'paleness, leanness, dryness' and 'the body bloodless and pale, a lean body, hollow eyes'.[31] In his letter to George and Georgiana in September 1819, Keats cites an entire passage about the blindness of love in Partition 3 'Love-Melancholy' of the *Anatomy* (*Letters*, II, 191). In the same section, Burton postulates that 'the symptoms of the mind in lovers are almost infinite, and so diverse that no art can comprehend them' and 'love is a plague, a torture, an hell'.[32] In this first stanza, Keats reiterates such incomprehensibility and pathology of love in the *Anatomy* not only by employing the word 'malady', but also by repeating the negative expression of 'could not' three times, which generates a sense of uncertainty, the oscillation between truth and untruth, indicating the malignant and oppressive nature of love that is not only beyond the control of human subjectivity, but also threatens it. Such indeterminacy of love has vicious effects on the couple's daily life: they 'could not ... dwell', 'could not sit at meal', and 'could not ... sleep'. The negative phrases of 'could not' insinuate the idea that love endangers and deactivates human functions of basic biological needs: habitation, food, and sleep. Moreover, the negative undertone of love invades the sphere of labours, which construct and fortify social identities. Thus, because 'their love grew tenderer', Lorenzo abandons his position in 'house, field, or garden', and Isabella 'spoilt her half-done broidery' (ll. 9–16). This depiction suggests that erotic love is the opposite of the secular order of working, which aims to boost production, accumulate resources, and sustain living. The opposition also resounds with Burton's proposition of 'labour, slender and sparing diet, with continual business' as the cure for love-melancholy, as 'love retires before business; be busy and you will be safe'.[33]

To aggravate this dangerous nature of erotic love, Keats transforms the prompt sexual union in Boccaccio to a trial of self-doubt and self-affliction before the consummation. Their nameless fear of sex is not caused by a sense of shame imposed by religious or social conventions, as in the cases of other romantic espousals of sexual passion, but is engendered by a prescience of destruction, as Lorenzo perceives in Stanza 8: 'Believe how I love thee, believe how near / My soul is to its doom' (ll. 60–61). Their hesitation is interwoven by confirmations and doubts; Lorenzo's affirmation of 'will I' in his two lines 'To-morrow will I bow to my delight, / To-morrow will I ask my lady's boon' is intercepted by Isabella's anxiety expressed by the doubtful 'may' and 'if' in her following lines: 'O may I never see another night, / Lorenzo, if thy lips breathe not love's tune' (ll. 27–30). The fluc-

---

31 Robert Burton, *The Anatomy of Melancholy*, vol. 3, ed. Holbrook Jackson (London: The Folio Society, 2005), 146.
32 Ibid., 155.
33 Ibid., 211–212. Burton is citing Avicenna's line in Latin: *Cedit amor rebus; res age, tutus eris*.

Fig. 1: John Everett Millais, Isabella, 1849. Walker Art Gallery.

tuation between restraint and fulfilment of erotic love once again triggers pathological symptoms, as Isabella 'Fell sick within the rose's just domain, / Fell thin as a young mother's, who doth seek / By every lull to cool her infant's pain' (ll. 34–35). The image of a young mother worried about her child seems a bizarre simile for Isabella's sickness, which is caused by her ungratified desire for sexual contact with Lorenzo. Keats will again cast Isabella as a mother figure in the digging scene from Stanza 44 to 48 as a symbolic process of childbirth. Keats seems to suggest a problematic relationship between eroticism and reproduction that for women, sexual enjoyment is usually repressed and hindered by the social obligations of propagation and maternal cares.

The scene of the couple's consummation started in Stanza 7, under the cover of innocent love, is in fact imbued with latent violence and suggestive coercion. The consummation is supposed to be a manifestation of mutual affection and equality, but Lorenzo's speech dominates the entire pre-conjugal conversation. Keats's revision of this stanza intensifies this power relationship in terms of speech. The two original lines that conclude Stanza 7 present Isabella's utterance of active will for this sexual union in a complete sentence: 'Lorenzo I would clip my ringlet hair / To make thee laugh again & debonair – '.[34] In the final version, however, Keats replaces them with another two lines: 'Lorenzo! – here she

---

[34] The Poems of John Keats, 247.

ceas'd her timid quest, / But in her tone and look he read the rest' (ll. 55-56). Isabella's complete sentence is reduced to a single word 'Lorenzo', as she 'lisped tenderly' and 'ceas'd her timid quest' (ll. 54-56). The very word 'lisped' signifies Isabella's aphasic status, her loss of lingual ability, in the ensuing sexual interaction. Keats's revision deprives Isabella of her active voice and action; she becomes an object of Lorenzo's masculine gaze, subject to his power of arbitrary interpretation – 'in her tone and look he read the rest'. In her study of rape culture in eighteenth- and nineteenth-century England, Anna Clark points out that the fashionable libertinism in that time made male violators 'confident of their sexual prowess that they ignored women's resistance, portraying their victims' protests as coy acquiescence'.[35] The assumption that Lorenzo is attempting to rape a reluctant Isabella might appear thin, but Keats's manoeuvre here actually foreshadows Porphyro's sexual advance upon the sleeping Madeline in the later *The Eve of St. Agnes*. Keats's revision of Stanza 7 silences Isabella, who becomes a passive object of Lorenzo's active 'reading' and generates considerable ambiguity in the nature of this, seemingly romantic, sexual union (the same ambiguity in the erotic interaction between Porphyro and Madeline in *The Eve of St. Agnes*). In the following two stanzas, Lorenzo's speech dominates Isabella's muteness. Although Lorenzo asserts his respect of Isabella's will by saying 'I would not grieve / Thy hand by unwelcoming pressing' (ll. 61-62), his later lines – 'And *I must* taste the blossoms that unfold / In its ripe warmth this gracious morning time' (ll. 67-68, emphasis added) – demonstrates his relentless will to sexually consume Isabella, with a typical floral metaphor in the libertine tradition. All these potentially negative undertones of erotic love are entirely unrelated to Isabella's brothers, the supposed patriarchal antagonists, but are inherent between the protagonists.

Keats's depiction of the actual sexual intercourse is in the final four lines of Stanza 9, with only two lines describing the bodily actions:

> So said, his erewhile timid lips grew bold,
> And poesied with hers in dewy rhyme:
> Great bliss was with them, and great happiness
> Grew, like a lusty flower in June's caress. (ll. 69-72)

Keats restrains his narration by reducing the intercourse to a mere gesture of kiss, leaving what is left for the reader's imagination. The last two lines of this stanza about the couple's 'Great bliss' and 'great happiness' seem to redirect the previous course of amorous struggles to its supposed romance end of fulfilment, but this does not annul the ambiguity and the violent undercurrents in the erotic

---

35 Anna Clark, *Women's Silence, Men's Violence: Sexual Assaults in England, 1770-1845* (London: Pandora, 1987), 36.

relationship between Isabella and Lorenzo. The most significant part in this passage is the verb 'poesied', which means 'to produce poetry', according the *Oxford English Dictionary*, with this usage of Keats as the only example. His unique coinage of this verb as an equivalent of kissing reflects again his idea of the 'material sublime', which emphasises the crucial status of the body in artistic creation. The word 'poesied', therefore, also represents his equation of poetic creation and eroticism.

The ominous Stanza 12 and Stanza 13 pave the way for the upcoming tragedy brought forth by Isabella's two brothers. Keats raises a question about the couple's happiness: 'Were they unhappy then?' followed by an immediate answer ' – It cannot be – ' with a strong sense of doubt with those two dashes. The reason that Isabella and Lorenzo must be happy is because:

> Too many tears for lovers have been shed,
> Too many sighs give we to them in fee,
> Too much of pity after they are dead,
> Too many doleful stories do we see (ll. 90–93)

In these lines, Keats alludes bitterly to the sensational effects of romance tradition. Readers of romance, alongside the protagonists with whom they identify, suffer all these 'Too many' and 'Too much' in exchange for the final happy conclusion of romance. All the excessive 'tears', 'sighs', 'pity' and 'doleful stories' are the price to pay for the final wish-fulfilment. The more intense the suffering, the sweeter the outcome will be. In *Isabella*, however, Keats aims to counter this tradition and to break the economy of emotional exchange that it represents, in order to 'find the agonies, the strife / Of human hearts', as he declares in 'Sleep and Poetry'. In Keats's 'alternative romance', pain is not the price for, or foil of pleasure, but itself the very source of negative pleasure, as he affirms the 'truth' in Stanza 13 that 'Even bees, the little almsmen of spring-bowers, / Know there is richest juice in poison-flowers' (ll. 103–104), indicating the sadomasochist pleasure generated and intensified by bodily and mental suffering.

Boccaccio opens the story with 'In Messina there dwelt three young men, Brethren, and Merchants by their common profession, who becoming very rich by the death of their Father, lived in very good fame and repute'.[36] But not until Stanza 14 does Keats introduce Isabella's two brothers and their wealth and enterprise. This arrangement suggests that though the brothers' intervention physically separates Isabella and Lorenzo and intensifies the former's deterioration, the pre-existing pathology within the couple's romantic relationship is equally significant. Keats's depiction of the two brothers from Stanza 14 to Stanza 17 inspires George Bernard Shaw's famous remark: 'If Karl Marx can be

---

36 Boccaccio, *Decameron*, 160.

imagined as writing a poem instead of a treatise on Capital, he would have written *Isabella*.[37] Susan J. Wolfson regards these 'capitalist stanzas' as Keats's deliberate digression, through which 'literary and commercial riches, literary taste and commercial venture, wind up on the same axis of imagery'.[38] Kurt Heinzelman stresses Keats's innovation in these stanzas, as the 'institutionalized capitalism described in *Isabella* is foreign to Boccaccio's Italy'.[39] Keats's modification of the number of Isabella's brothers from three to two is also noted, as LaGory argues that it intensifies 'the contrast between brothers and lovers' and the former are of a 'barren relationship' that 'brings forth only money'.[40] However, despite the apparent dichotomy between sophisticated and ruthless commercialism and naïve sentiment/innocent love, Keats eroticises the brothers' reaction to the relationship between Isabella and Lorenzo:

> How was it these same ledger-men could spy
> Fair Isabella in her downy nest?
> How could they find out in Lorenzo's eye
> A straying from his toil? (ll. 137–140)

Deviating from Boccaccio's story, in which the eldest brother accidentally sees Isabella sneaking to Lorenzo's place, Keats subtly replaces this crucial and concrete incident with ambiguous speculations. The disclosure of the amorous affair does not, as in Boccaccio, result from Isabella's coincidental recklessness, but is the necessary outcome of the brothers' habitual voyeurism on their sister, and with a homoerotic hint, on Lorenzo. After two stanzas of digression apologising to Boccaccio, Keats resumes his narrative of the brothers' action. They confide to each other their 'bitter thoughts' that are 'well nigh mad' over the fact that Lorenzo 'Should in their sister's love be blithe and glad' (ll. 164–166). Indeed, Keats makes it clear that the brothers' 'bitter thought' originates from their 'plan to coax her by degrees / To some high noble and his olive-trees' (ll. 167–168). However, in the next stanza, he suggests that in addition to the pragmatic reason of seeing Isabella as a commodity to propel their economic exchanges, the brothers' frustration and anger result from their erotic attachment to both Isabella and Lorenzo, as 'many a *jealous* conference had they' (l. 169, emphasis added). With the brothers' voyeurism and jealousy, fixing upon both Isabella and Lor-

---

[37] George Bernard Shaw, 'Keats' in *The John Keats Memorial Volume*, ed. George Charles Williamson (New York: John Lane, 1921), 175.
[38] Susan J. Wolfson, 'Feminizing Keats', in *Critical Essays on John Keats*, ed. Hermione de Almeida (Boston: G. K. Hill, 1990), 257.
[39] Kurt Heinzelman, 'Self-Interest and the Politics of Composition in *Isabella*', *ELH* 55.1 (1988): 162, doi: 10.2307/2873115.
[40] LaGory, 'Wormy Circumstance', 325.

enzo, Keats perplexes their murderous motive and subtly undermines the erotic love/capitalist calculation dualism assumed by many critics.

Keats's pathological poetics of eroticism continues in the murder scene. As they walk deep into the forest, 'Sick and wan / The brothers' faces in the ford did seem' (ll. 213–214). The brothers' 'Sick and wan' complexions resound with the 'sick longing' and 'cheeks paler' of Isabella and Lorenzo in the prime of their love. After they slay Lorenzo, the brothers 'dipp'd their swords in the water' and ride homeward 'with convulsed spur' (ll. 222–223). The image of phallic swords penetrating the soft and receptive water is an obvious metaphorical picture of sexual violence, and the ecstatic state of 'convulsed spur' overlaps sexual pleasure with murder and death. Keats's eroticisation of the murder scene, extended from the simple description in Boccaccio's story, corresponds to the brothers' ambiguous complex for Isabella and Lorenzo, which is engendered by Keats's deliberate designs of voyeurism and jealousy.[41] Again, we can observe that Keats connects erotic love with sickness, violence, and even death.

Isabella's reaction to the ill news of Lorenzo's disappearance also highlights Keats's deviation from Boccaccio. In Boccaccio's story, Isabella 'fell into abundance of tears, where-among she mingled many sighes and groanes, such as were able to overthrow a farre stronger constitution: so that, being full of feare and dismay'.[42] Keats, however, apart from continuing the pre-existing pathological poetics, presents a double-layered structure of pain and erotic pleasure in Stanza 30:

> She weeps alone for pleasures not to be;
> Sorely she wept until the night came on,
> And then, instead of love, O misery!
> She brooded o'er the luxury alone:
> His image in the dusk she seem'd to see,
> And to the silence made a gentle moan,
> Spreading her perfect arms upon the air,
> And on her couch low murmuring 'Where? O where?' (ll. 233–240)

R. S. White interprets this passage as a typical Freudian pattern of grief and mourning.[43] But I also observe Keats's deliberate indication of autoeroticism. After enduring sheer sorrow for the absent love in the day, in the night Isabella indulges in 'luxury'. Tontiplaphol regards Keats's 'luscious poem' as the embodiment of the nineteenth-century 'poetics of luxury', which focuses on 'tactile

---

41 Boccaccio's account (*Decameron*, 160.) of the murder has only one sentence: 'they ran sodainly upon Lorenzo, slew him, and afterward enterred his body, where hardly it could be discovered by anyone'.
42 Ibid., 160.
43 White, 'Keats, Mourning, and Melancholia', 143.

and oral experiences', 'rich indulgences nourished by the proximity that attends touching and tasting', and 'circumscribed spaces crowded with sensory stimuli'.[44] Stemming from such somatic and sensory connotations, 'luxury' here goes beyond mere extravagant dress, furniture, or food, and denotes lasciviousness and lust, as Rachel Schulkins also agrees that 'luxury' represents 'her dream of sexual consummation with Lorenzo's image'.[45] The association between autoeroticism and Keats can be traced as early as Byron's derogatory comment on his works as 'the Onanism of poetry' and 'a sort of mental masturbation' and Keats himself a 'miserable Self-polluter of the human Mind'.[46] Marjorie Levinson proposes that Byron's remarks suggest 'the subjective vacancy of Keats's writing', the internal emptiness beneath the latter's poetic language of 'finery'.[47] In her discussion of 'La Belle Dame Sans Merci', Levinson further points out that the age's fear of masturbation lies in its 'image of productive self-alienation'.[48] Though she does not take this passage in *Isabella* into consideration, Isabella's autoerotic 'luxury' conforms to Levinson's observation of the poem's sentiment as 'the self-conscious feeling of *having* a feeling: a reflexive address to a fetishized feeling'.[49] It also evokes Marianne Dashwood's painful disorder after being abandoned by John Willoughby in Jane Austen's *Sense and Sensibility*, published a few years before Keats's volume that contains *Isabella*. In Marianne's similar traumatic experience of her love object's absence, Eve Kosofsky Sedgwick discerns her erotic identity as 'the masturbating girl', which is beyond the conventional categorisation of heterosexual and homosexual relationships.[50] This heterogeneous identity of autoeroticism, in her agitation and 'excessive affliction', finds a violent outlet in literary creation, a sort of imaginary interaction with her lost love object: 'writing as fast as a continual flow of tears would permit her...for the last time to Willoughby'.[51] In Stanza 30 of *Isabella*, Keats has the heroine call for the feeling for her love object's absence and picture Lorenzo's image, in order to have an imaginary consummation with it, as she 'made a gentle moan, / Spreading her perfect arms upon the air'. Her autoerotic complex, confirmed by the capitalised 'Selfishness' in the opening line

---

44 Tontiplaphol, *Poetics of Luxury in the Nineteenth Century: Keats, Tennyson, and Hopkins* (Burlington: 2011, Ashgate), 7–8.
45 Schulkins, *Keats, Modesty and Masturbation*, 81.
46 Byron and Thomas Moore, *The Life, Letters and Journals of Lord Byron* (London: J. Murray, 1866), 217, 225.
47 Marjorie Levinson, *Keats's Life of Allegory* (New York: Basil Blackwell, 1988), 16.
48 Ibid., 46.
49 Ibid., 144.
50 Eve Kosofsky Sedgwick, 'Jane Austen and the Masturbating Girl' in *Sense and Sensibility: Norton Critical Edition*, ed. Claudia L. Johnson (New York: W. W. Norton & Company, 2002), 395.
51 Jane Austen, *Sense and Sensibility*, 27.

of the next stanza, is produced by poetic imagination, echoing Marianne's hysterical writing to Willoughby. In this typical Keatsian trance, Isabella undergoes a process of self-disintegration, splits her subject into two to form an image of her lover for the masturbatory 'luxury alone'. Isabella's sorrow in the day, which is a justified emotion that constitutes positive romantic love, contrasts with her obscene pleasure in the night, which is pathological, autoerotic, anti-social, and unnameable.

In Stanza 40, after disclosing the murder, Lorenzo's ghost takes heed of Isabella's decaying outward features, which is another deviation from Boccaccio's account. Surprisingly, her suffering pleases him: 'That paleness warms my grave... thy paleness makes me glad; / Thy beauty grows upon me, and I feel / A greater love through all my essence steal' (ll. 316–320). Lorenzo feels comforted and satisfied to see Isabella pining away because of him. In addition to Keats's remark of 'Selfishness' on Isabella's nightly autoeroticism, here is another manifestation of selfishness. Instead of an ideal depiction of love as self-sacrificing affection for the other, Keats presents a realistic observation of erotic love as selfish that Lorenzo still seeks to possess Isabella's body and mentality even beyond his grave. Daniel P. Watkins notes that in this dream, by learning the cause of Lorenzo's death, Isabella is 'school'd' by the cruelty of human crime, in the way politics controls even the most private human experience.[52] But at the same time, she and the reader is 'school'd' by the complicated reality of erotic love, which is far from the naïve sentiment of mutual affection. Once again, Keats insinuates that although the physical separation and the deprivation of love are caused by the brothers' violent interference, there is innate negativity in such a romantic relationship.

In the digging scene from Stanza 44 to 48, Keats's unique design again deviates from Boccaccio's story. In Florio's translation of Boccaccio's original account, the whole process of digging does not take much time and effort, as 'they digged not farre' and 'found the body of murthered Lorenzo'.[53] However, in Keats's version, it is a long and strenuous trial that lasts for three hours: 'Three hours they labour'd at this travail sore' (l. 382). Watkins interprets Keats's design in Stanza 48 as a representation of 'manual labour under oppressive condition' and 'caricature of the relations of production'.[54] Smith notes that Isabella's 'eager digging' reminds readers of the brothers' greed.[55] Heinzelman sees in Isabella an image of 'a miser prodigiously digging up his hoard'.[56] In addition to these

---

52 Daniel P. Watkins, 'Personal Life and Social Authority in Keats's *Isabella*', *Studies in Romanticism* 13.4 (1974), 40.
53 Boccaccio, *Decameron*, 161.
54 Watkins, 'Personal Life and Social Authority', 41.
55 Smith, 'The Material Sublime', 309.
56 Heinzelman, 'Self-Interest and the Politics of Composition', 165.

readings, the entire digging scene has a symbolic meaning. Keats's modification of 'trusty Nurse' in Florio's translation to 'an aged nurse' evokes an image of midwife, noted by LaGory as the 'descendent of Juliet's Nurse and Spenser's Glause'.[57] The words 'labour' and 'travail' – 'a dismal labouring' and 'Three hours they labour'd at this travail sore'– reinforces this implication. That is, Isabella's excavation of Lorenzo's corpse with the help of a nurse/midwife is a potential process of childbirth. In this sense, Isabella is both love object and mother figure for Lorenzo, predating the Oedipal familial procedure. The eroticism of latent mother-son incest is suggested strongly in Stanza 47, where Isabella kisses the corpse:

> ... with a lip more chill than stone,
> And put it in her bosom, where it dries
> And freezes utterly unto the bone
> Those dainties made to still an infant's cries (ll. 371–374)

Douglas Bush notes that for earlier critics these lines 'embodied all the poignancy of thwarted motherhood', but Keats's 'amatory falsetto of "dainties"' spoils this idea.[58] For C. L. Finney and Amy Lowell, the word 'dainties' is infelicitous, vulgar, and inappropriate in the context of a tragic death.[59] LaGory reads this quasi-breastfeeding scene not only as 'thwarted motherhood' but also 'thwarted sexual love' and the destined failure of 'sexual love unperplexed from marital love and parenthood'.[60] What Keats presents through this scene from Stanza 43 to 48 is how erotic love generates the affinity between life and death, as Hoeveler discerns correctly that the scene 'might have been written by someone who could only imagine birth as a form of death' and how it dissolves the social boundary constructed by incest taboo.[61] Through the metaphorical images of childbirth and breastfeeding, Keats defies the maternal obligation of reproduction, mixing delivery throes with the perverse pleasure of oral eroticism on Isabella's breasts. In Stanza 47, her breasts do not produce milk, the necessary, non-sexual, socially approved subsistence for infants, which are the fruits of reproduction and the guarantee of human existence. As the bodily zone of mutually exclusive maternity and eroticism, the image of Isabella's breasts responds to the social antithesis stemming from the eighteenth-century 'Cult of Domesticity', an ideology that ideal motherhood and successful propagation must exclude any

---

57 LaGory, 'Wormy Circumstance', 329.
58 Douglas Bush, *John Keats: His Life and Writings* (New York: Macmillan, 1966), 78.
59 See Claude L. Finney, *The Evolution of Keats's Poetry* (Cambridge: Harvard University Press, 1936), 377.
60 LaGory, 'Wormy Circumstance', 328.
61 Hoeveler, 'Decapitating Romance', 333.

trace of female sexual desire.[62] Isabella's milk-less 'dainties' thus subvert this ideal, and signify the idea of unnecessary, anti-living, pathological, and excessive consumption of erotic love, so intimate to 'the horrid thing' and approximating to the experience of death.

In Stanza 49, Keats digresses to a personal reflection on the disparity between 'this wormy circumstance' of Isabella with 'the gentleness of old Romance, / the simple plaining of a minstrel's song!' (ll. 387–388). A similar disparity can be seen in 'Sleep and Poetry', as discussed previously, and in 'On Sitting Down to Read King Lear Once Again'. In both poems, Keats aspires to dismiss romance; he says farewell to 'flowery bays' and 'o'erwhelming sweet' in the former, and bids 'golden-tongue romance' to 'Shut up thine olden pages, and be mute' in the latter. In this stanza of digression in *Isabella*, Keats once again distances his poem from romance. Furthermore, unlike 'a nobler life' and more than 'the fierce dispute / Betwixt damnation and impassion'd clay', it is a 'wormy circumstance' displayed in *Isabella*. Despite the sudden stop of narrative, Keats's word choice of 'wormy' more than sufficiently summarises the previous digging scene and Isabella's following actions. 'Wormy' means not only 'resembling a worm, worm-like' but also 'of earth, soil, the grave' and 'infested with worms, full of worms', as defined in the *Oxford English Dictionary*. On the one hand, the word alludes to the calculation and cruelty of Isabella's brothers. On the other hand, it reflects the sensuousness of decadence and death and the eroticism generated by Isabella's intimacy with Lorenzo's corpse. Though aiming to 'find the agonies, the strife / Of human hearts', Keats displays darker aspects, a less 'nobler life' of human suffering. He reveals the often-unpresented reality of tragedy, which is the abjectness and decadence of physical death, and eroticises this unsightliness, 'this wormy circumstance', to represent the negative pleasure of endangered subjectivity and disintegrated self. And in the last line of Stanza 49, Keats invites the 'Fair reader' to relish this negative pleasure, to 'taste the music of that vision pale' (l. 391), by combining three somatic sensations – gustatory, auditory, and visual. As in Stanza 9, where Lorenzo's lips 'poesied' Isabella's 'in dewy rhyme' (l. 70), in Stanza 49 Keats manifests the intense correlation between poetic imagination and erotic love, and how its 'intensity' becomes highest when dealing with the human experiences that are pathological, anti-living, and self-destructive.[63]

---

62 Felicity A. Nussbaum, *Torrid Zones: Maternity, Sexuality, and Empire in Eighteenth-Century English Narratives* (Baltimore: The Johns Hopkins University Press, 1995), 24–25.
63 For Keats, 'intensity' signifies the artistic drive moving constantly away from the experience 'that is fundamental to our general awareness of life' (Sperry, 'The Epistle', 588) and 'a power to generate in an audience strong and comprehensive response, which sometimes includes erotic overtones' (Radcliffe, 'Keats, Ideals, Isabella', 257).

After unearthing Lorenzo's body, Isabella severs its head with 'duller steel than the Perséan sword' (l. 393). There has been ample critical discussion about the decapitation's significance, especially about Keats's replacement of the omitted phrase 'no foul Medusa's head' with 'no formless monster's head' (l. 394). Smith argues that the change 'complements the "duller steel"' by emphasising that these are real people, not mythical fantasies.[64] Hoeveler reads the decapitation as still a variation of castration reflecting Keats's own anxiety, despite the deletion of 'foul Medusa's head'.[65] Aside from these interpretations, I would highlight an unnoticed and subtle omission of Boccaccio's original description. In Florio's translation of this passage, despite such a profound distress:

> Wisedome and government so much prevailed with her, as to instruct her soule, that her teares spent there, were meerley fruitless and in vaine, neither did the time require any longer tarrying there. Gladly would she have carried the whole body with her, secretly to bestow honourable enterment on it, but it exceeded the compasse of her ability.[66]

In Keats's source, Isabella's decision to decapitate Lorenzo's corpse is based on concrete reasons. She acknowledges that her excessive grief in this moment provides no practical help, and she is fully aware of her inability to carry her lover's entire body away. This highly functional reasoning is supported by her 'Wisedome and government'. In other words, Isabella severs Lorenzo's head because she *has to*, because it is *necessary*, in a context of reality and pragmatism. By disregarding this original account, and by directly presenting the decapitation without any reasons, Keats deprives Isabella of her 'Wisedome and government'. In *Isabella*, the decapitation is no longer a practical and necessary resort reached by Isabella's reasoning, but only a manifesto of her sheer erotic obsession that follows her pathological signs and leads to her eventual madness. In terms of this omission, the transition from Boccaccio's story/Florio's translation to *Isabella* indicates that for Keats, versification, or poetical creation, is an erotic process of forsaking 'Wisedome and government' – instrumental reason and self-control – and deteriorating into madness and oblivion.

The subsequent scene focuses on Isabella's interactions with the severed head, 'whose gentleness did well accord / With death, as life' (l. 396). She cleans the head, places it in the pot of 'Sweet Basil' and nourishes it with her tears. This series of necrophiliac actions, as the central part of *Isabella*, has already generated abundant critical interpretations. Smith reads Isabella's tears here as 'regenerative grief' that 'prevents Isabella from being destroyed' and her cleaning as 'artistic devotion'.[67] She concludes that the basil's flourishing rep-

---

64 Smith, 'The Material Sublime', 309.
65 Hoeveler, 'Decapitating Romance', 332.
66 Boccaccio, *Decameron*, 161.
67 Smith, 'The Material Sublime', 310.

Fig. 2: Frans van der Neve, Narcissus and Echo, 17th Century. Metropolitan Museum of Art.

resents, to some extent, the eternity of love, and 'Isabella and her plant are immortalized in legend'.[68] Watkins views Isabella's actions as 'abstractions which stand above the injustice and contradictions of social life' and achieve 'spiritual truth'.[69] Radcliffe observes another form of the 'deep desire for idealized objects' and highlights the danger of worshiping them blindly.[70] Referring to Hélène Cixous and Julia Kristeva, Hoeveler regards the head as 'partial object ... the essence of fetishism' and as 'a seed in a pod, a child in a perpetually growing womb', signifying that 'Isabella has eroticized her abjection'.[71] White maintains that Isabella's behaviour attest to Freudian melancholia, as Lorenzo's head functions as a 'substitute object' for her lost lover.[72] According to the above interpretations, Isabella's actions constitute a sort of artistic creation that revives and preserves her romantic love, though in a psychotic manner. Isabella's 'work' of the pot of basil as a piece of art transcends the social context of her misery, as

---

68 Ibid., 311.
69 Watkins, 'Personal Life and Social Authority', 41.
70 Radcliffe, 'Keats, Ideals, and Isabella', 257.
71 Hoeveler, 'Decapitating Romance', 334.
72 White, 'Keats, Mourning, and Melancholia', 144.

well as time and space, and eternalises itself in both Boccaccio's and Keats's literary texts. Agreeing that Isabella's actions represent a form of 'artistic devotion', I would further propose that they embody Keats's notion of writing poetry and exemplify his idea of the 'material sublime', thus corroborating my major argument of this paper – for Keats, poetic imagination is in essence an erotic process of self-annihilation.

In my reading of 'Epistle to John Hamilton Reynolds', I have argued that the 'material sublime' evokes Keats's possible medical construal of the word 'material' as pertaining to corporeal disease, which then symbolises general human suffering, especially in a somatic sense. Furthermore, that poetic imagination is 'yet still confin'd, / Lost in a sort of Purgatory blind' points to Keats's understanding that poetry does not stand for an alternative epistemological order other than reason and science to redeem human sufferings. Poetry, on the contrary, aestheticises and eroticises them to generate negative pleasures. In Isabella's case, her treatments of Lorenzo's head not only represent an idealisation of a love object that preaches a superficial motto: 'Love never dies, but lives, immortal Lord' (l. 397). Lorenzo's head is the raw material for the poet Isabella/Keats, representing the ultimate outcome of human suffering, the primitive source of the sublime – death. Isabella/Keats beautifies death, 'the horrid thing', with bodily and 'material' poetics. In this embodiment of 'material sublime', she 'kiss'd it, and low moan'd', tidies up its hairs 'with a golden comb', and:

> Then in a silken scarf, – sweet with the dews
> Of precious flowers pluck'd in Araby,
> And divine liquids come with odorous ooze
> Through the cold serpent-pipe refreshfully, –
> She wrapp'd it up; and for its tomb did choose
> A garden-pot, wherein she laid it by,
> And cover'd it with mould, and o'er it set
> Sweet Basil, which her tears kept ever wet. (ll. 409–416)

Isabella/Keats's versification of death as a poetic subject is based on erotic contacts, bodily fluid, and material luxuries, contradicting what Watkins regards as 'her very dearest hope and sincerest spirituality'.[73] Conceptually, Keats is anticipating the last stanza of 'Ode on Melancholy', in which Beauty must die, Joy is forever bidding adieu, Pleasure comes with poison, and 'him whose strenuous tongue / Can burst Joy's grape against his palate fine' (ll. 21–23, 27–28). For Isabella, Lorenzo (Beauty) is dead and her desire (Joy and Pleasure) is mingled with poisonous madness. She, as a 'poet', 'writes a poem' on Lorenzo's head with somatic fluid and contacts, echoing the 'strenuous tongue' that bursts Joy's grape, a potential image of laceration of flesh and its overflowing fluid.

---

73 Watkins, 'Personal Life and Social Authority', 41.

As Isabella falls into utter oblivion of space and time, she forgets 'the stars, the moon, and sun', 'the blue above the trees', 'the dells where waters run', and 'the chilly autumn breeze', and fails to recognise 'when the day was gone' (ll. 417–421). Such a symptom is Keats's self-awareness of and fear for poetic creation as a descent into 'a Mist', 'the burden of Mystery' (*Letters*, I, 277), where 'I am in a very little time annihilated' (*Letters*, I, 388). Moreover, the symptom of oblivion and self-annihilation extends from the mental to the physical. The poetic images of Isabella's erotic contacts with Lorenzo's head, her bodily fluid and material luxuries are all images of excessive consumption. Exploiting them means the self-wasting of bodily energy and resources. Consequently, Isabella as a poet 'is soon to be / Among the dead: She withers, like a palm / Cut by an Indian for its juicy balm' (ll. 446–448). Her artistic creation of 'the pot of basil' attests to my argument that, for Keats, writing poetry is itself a pathological and erotic process of self-annihilation, mentally as well as physically. Echoing Keats's confession to Reynolds that 'never will the prize, / High reason, and the love of good and ill, be my award!' (*Letters*, I, 262), the line 'And then the prize was all for Isabel' (l. 502) suggests that what a poet can achieve through poetry is poetry itself – as the 'cloudy trophies' at the end of 'Ode on Melancholy' (l. 30) – not an alternative 'spiritual truth' complementing the rationalist, scientific, and moral truths. In *Isabella*, Keats indicates that poetry does not aim to signify a timeless epistemological order that transcends history, or to reflect the historical context of his time. Poetry itself is both signifier and its signified; it opens a disruptive cavity in the very moment of writing, deviating from the linear process of narrative. In such a unique space the poet relinquishes his previous identity and indulges in a ceaseless cycle of erotic desire – from pursuit, fulfilment, to denial, and over again, and again – as in Isabella's creation of 'the pot of basil' and Keats's creation of *Isabella*.

In conclusion, *Isabella* epitomises Keats's equation of erotic love and poetic imagination as both self-annihilating experiences. Keats himself is aware of the dangerous nature of this poem, as he describes it as 'mawkish' and 'too smokable' (*Letters*, II, 174). The word 'mawkish', meaning the inclination to sickness and feeble sentiments, reflects Keats's awareness of the pathological poetics that is vulnerable to ridicule for its apparent 'effeminacy'. However, by insinuating a series of unhealthy and malignant signs imbued in the 'romantic' relationship between Isabella and Lorenzo with such pathological poetics, Keats underlines the innate danger in erotic love, which is then worsened by the brothers' violent interference, as well as in poetic imagination. Moreover, Isabella's necrophilic treatment of Lorenzo's head also realises Keats's idea of the 'material sublime' and represents a somatic form of poetic creation. In *Isabella*, Keats demonstrates the self-annihilating negativity in romantic eroticism, and for Keats, such negativity is entailed in writing poetry itself.

D. Gareth Walters
(Swansea University)

Espronceda's *The Student of Salamanca* and Chopin: Poetry and Musical Structures

Abstract

The influence of literature upon music was especially marked in the nineteenth century, notably with the vogue of programme music. Rarely is there a movement in the opposite direction, however, such as we find in some of the works of George Sand. Accordingly, this article explores how José de Espronceda's narrative poem *El estudiante de Salamanca* bears striking formal affinities with Chopin's second piano sonata, the 'Funeral March' sonata. Although both artists were resident in exile in Paris at the same time it is highly improbable that they would have been familiar with each other's work. Nonetheless, the article suggests how structural details and devices in Espronceda's poem betray characteristics both of Chopin's sonata and other music of the period in such features as sonata-form, the 'turbulent' nocturnes of Chopin, and thematic metamorphosis, a technique often employed by Liszt.

Keywords
Espronceda, Chopin, Programme music, Sonata-form, Thematic metamorphosis

Of all the arts it is perhaps music and literature that offer the least obvious scope for affinity. By contrast it is not uncommon to encounter and accept analogies between literature and painting. A poet or a novelist may often be described as painting a picture in words; the casual, but not careless, employment of a verb such as 'depict' is evidence of this. When it comes to music and literature, however, we are on less sure ground. An instance is when commentators observe that writers, and poets especially, betray 'musicality' in their works. I suggest, however, that on closer examination, this is at best a limited mode of affinity. What is often regarded as a musical quality is the employment – sometimes the abuse – of purely poetic devices such as alliteration or assonance. Moreover, there is a danger that a fixation with such effects can lead to the belief that this so-called musicality can of itself bear a meaning: that phonetic effects could fulfil a semiotic function.¹ A crucial factor then is meaning and context, for which one could find an analogy in music, whereby a single given note does not of itself communicate a mood. For instance, the note of E flat cannot be said to have a distinctive emotive value: as the tonic of E flat major it fulfils a different function from its effect as the third of C minor, which in turn is also distinct from its 'meaning' as the major third of B major, written as D sharp.

The danger in attempting to draw parallels between literary and musical detail emerges in Erika Reiman's interesting study of connections between the music of Robert Schumann and the novels of Jean Paul. To take one instance, Reiman suggests that the composer envisaged the B section of 'Valse noble' from *Carnaval* as a high point in the cycle, one comparable to an episode in Jean Paul's *Titan* when, in a moment of amorous tension, Albano flees in embarrassment from an avowal of love by Liane.² In a review of Reiman's study, however, David Ferris pointedly wonders how these two events could be similar: 'If it is just a question of creating an emotional climax that resolves unexpectedly, then the comparison is so vague and general that it is meaningless'.³

Analogy is no more straightforward either when we move from what we could term this micro-level to a macro-level. Such an issue is well exemplified in a recent book by Nelson R. Orringer that aims to interpret compositions by Manuel de Falla by juxtaposition with poems by his compatriot Federico García Lorca.⁴ There are, however, evident shortcomings in this approach. On the one hand the author takes no account of the scale of individual works, as when he compares Falla's one-movement sonata-form *Fantasia baetica*, which lasts around fifteen minutes, to a short poem entitled 'Baladilla de los tres ríos' from one section of Lorca's *Poema del Cante Jondo*. There is, too, a manifest lack of precision in the

---

1 A cautionary note in this respect was struck as long ago as 1942 in a lecture by T.S. Eliot delivered at the University of Glasgow: 'the music of poetry is not something which exists apart from the meaning. Otherwise, we could have poetry of great musical beauty which made no sense and I have never come across such poetry'. 'The Music of Poetry', in *Selected Prose*, ed. John Hayward (Harmondsworth: Penguin Books, 1953), 56. As a demonstration of how phonetic features can only reinforce meaning and never supply it, let us consider the voiceless sibilant [s] in two hypothetical lines of poetry. In 'the silken maidens seek the sylvan sward' one would deduce that that the phoneme in question communicates a sense of calm. However, in 'the spiteful serpent sinks in the slough of sin' we would hardly think that we have a similar feeling of repose even though the alliterative detail is the same.
2 Reiman's analysis is minutely detailed: she suggests that Schumann returns from the dominant of G minor to the opening, in B flat major, by unexpectedly reinterpreting an F sharp enharmonically as the 'slightly startling' G flat that begins the piece. On this basis she alleges a similarity with Albano's flight from Liane. Erika Reiman, *Schumann's Piano Cycles and the Novels of Jean Paul* (Rochester NY: University of Rochester Press, 2004), 87.
3 David Ferris's review appears in *Music and Letters*, 87. 2 (2006): 326–328.
4 Nelson R. Orringer, *Lorca in Tune with Falla: Literary and Musical Interludes* (Toronto/Buffalo/London: University of Toronto Press, 2014).

attribution of analogous works as in the observation made about another of the poems in the same collection, 'Danza. En el huerto de la Petenera', when he states that '*any* of Falla's three nocturnes from *Noches [en los jardines de Espana]* could have inspired it' (my emphasis).[5]

A different kind of problem comes to the fore in another – more ambitious and sophisticated – endeavour to connect music and literature by Peter Dayan.[6] This concerns a consideration also of secondary literature in the form of critical writing about these artistic activities. Drawing heavily on French twentieth-century theorists such as Barthes and Derrida, Dayan's survey emerges as a philosophical meditation on the potentialities and limitations of the interrelationship of the two arts. In the process, Dayan tends overwhelmingly to the kind of gnomic aphorism, which by its very nature is neither easy to endorse nor to refute, supplying answers to questions that either have not been asked, or do not require posing.

A seemingly fruitful area for analogy between music and literature has tended to reside in what could be termed rather loosely atmospherics. This admittedly modest mode of comparison envisages an understanding that has regard for reader-response theory. It postulates the importance of the reader or the audience for realizing the ultimate significance of the work in question and consequently rather downplays the purity, or even the primacy of the text itself. Applied to music, this could be seen as the attempt to interpret or 'explain' pure music in literary, or at least verbal, terms. An instance of the former is evident in Marcel Brion's study of Schumann, when he compares a description of the natural world in one of Tieck's stories to certain passages from the music, specifically the second movement of his Third Quartet and the 'romance' from the Symphony in D minor. Brion suggests that 'in both cases we are presented with a plastic transposition of feeling, which emerges from a sort of duologue, conscious or unconscious between man and nature'.[7] A case of the latter – a verbal equivalence of music without appeal to a specific writer or work – can be seen in the response to the music of Chopin by the nineteenth-century American commentator James Huneker, which is highly colourful and rhapsodic. He seldom misses an opportunity to introduce imagined situations or even narrations into his analyses, although he does concede that his flights of fancy are in the eye of the beholder, as, for instance, with his observations on the G minor Ballade, Op. 23:

> As in some fabulous tales of the Genii, this Ballade discloses surprising and delicious things. There is the tall lily in the fountain that nods to the sun. It drips in cadenced monotone and its song is repeated on the lips of the slender-hipped girl with the eyes of

---

5 Orringer, *Lorca in Tune with Falla*, 27.
6 *Music Writing Literature: from Sand via Debussy to Derrida* (Aldershot: Ashgate, 2006).
7 Marcel Brion, *Schumann and the Romantic Age*, trans. Geoffrey Sainsbury (London: Collins, 1956), 31 (Original title: *Schumann et l'âme romantique*).

midnight – and so might I weave for you a story of what I see in the Ballade and you would be aghast or puzzled. With such a composition any programme could be sworn to ....[8]

In defence of Huneker it has to be admitted that Chopin himself was quite often keen to tease his audience with putative programmes, as when he suggested that his G minor Nocturne, Op. 15. No. 3 was 'after Hamlet', only to later retreat with the comment 'Let them guess for themselves'.[9] Moreover, what is striking about some of Chopin's compositions is that they sometimes appear to embody an extra-musical inspiration rather than fulfilling what could be defined as a more obvious musical form or logic. A case in point is the B major Nocturne, Op. 37. For the most part this is a serene composition with subjects that complement rather than contrast with each other. Towards the end of the piece, however, the mellifluous singing line is interrupted by a dramatic recitative that leads to a dismissive conclusion of two staccato chords over a tonic bass note – the most evident indication of an idyll that has been shattered. One will have recourse to such language because there is no intrinsically musical expectation or anticipation of such an ending.

It was during the romantic era or, less narrowly, the nineteenth century that the relationship between music and literature was closest. Before this time, the influence of the written word on music was principally confined to such outputs as opera and oratorio, mainly prompted by the institutions of the court and the church. A crucial factor in the emergence of literature as inspiration for music was the development of programme music, embryonic in Beethoven's *Pastoral Symphony* and fully-fledged some twenty years later in Berlioz's *Symphonie Fantastique*. Later in the romantic era, with the piano music of Schumann and the symphonic poems of Liszt, the vogue developed to such an extent that 'pure' music was no longer a norm, so that a composer like Brahms could be viewed as old-fashioned or atypical of his age – if not an anomaly then certainly not a full-blown romantic.

In this relationship between music and literature, however, the movement is overwhelmingly one-way: a poem or other literary work will be the germ or point of reference for the musical composition, which may range from the precisely detailed to the vaguely atmospheric in its depiction of the literary precursor. Furthermore, even when composers did not specify a programmatic or a literary stimulus this did not deter others from making claims on their behalf. A classic instance is provided by Schumann's comment on Chopin's Ballades, when he stated in what appears to be a casual remark that these compositions, so Chopin had told him, had been inspired by 'certain poems of Mickiewicz' ('angeregt

---

[8] James Huneker, *Chopin: The Man and His Music* (Teddington, Middlesex: Echo Library, 2006), 105.
[9] Ibid., 99.

durch Dichtungen con Mickiewicz').[10] On the basis of this vague indication, however, future generations of critics were led to suggest a variety of putative sources and parallels in the poetry of Chopin's fellow Pole, even though only two of the four Ballades had been composed when Schumann made the observation. This issue is explored in detail by Jonathan D. Bellman, and the same critic appropriately argues that these compositions should be assessed *qua* musical forms rather than products of a literary stimulus that would comprise mere speculation.[11]

In this essay I aim to explore what could be seen as an inversion of the process implicit in programme music by arguing that a given literary work possesses a structure that can be well understood in terms of a distinctively musical form. The normal direction of influence, as we have seen already, has been from the literary work to the musical composition, but a rare exception is provided by the work of George Sand. Apart from her celebrated relationship with Chopin, it would not be inappropriate to refer to her in terms of a 'musicien manqué'. David A. Powell, in particular, has drawn attention to the direct impact of music on her output.[12] Moreover, Peter Dayan has described how Liszt's paraphrase/arrangement in the form of a *rondo* composition of a song by Manuel García was the basis, indeed the programme, for Sand's story 'Le contrebandier'. What I propose in this article is an endeavour along the lines of these studies by Powell and Dayan, but by paying particular attention to structures and devices in the music of the period, specifically, (i) sonata-form, (ii) the Chopin nocturne, and (iii) thematic metamorphosis.

As a result of the need to provide a title for this article the surprise, which I might have hoped for with my summary of the work in question, will inevitably be lost. In order to maintain as much suspense as possible, however, I will in what follows employ terminology that is as far as possible not genre specific. I have in mind a work of the romantic era, dating from the late 1830s. It does not belong to any of the main nations associated with the romantic movement, that is the creator is neither English, nor French, nor German. It is the product of an artist who is regarded as the leading exponent of romanticism in his country. Furthermore, as a result of the political situation in his native country he moved as an exile to Paris in the period around 1830 where he associated with his compatriots. The work concerned is an extended one in four sections. The first operates by contrasting variously darkness and light, energy and stillness, and in the conventional understanding of the terms, masculine and feminine. One of the

---

10 Cited in Arthur Hedley, *Chopin* (London: J. M. Dent, 1963), 172.
11 Jonathan D. Bellman, *Chopin's Polish Ballade: Op. 38 as Narrative of National Martyrdom* (Oxford: Oxford University Press, 2010), 19–34.
12 David A. Powell, *While the Music Lasts: the Representation of Music in the Works of George Sand* (Lewisburg: Bucknell University Press, 2001).

parts is more playful, albeit in a somewhat sardonic fashion. The work also contains an explicit mention of a funeral procession, and it concludes in an uncannily bizarre and eerie fashion. From this description there would be to two groups of specialists an immediately obvious answer. Had I indeed referred to 'movements' rather than 'parts' in my summary, perhaps even non-musicologists might have posited Chopin's Second Sonata as their response, the so-called 'Funeral March Sonata'. But if we restore the term 'parts' then an audience of Hispanists might just as readily identify the work in question as a narrative poem entitled *El estudiante de Salamanca* (*The Student of Salamanca*) by the Spanish writer José de Espronceda.

Fig. 1: August Kneisel, Frederic Chopin, 1830–1840. Eötvös Loránd University, Budapest.

My main focus is on the structures of these two works and formal issues arising from them, while my aim is to demonstrate how a literary work (Espronceda's narrative poem) operates by principles that are highly characteristic of music (Chopin's Second Sonata principally but also other compositions). I begin with an important clarification. Unlike with the case of Sand and Liszt, it is not my intention to demonstrate influence. Consequently, I can dispense with the need to explore biographical elements, such as the fact that the two artists both resided in Paris at around the same time. Indeed I work on the assumption that Chopin and

Espronceda would have no knowledge of the other's work; certainly Chopin would not have had the linguistic capability to have read the Spanish poet's as yet untranslated works, while there is no evidence Espronceda had any interest in music even if Chopin might have been known to him as a name.[13] I am happy as a consequence to follow the principle adopted by Theodor Adorno when he compares Proust's *A la recherche du temps perdu* with Mahler's *Das Lied von der Erde:* 'the unity of the years [of composition of these two works] throws an unsteady bridge between two artists who knew nothing of each other'.[14] Such a lack of mutual acquaintanceship is emphasized, too, in the opening remarks of a comparative essay on the same two figures by Julian Johnson, whose essay pursues what is also my aim: merely 'a parallel at the level of literary and musical structure'.[15] What I am suggesting specifically in the case of the two works that I am considering is that their shared romantic sensibility has led to the creation of products that coincidentally possess a structural kinship, with the further implication that this comparison may serve to encourage us to conceive of literature on other occasions also in terms of musical form.

The Student of Salamanca was probably begun in 1835 and completed in late 1839, not long before its first publication.[16] It recounts the tale of Don Felix de Montemar, a notorious womanizer and libertine. As such, he represents another version of the Don Juan myth, so prominent in Spanish culture and literature, though best known perhaps in Mozart's Don Giovanni.[17] Espronceda's eponymous hero is additionally given a distinctive romantic stamp: towards the end of the poem especially when he is converted into a defiant figure, variously Satanic and Promethean in his challenge to supernatural forces and to God. The plot is centred on Felix's seduction and abandonment of a noblewoman, Doña Elvira,

---

13 For detail on the periods spent by the two in Paris see Hedley, *Chopin*, 41–59; and Robert Marrast, *José de Espronceda y su tiempo; literatura, sociedad y política en tiempos del Romanticismo*, translated into Spanish by Laura Poca (Barcelona: Editorial Crítica, 1989), 132–177. A basic English-language summary of Espronceda's life, including the time spent in Paris, is to be found in the introduction to the text from which I shall quote in this essay: *José de Espronceda, The Student of Salamanca*, translated by C. K. Davies, with an Introduction and Notes by Richard A. Cardwell (Warminster: Aris and Phillips, 1991), 1–9.

14 T. W. Adorno, *Mahler: A Musical Physiognomy*, trans. Shierry Weber Nicholson (Chicago: Chicago University Press, 1992), 145.

15 Julian Johnson, 'Rehearsing Lost Time: Proust and Mahler', *Romance Studies* 32. 2 (2014): 88, doi: 10.1179/0263990414Z.00000000060.

16 For fuller detail on the composition and publication of the work see Cardwell's Introduction to *The Student of Salamanca*, 9–10.

17 The literary prototype for the various representations of Don Juan is a play by Tirso de Molina (1579–1648), *El burlador de Sevilla*, which predates another theatrical version of the figure by Molière by several decades. Byron's long poem on the eponymous hero (1819–1824) is perhaps the most notable Romantic depiction of this character. Another Spanish version of the Romantic era is José Zorrilla's play *Don Juan Tenorio* (1844).

who dies of a broken heart. Her brother, Don Diego, challenges Felix to a duel and is killed. Shortly after killing the brother, Felix catches sight of a hooded female figure in the dark streets of Salamanca. Unable to resist what he presumes may be another conquest, he follows her on a long trek through the city. In the course of this, he comes across a funeral procession and sees that the two cadavers thus borne are those of Diego and of himself. Unperturbed by this vision he continues his pursuit of the mysterious, cloaked woman and eventually is led into a large mansion that is described in a classic Gothic-horror fashion. The house is inhabited by ghostly apparitions that mock Felix, and the figure he has been pursuing is revealed to be Elvira, but now a putrefying skeleton whom Felix is compelled to take as his wife in a macabre marriage ceremony accompanied by an epithalamium from the spectral witnesses, thus fulfilling the broken promise made while Elvira was alive. Finally, he is embraced by the skeleton, and as the breath is squeezed out of his body he collapses and dies.

This is a bare résumé of what happens in the poem. The kinship with the romantic manner of such writers as Edgar Allan Poe is evident. It does not, however, do full justice to the descriptive detail nor, more crucially, the narrative sequence. Indeed, around half the poem comprises a flashback that reverts to present time only at the start of the final lengthy part describing the pursuit of the mysterious woman. In place of a linear narrative there is a structure that possesses some of the features of larger-scale musical works of the classical and romantic eras. After an evocative scene-setter, highlighting the sense of horror and the supernatural, the tale begins *in medias res* with the violence of the duel between Felix and Diego, as yet unidentified:

> Súbito rumor de espadas
> Cruje y un «¡ay!» se escuchó;
> un «¡ay!» moribundo, un «¡ay!»
> que penetra el corazón,
> que hasta los tuétanos hiela
> y da al que lo oyó temblor,
> Un «¡ay!», de alguno que al mundo
> Pronuncia el último a Dios.

> [A clash of swords, unexpected,
> Strident, sounds; a cry is heard.
> A shriek of death, awful, final.
> Penetrating to the very heart,
> Chilling to the very marrow,
> Causing dread in those who hear.

> The cry of a man pronouncing
> His last farewell to the earth.][18]

The remainder of the first part is by contrast an extended description of Elvira and her love for Felix. It begins:

> Bella y más pura que el azul del cielo,
> con dulces ojos lánguidos y hermosos,
> donde acaso el amor brilló entre el velo
> del pudor que los cubre candorosos;
> tímida estrella que refleja al suelo
> rayos de luz brillantes y dudosos,
> ángel puro de amor, que amor inspira,
> fue la inocente y desdichada Elvira. (ll.140-147)

> [So beautiful, purest blue of heav'n paling
> Before her soft, sweet, lovely, languid, glances,
> Through which, their veil of modesty assailing,
> The brightly shining light of love entrances;
> A timid star whose rays come earthward, quailing,
> Tremulous arrows of light, gleaming lances:
> Luckless Elvira, to be happy never,
> She was love's armoury, angelic ever.] (ll.140-147)

The juxtaposition of these two passages suggests one of the hallmarks of a large-scale musical work of the period: sonata-form. This originally and typically entailed the presence of two contrasting themes or subjects as the structural foundation of first movements of symphonies, concertos, quartets, and sonatas. In the works of classical composers – that is from Haydn to Schubert – such contrasts are best defined in purely musical terms.[19] In the romantic era, however, the contrast could be often described in non-musical ways, as conflicting or sharply divergent moods of the kind we encounter in the first movement of Chopin's 'Funeral March' sonata and as conveyed through the descriptions of the two characters in *The Student of Salamanca*.

Developing the analogy with a large-scale musical composition, the second part of Espronceda's poem fulfils the function of a slow movement of a sonata or symphony, and, more precisely than this, it also brings to mind the procedure seen for instance in the second movement of Chopin's second Piano Concerto in F minor. Such a feature is also a minor trademark of a number of this composer's

---

18 *The Student of Salamanca. El estudiante de Salamanca*, 45, ll. 41-48. Further references are drawn from this edition and incorporated as line references only.
19 For example, in the opening movement of Beethoven's 'Waldstein' Sonata (Opus 53) the first subject takes the form of *moto perpetuo* quavers, providing a sense of rapid movement. By contrast the second subject is characterized by stillness by the emergence of a chorale-like melody that is richly harmonized.

Nocturnes, in particular in the first and second of the Opus 15 set. What this process involves is the incorporation of a turbulent section as the central component of an otherwise tranquil piece. In like fashion, the second part of *The Student of Salamanca* begins with a gentle, idyllic evocation of night:

> Está la noche serena
> de luceros cooronada,
> terso el azul de los cielos
> como transparente gasa.
>
> Melancólica la luna
> va trasmontando la espalda
> del otero su alba frente
> tímida apenas levanta,
>
> y el horizonte ilumina,
> pura vírgen solitaria,
> y en su blanca luz süave
> el cielo y la tierra baña.
>
> Deslízase el arroyuelo
> fúlgida cinta de plata
> al resplandor de la luna,
> entre franjas de esmeralda. (ll.180-191)
>
> [The night wears a crown in silence
> A chaplet of starry twinklings,
> The lambent blue of the heavens
> Like gauze, diaphanous, limpid.
> The moon, melancholy, rises,
> Ascending the hillside, climbing
> On his shoulder: her pale forehead
> Apprehensively uplifting,
>
> Laving the skyline with brightness,
> A discreet and lonely virgin,
> Bathing both the earth and heaven
> In her pallid silken twilight.] (ll.180-191)

Equally luminous is the description of Elvira herself:

> ¡Una mujer! Es acaso
> blanca silfa solitaria,
> que entre el rayo de la luna
> tal vez misteriosa vaga?
>
> Blanco es su vestido, ondea
> suelto el cabello a la espalda;

hoja tras hoja las flores
que lleva en su mano arranca. (ll.212-219)

[A woman! Or is it maybe
A sylph white as any lily
Walking alone in the moonlight,
Wandering, shadowy, mystic?

Dressed in white, her hair loose hanging,
Curls upbraided floating lightly,
From her flowers with her fingers
One by one the petals twitching...] (ll.212-219)

We soon discover, however, that she is heartbroken, abandoned by her feckless lover. Consequently, the narrative assumes a much darker metaphorical tone with imagery that correlates to the forlorn woman's fate:

¡El corazón sin amor!
¡Triste páramo cubierto
con la lava del dolor,
oscuro inmenso desierto
donde no nace una flor!

Distante un bosque sombrío,
el sol cayendo en la mar.... (ll.273-280)

[The heart love-less and dismayed!
A sad desert overlaid
With the hot lava of pain,
A dark waste, an open plain,
Where no flower blooms, to fade.

A wood remote and dark,
The sun swimming out of reach....] (ll.273-280)

The equivalent for the second-movement Scherzo in the Chopin sonata is the poem's third part, which is cast in the form of a short dramatic sketch, the dialogue serving to detail Don Diego's confrontation with his sister's seducer as he interrupts a card game in which Felix is participating. He confronts his sister's seducer, but this merely provokes a dismissively cynical response:

D. DIEGO (desembozándose con ira)
Don Félix, no conocéis
A don Diego de Pastrana?

D. FÈLIX
A vos no, mas sí a una hermana
Que imagino que tenéis.

D.DIEGO
Y no sabéis que murió?

D. FÉLIX
Téngala Dios en su gloria.

D. DIEGO
Pienso que sabéis su historia,
Y quién fue quien la mató.

D. FÉLIX (con sarcasmo)
¡Quizá alguna calentura!

D.DIEGO
¡Mentís vos! (ll.601-610)

[D. DIEGO (*angrily unwrapping himself*)
Is Don Diego de Pastrana.
Don Felix, unknown to you?

D. FELIX
Yes, but your sister I knew.
Let me see ... Her name is Ana.

D. DIEGO
'Twas Elvira. She is dead.

D. FELIX
May God keep her in His Glory.

D. DIEGO
You must know, I think, her story,
And whose hand to death her led.

D. FELIX
Haply 'twas by fever's fingers.

D. DIEGO
You lie. (ll.601-610)

The gamblers intervene in the dispute and demand that the antagonists leave if they wish to continue the brawl. The impetuosity inherent in this scene and the air of short-breathed, sardonic menace are characteristics of the corresponding movement in the Chopin sonata. There is, however, a structural distinction in this instance. In Chopin's work the contrast of violence and serenity, evident in the sonata-form first movement, is maintained through the presence of the major-key trio with its lulling melody. There are no such moments of relaxation in this part of the poem; indeed, there is an increase in tension, preparatory to the duel, already described as a flashback at the start of the poem and whose fateful outcome is recapitulated as the final section begins.

Fig. 2: Henri Fantin-Latour, The Evening Star, 1877. Cleveland Museum of Art.

In my analysis of these two works I have, until now, concentrated on affinity and equivalence. But, as my observation regarding the trio section of the Scherzo implies, there are also divergences. Especially notable, having regard for the overall structure of the works is the character and role of the final sections of both. Chopin's last movement is a *moto perpetuo*, marked pianissimo throughout up to the final two chords. It is a brief as well as a rapid piece and has been described as 'night winds sweeping over the churchyard graves'.[20] While there is a funeral procession in The Student of Salamanca in which the bodies of Felix and Diego are carried through the streets, this is merely one detail in what is an eventful and complex final section. If we compare this concluding part of the poem structurally with musical counterparts, then the analogy would not be especially suitable for contemporaneous examples of large-scale works. In the symphonies of the

---

20 Huneker, *Chopin* (114) indicates that such was the title suggested for this movement either by Carl Tausig or Anton Rubinstein.

classical and early romantic eras the intellectual weight of the composition was in its first half: a sonata-form first movement (often including repeats), commonly the longest movement of the piece, followed by a substantial slow movement. The third and fourth movements, however, were less imposing or even slight by comparison: a minuet (later a scherzo) and trio, rounded off by a finale, predominantly a rondo, which was in the main not as intense as the first movement. In the course of the nineteenth century this kind of model tended to change so that the last movement, far from being a light or witty leave-taking, became at least the equal of the first movement in its emotional significance. Indeed, Espronceda's poem resembles more a model of symphonic structure that envisages the final movement as its high point.[21]

The final part of *The Student of Salamanca* depicts Felix 'sword in hand' (l.695), having just despatched the unfortunate Diego in a duel. Almost immediately he hears a sigh from a figure nearby: 'a flowing shape draws nigh, his progress baulking,/ A vision wrapped in flowing raiment white' (ll. 719-20). He discerns that it is a woman. He addresses her but receives no response other than a groan. A second approach to the mysterious figure in which he propositions her prompts a reply in a smooth, melodious voice in which she indicates that she is no longer of this world. She warns Felix against pursuing her, but her words fall on deaf ears. He continues his pursuit, but the familiar surroundings momentarily appear different and he hears ghostly voices echoing his name. He attributes such fancies to having drunk too much while gambling earlier, but shortly after he comes across the funeral procession in which his own body, as well as that of Diego, are displayed. Undeterred, he exchanges words with the cloaked woman, and despite her repeated warnings of the threat to his life doggedly continues to go after her. His pursuit has now changed from the quest for another amatory escapade into a matter of following his destiny, come what may. The erotic urge has seemingly been transformed into a metaphysical one:

«Seguid, señora, y adelante vamos:
tanto mejor si sois el diablo mismo,
y Dios y el diablo y yo nos conozcamos,
y acábese por fin tanto embolismo.

Que de tanto sermón, de farsa tanta,
Juro, pardiez, que fatigado estoy;
nada mi firme voluntad quebranta,
sabed en fin que donde vayáis, voy.

---

21 A notable early example of such a shift in gravity is provided by Beethoven's Ninth Symphony with its choral finale. It also becomes a feature in some, though not all, of the symphonies by Bruckner and Mahler. Among twentieth-century composers Shostakovich occasionally transfers the weight of the symphony into its last movement.

Un término no más tiene la vida,
término fijo; un paradero el alma;
ahora adelante.» Dijo, y en seguida
camina en pos con decidida calma. (ll.1185-1196)

['Lead on, my lady, let us now be going,
Be you the Devil, well, could not be bettered,
For God, the Devil and I would then be knowing
Each other, and this confusion well fettered.

For with farce and religious elocution
God knows I have reached satiety,
Know that you cannot break my resolution,
Where you go, I will follow, so lead me.

To man there is assigned a span for living:
Only the one: his soul one destination:
On our way!' he said. Not showing misgiving
He dogged her steps, devoid of hesitation.] (ll.1185-1196)

The veiled lady knocks at the door of a mansion, and it opens as though of its own accord. Felix enters too and follows her, crossing 'long galleries, strange, desolate and lonely' (l. 1204). Gradually, Felix has been converted into a character, far removed from the callous and cynical seducer of before. He is now seen in transcendental terms:

Grandïosa, satánica figura,
alta la frente, Montemar camina,
espíritu sublime en su locura
provocando la cólera divina:
fábrica frágil de materia impura,
el alma que la alienta y la ilumina,
con Dios le iguala, y con osado vuelo
se alza a su trono y le provoca a duelo. (ll.1245-1252)

[Grandiose, puffed with satanic vanity,
Proudly advancing, Montemar comes striding,
A spirit of sublime insanity
In sheer madness all Providence deriding –
Just a frail parcel of humanity
The life in the bright soul therein residing
He equals with God, and with daring flight
Soars up to challenge the Almighty to fight.] (ll.1245-1252)

Described as a 'second Lucifer' (l.1253), he is, in short, the epitome of the romantic hero, shaking his fist at fate and ready to challenge God. His daring can at this point be justly described as Promethean, reminiscent of the ideal rebel or revolutionary, so beloved of romantic writers and artists.[22] This final portrait of the eponymous hero differs certainly in emphasis from Espronceda's initial presentation of him:

> Segundo don Juan Tenorio,
> alma fiera e insolente,
> irreligioso y valiente,
> altanero y reñidor:
> Siempre el insulto en los ojos,
> en los labios la ironía,
> nada teme y todo fía
> de su espada y su valor. (ll.100-107)

> [A second Don Juan Tenorio,
> A contemptuous desperado,
> Truculent, reeking bravado,
> Arrogant, spurning the Lord.
> Scorn from his eye never absent:
> Irony on his lip lusting,
> Fearing nothing, all entrusting
> To his daring and his sword.] (ll.100-107)

The courage is there all along, but the essence of his character has changed. It would be appropriate, in fact, to describe what has happened to Felix as a metamorphosis. I use this term advisedly in order to establish another parallel with music, again especially of the period in which Espronceda was writing. I am thinking specifically of a procedure cultivated notably by Franz Liszt, in a number of compositions: thematic metamorphosis. By way of analogy with what happens to Felix one could point to a work such as Liszt's second piano concerto (drafted mainly in 1839-40) where a dreamy, wistful theme at the start is transformed into an assertive and triumphant march-like tune towards the end. The difference between music and poetry in this instance is that in music metamorphosis is essentially a technical device, melodic in nature, for spawning new and unexpected thematic material.[23] In the case of the written text, however, language provides an opportunity, if not a necessity, for an explanation of any transformation. With Felix there is an indication, especially during the gambling scene in part three, that he is changing as a result of disillusion with life, even with its

---

22 The conception of the Romantic hero in such terms and his depiction as an image of the artists themselves is explored with particular reference to paintings of the period by Hugh Honour, *Romanticism* (Harmondsworth: Penguin Books, 1979), 217-275.
23 Critical opinion is divided on the merits of the metamorphosis in Liszt's concerto, with opinions ranging from 'masterstroke' to 'vulgar'.

hedonistic potential. Hence, there is not the feeling of randomness that we get with Liszt's concerto and other examples of thematic metamorphosis in music.[24]

As I approach the conclusion of this essay, I appreciate how this divergence together with others I have indicated may seem to be stumbling blocks in an attempt to suggest a parallel between these works of Chopin and Espronceda. My counter-argument entails considering the issue of affinity from a different angle, which involves hypothetically taking *The Student of Salamanca* as the programme for Chopin's sonata. As we examine the programmatic works of the nineteenth century based on literary works, we discover that the connection between the precursor and the musical composition is often neither close nor precise. To take one instance: the title of Liszt's 'Dante' sonata ('Sonata après une lecture de Dante') gives apparently very little away. The piano composition itself focusses on two aspects of one part of one work (admittedly the most famous) of the Italian writer, from the first part (Inferno) of his *Divina Commedia:* the evocation of the souls in torment and the doomed love of Francesca da Rimini. In the process he establishes a contrast between anguished turbulence and amatory lyricism such as might be encountered in a sonata-form movement of the era, similar to what we encounter in the opening movement of Chopin's 'Funeral March' Sonata. In the case of programme music, composers were very selective in their treatment of the literary source. This feature is also evident in some overtures by Tchaikovsky. He too, like Liszt, was drawn to the tale of Francesca da Rimini, the subject of one such composition. In like manner, he would be stimulated by the plays of Shakespeare, as witness his overtures on Romeo and Juliet and, towards the end of his life, Hamlet.[25] Again the key is selectivity; there is no attempt to duplicate all the material of the precursor text. Thus, in *Romeo and Juliet*, after an initial section depicting Friar Lawrence, the bulk of the composition contrasts the violence deriving from the family feud with the amorous ecstasy of the doomed lovers.

With such parallels in mind I shall now seek to summarize how *The Student of Salamanca* could serve as a programme for Chopin's sonata. The *agitato* first subject of the opening movement depicts the duel; the contrasting second subject hints both at the beauty of Elvira and, in its more expansive rendering, the latent nobility of spirit that Felix will ultimately demonstrate. The second move-

---

24 Cardwell (*The Student of Salamanca*, 10) reminds us that the poem was written over a period of four years during which Espronceda's outlook was rapidly changing. One such consequence, in his view, is that the character of Felix is not as consistent as critics suppose. He thus contends that it is a mistake to see the poem as a 'single unified narrative'. On the other hand, the poet was content to publish it as it stands and we can only assess what we have before us.
25 Such works are in fact of a kind that contemporary and later composers such as César Franck and Richard Struss would designate symphonic poems.

ment communicates his brio and impetuosity, while the trio reiterates the gentleness and grace of Elvira. The third movement obviously alludes to the supernatural apparition of the funeral procession of the bodies of Diego and Felix, while the trio offers a final evocation of the essence of Elvira. Finally, the fourth movement is a sound-picture of the grotesque and macabre visions that assail Felix, leading to his death, which is musically represented by the hammer blows of the last two chords as a graphic indicator of his fatal collapse. Indeed, such a narrative has arguably supplied a greater number of specific points of contact between the poem and the musical work than we encounter in the examples of programme music cited above.

In conclusion, my ability to supply such a putative narrative for the Chopin Sonata has not arisen essentially from any emotional response to the music along the lines of Huneker, facilitating a rough and ready adaptation to the poem. On the contrary, rather than gut reaction it has been a musically centred awareness of form and structure that has enabled this reading. As good as any justification for what I have sought to demonstrate to be the principal aim of this article is afforded by T. S. Eliot's *Four Quartets*, for which the poet himself saw an equivalence in Beethoven's late quartets.[26] Many commentators of Eliot's work have explored this inspiration to good effect. Indeed, for the justification of such approaches, as well as my own in this essay, one could not do better than refer to Eliot's friend and mentor Ezra Pound when he suggests that 'the value of music as elucidation of verse comes from the attention it throws on detail'.[27]

---

26 In 1931, many years before he started *Four Quartets*, Eliot wrote to Stephen Spender while listening to Beethoven's A minor Quartet, Opus 131, and commented that he would like 'to get something of that into verse' before he died.
27 Ezra Pound, *ABC of Reading* (New Haven: Yale University Press, 1934), 140.

Marie-Louise Svane
(University of Copenhagen)

Tragedy or Melodrama? The Greek War of Independence in European Theatre

Abstract

The Greek War of Independence against Ottoman dominion (1821-1830), sparked a wave of philhellenic sympathy across Europe. In liberal circles, initiatives in support of the Greek revolution were taken, whereas the European governments stayed out of the conflict and took measures to control the public sentiment in their countries. Dramatic treatments of the Greek struggle became popular in many European theatres. This article examines a selection of philhellenic plays performed in Paris and London in the 1820s. My interest lies with investigating how the contemporary Greek war was transferred onto the stage using the dramatic genres and conventions of the time whilst negotiating the control of national censorship. In the context of political pressure and a demand for dramaturgical efficiency, I focus on the problems of documentarism in plays about the Greek war. At a general level, the philhellenic plays are seen to contribute to the larger process of European cultural self-identification along the dividing lines between East and West, although this agenda is often in tension with the dramatic handling of the subject, which calls for intrigue and characters crossing the border lines.

Keywords

Greek War of Independence, Revolution, nineteenth-century theatre, nationalism, censorship.

1. War and the Theatre

The repertoires of the London and Paris theatres of the 1810s and 20s indicate a clear connection between war, nation, and the theatre. In these turbulent decades, when Napoleon's continental wars and various national revolts were drawing new borders between European states, news of victories and losses in famous battles was regular fodder for the press and a source of fascination for the general public. Enormous new stage grounds were established for the purpose of celebrating patriotic victories, such as Astley's Amphitheatre and Saddler's Wells, in London, and the Cirque Olympique and Salle des Jeux Gymniques, in Paris. Military parades with cavalry and canon were performed, and scenes of naval battles complete with burning frigates staged. Performances such as *La Bataille d'Aboukir* and *Napoléon en Égypte* would celebrate the victories of the French over the English in Egypt, while the British would recall their victory over Napoleon in *The Battle of the Nile,* and *The Battle of Waterloo,* and would celebrate their conquest of Indian Mysore in *Tippoo Sahib, or The Storming of Seringapatam* and *El Hyder*.[1] The military plays were a remarkable feature of the theatre of the first decades of the nineteenth-century.

Representations of war on stage were nothing new. In fact, the oldest preserved tragedy, Aeschylus' *The Persians* (472 BC), relates the victory of the Greeks over the Persian King Xerxes at the Battle of Salamis. In Aeschylus, as in the military plays of the Napoleonic period, the subject is a war quite recently fought featuring a patriotic victory over an enemy aggressor. Nevertheless, the Classical play is not a piece of propaganda in the same way as the military plays of the Napoleonic era. The tables are turned, and what we witness is not the self-glorification of the victors, but, on the contrary, the results of war as seen through the reactions of the vanquished enemy: the horror of the war, the pain of defeat, and the Persian dynasty in the tragic moment of its dissolution.

The Greek War of Independence (1821-1830) also quickly became a subject on the theatrical stage. Theatre life in the first decades of the nineteenth-century was teeming and varied. The patent national theatres reserved the privilege of playing the Classics, while private theatres competed on a broad scale of genres and sensational contents appealing to the eye and the senses. The Greek War drama was readily adapted to various contemporaneous genres, significantly to the military drama as enacted in spectacular performances on the new stages in London and Paris. It was furthermore influenced by the popular trend of oriental melodrama, itself a part of the larger orientalist vogue of the century. Since the beginning of the century, widely popular tales from *The Arabian Nights' Entertainment*, amongst other oriental tales, had been staged in lavish productions that evoked the splendours of the East: Sultans' palaces, harem interiors, and interludes with dancing slave girls, etc.

Such projections of fantasy came to characterize this genre and contributed to the construction of a sort of theatre-Orient, which was easily replicable and thus also employed by other genres of the theatre, including the military plays of the period. Indeed, there were good historical grounds for this adaptation. In Napo-

---

1 See Edward Ziter, *The Orient on the Victorian Stage*, Chap. 5 'The geography of imperial theatre' (Cambridge: Cambridge University Press, 2002); Heidi Holder, 'Melodrama, Realism, and Empire on the British Stage' in *Acts of Supremacy: The British Empire on Stage, 1790-1930*, ed. J. S. Bratton et al. (Manchester: Manchester University Press, 1991); Angela Pau, *Orient of the Boulevards: Exoticism, Empire and Nineteenth-Century French Theater*, Part II. *Dramatic Campaigns* (Philadelphia: University of Pennsylvania Press, 1998). doi.org/10.7765/9781526123619.00008.

leon's first military campaign as well as in British colonial expansion, the main target was the conquest of territories in the Eastern hemisphere: Napoleon in Egypt and the British in India. Accordingly, many of the military plays have an Eastern backdrop: Cairo, the Nile, Mysore, Bengal, etc. Local shahs, sultans, mahdis, and chieftains of the region presided over their palm courts, harems, and camels, acting either as loyal supporters of the local French or British administration, or as fanatical warlords who opposed their colonial rulers only to be overcome by French or the British forces. Typically, a denouement of military bravura, complete with cavalry and canon, culminated in a tableau of British or French heroes, posing before the ruins of a rampart, waving the Union Jack or the Tricolore.

2. The Greek War and Theatre Convention

The connection between the markers of the theatre-Orient and the codes of the patriotic-military drama is also relevant to the staging of philhellenic drama in the European theatre during the 1820s, as both the colonial drama and the philhellenic drama imply an encounter or a clash between West and East. The difference, of course, was in the nature of the clash; plays about the Greek War presented to their audiences a 'colonised West' (Greece under Ottoman dominion), whereas in the colonial plays, 'the West' was identified as being the victorious colonial power. In the Greek plays, the watchwords were 'liberty' and 'liberation' from oriental dominion, whereas the colonial plays generally suggested that it was Western civilisation that conferred 'liberty' and progress onto a backward Orient. In British and French colonial plays the Orient thus had to be conquered and Europeanized. Contrary to this, in the philhellenic plays, the Orient had to be cleansed from Greece and from Europe. In other words, the borders between East and West were crossed along different lines in the two types of war-drama, even if both were drawing on a common stock of patterns and dramaturgic rules.

In any case, the wave of sympathy and interest in the Greek cause that was spreading all over Europe during the war years of 1821–1830 also clearly manifested itself in theatre productions, as well as in other areas of cultural production. Amy Muse, for instance, has identified a wave of philhellenic titles appearing in the repertoires of London stages in these years. With reference to the observation made by Edith Hall and Fiona Macintosh in their *Greek Tragedy and the British Theatre 1660–1914*, she observes that 'the crop of War of Independence dramas was the most conspicuous feature of the 1820s' British theatre'.² As we shall see, the tendency is the same in France, even though regulations of censorship and other conditions contributed to profiling the philhellenic drama differently in different countries.³

In the following I wish to address the question of how the Greek War of Independence was narrated on the European stage, and especially how it *could* be narrated using the dramatic forms and genre conventions typical of the time. Related to this are a number of questions about the relationship between war, theatre, and politics: What can be said about the real war fought between 1821 and 1830 in the far South-Eastern corner of Europe and about the transposition of its subject and events into a war fiction staged before audiences in London and Paris? What sort of historical documentation and political values are the plays premised upon? How did audiences respond? What sort of problems could censorship cause for the philhellenic plays? What kind of dramaturgic problems and solutions could be caused by the fact that the war was going on in the contemporary present and with an uncertain outcome? Some of the answers are to be sought in the theatre archives, others in the contemporary history, but first and foremost in the plays themselves. In the following discussion six or seven plays have been selected as typical examples of the philhellenic drama of the period.

3. Censorship

The two French plays I will discuss are *Parga, ou le Brûlot* [Parga, or the fireship] written by Pierre-Frédéric-Adolphe Carmouche and performed in 1827, and *Le Dernier Jour de Missolonghi* [The last day in Missolonghi] written by Georges Ozaneaux and performed in 1828. The British plays are C. E. Walker's *The Revolt of the Greeks; or, The Maid of Athens* (1824), J. B. Buckstone's *The Revolt of the Greeks; or, The Maid of Athens* (1829) (distinct from Walker's piece, notwithstanding the identical titles) and William Barrymore's *The Suliote; or, The Greek Family* (1829). The two philhellenic dramas in German, which will only be mentioned in passing here, are both productions by the Danish born Harro Harring,

---

2 Amy Muse, 'The Great Drama of the Revival of Liberty: Philhellenic Drama of the 1820s' in Gioia Angelletti (ed.), *Emancipation, Liberation, and Freedom. Romantic Drama and Theatre in Britain 1760-1830* (Monte Universita Parma Editore, 2010) 140-41; Amy Muse, 'Encountering Ali Pasha on the London Stage: No Friend to Freedom?' *Romanticism* 17.3 (Edinburgh University Press 2011) 340; Edith Hall and Fiona Macintosh, *Greek Tragedy and the British Theatre 1660-1914* (Oxford: Oxford University Press, 2005). doi.org/10.3366/ROM.2011.00 47.

3 See John McCormick, *Popular Theatres of Nineteenth Century France,* Chap 7 Censorship, 99ff. (London: Routledge 1993); *Censorship: A World Encyclopedia* ed. Derek Jones (Routledge, 2001, 2015). doi.org/10.4324/9780203168110.

Die Mainotten [The Maniotes], performed in 1824, and *Der Renegat auf Morea* [The Renegade in the Morea] performed in 1831.[4] These selections were based on two primary criteria: that a text in print or manuscript has survived and is available; and that the play is known to have been staged at a prominent theatre, and mentioned in contemporary theatre criticism.

While these plays have largely disappeared from public memory, they are sporadically mentioned in volumes of theatre history from the nineteenth-century. Several titles can be traced back to the surviving yearbooks or playbills of individual theatres; others may be found in collections of posters and advertisements in theatre archives.[5] Of the plays to be discussed, two British melodramas, C. E. Walker's *The Revolt of the Greeks* (1824) and William Barrymore's *The Suliote* (1829), exist only in manuscript, and both are kept in the archive of the Lord Chamberlain's Office, the institution of censorship, which from 1731 decided on behalf of the British government what could be played in the national theatres as well as on private stages. The theatre was, along with the press, the popular mass media of the time, and the aim of theatre censorship was to ensure that performances offended neither the government nor the authorities, and generally to prevent offensive ideas from being disseminated. French censorship, re-established in 1807 by Napoleon and continued, although with restorative goals, by the Bourbon regime in the 1820s, intervened more firmly than its English equivalent. This, among other things, was due to a strict surveillance and regulation of theatre licences in Paris, whereas in London numerous small, private theatres opened for a season or two without being consistently recorded by the authorities.[6] The Greek Revolution attracted considerable public interest, and was thus politically sensitive, which can be seen from the frequent inter-

---

4 Pierre-Frédéric-Adolphe Carmouche, *Parga, ou le Brûlot, Mélodrame en trois actes, à spectacle*, first performance at Théâtre de Porte-Saint Martin 1827; Georges Ozaneaux, *Le Dernier jour de Missolonghi, Drame héroïque en trois actes, en vers, avec des chants*, first performance at Théâtre Royal de l'Odéon, 1828. C. E. Walker, *The Revolt of the Greeks; or, The Maid of Athens*, first performance at Royal Theatre Drury Lane, June 1824; J. B. Buckstone, *The Revolt of the Greeks; or, The Maid of Athens, A Romantic Drama in four Acts*, first performance at Royal Theatre Drury Lane, June 1829; William Barrymore and J. Raymond, *The Suliote; or, The Greek Family, a Melo-Drama in Three Acts*, first performance at Royal Theatre Drury Lane, October 24, 1829. Harro Harring, *Die Mainotten, Dramatisches Gedicht in drei Aufzügen*, first performance at Theatre of the Court, Munich 1824 and *Der Renegat auf Morea*, 1831, locality of first performance unknown.
5 Until now no comprehensive overview of European philhellenic theatre production has been published. A tentative but useful overview of French philhellenic plays can be found in Fridériki Tabaki-Iona: *Poésie philhellenique et périodiques de la Restauration* (Athens: Société des archives helléniques, littéraires et historiques, 1993). Tabaki-Iona establishes a list of plays mentioned in the periodical press, some of them with reference to published text editions, others only titles without secure reference.
6 See note 3.

vention of the censors. In 1825, for example, two plays with Greek topics were rejected by Parisian censors. One of these, Népomucène-Louis Lemercier's *Les Martyrs de Souli, ou l'Épire Moderne* [The martyrs of Suli, or modern Epirus], was never actually produced for the stage, but published in a book edition and performed to audiences at private readings. The other, Auguste Fabre's *Irène, ou l'Héroïne de Souli* [Irene, or the heroine of Suli], suffered the same fate. Fabre's play was also banned by the censors in 1825, despite the fact that it had been unanimously accepted by the management of the Théatre de l'Odéon.[7] It also appears from correspondence between the censor and theatre managers that a given play might have been accepted and performed only on condition that certain lines be removed or specific words replaced. The manuscript of *The Revolt of the Greeks; or, the Maid of Athens* (1824) shows traces of the author's deletion of problematic expressions and the addition of replacement dialogue for the characters in the play.[8]

By tracing the censor's remarks in the margin of the text and noting subsequent corrections and adjustments made by the author, we gain a picture of the larger political pattern emerging in the 1820s, of which theatre was a part. In particular, we can observe the way in which the Greek cause crystallised political reactions within the respective European governments, as censorship either allowed or interdicted certain characters or lines in the plays about Greece. In general, the censor's examination would pounce on terms of abuse of a distinctly racial or anti-Muslim nature as being out of step with the government's diplomatic considerations vis-à-vis the Porte, i. e. the Ottoman government in Constantinople. Also, pejorative designations of the fictive rulers in the plays, such as 'despot', 'tyrant', and 'monster', which might be associated with a general criticism of governmental systems in contemporary Europe, would be cancelled. Finally, examination could result in the banning of a play, as was the case in 1825 with Auguste Fabre's *Irène ou l'Héroïne de Souli*, despite the fact that the author

---

7 *Oeuvres choisies d'Auguste Fabre, mises en ordre et augmentées de la vie de l'auteur*, Tome 1, Paris 1848, 407–408.
8 Besides the limited amount of modern research, principally represented by Amy Muse's contributions (see notes 2 and 21), my search and retrieval of dramatic representations of the Greek War of Independence from the period 1821–1830 have been guided by Loukia Droulia's extensive survey from 1974 (see below) and directed to the online theatre archives of Bibliothèque Nationale Francaise and British Library (see below). Loukia Droulia, *Philhellénisme. Ouvrages inspirés par la guerre de l'Indépendance grècque. Répertoire bibliographique* (Athens 1974). *Almanach des spectacles* Paris 1822–1828 http://gallica.bnf.fr/ark:/12148/cb32688157h/date. *Lord Chamberlain's Plays. Vol. III. May–July 1824.* May 1824–Jul. 1824. MS Lord Chamberlain's Plays, 1852–1858 Add MS 42867. British Library. Nineteenth Century Collections Online, http://tinyurl.galegroup.com/tinyurl/6gsE82. Accessed 26 June 2018. *Lord Chamberlain's Plays. Vol. XXXIII. Sept.–Oct. 1829.* Sep. 1829–Oct. 1829. MS Lord Chamberlain's Plays, 1852–1858 Add MS 42897. British Library. Nineteenth Century Collections Online, http://tinyurl.galegroup.com/tinyurl/6gsLD3. Accessed 26 June 2018.

submitted several rewritings to the censors. In this particular case, the replacement of a few problematic lines was not enough to alter the examiner's ruling that Fabre's play took a generally revolutionary stand on the Greek question, and that a licence would be inconsistent with France's neutral foreign policy.

During the first five years of the Greek War of Independence, the European powers remained neutral and strategically kept out of the conflict, while the liberal opposition and intelligentsia in these countries joined in solidarity with the Greek cause. The liberal press overflowed with news and reactions to the war, and private collections were organised in support of the insurrection, most importantly by the powerful Greek Committees in London and Paris. The censorship of Greek plays thus had a dual motivation: on the one hand, it functioned as the government's control of impulses towards insurrection within its own population; on the other hand, it monitored the nation's diplomatic and pragmatic strategies in European geopolitics relevant to 'the Greek question'.

A discussion of the philhellenic drama of the period necessarily involves a focus on the way in which the Greek struggle against Ottoman dominion is narrated and interpreted in the Greek plays performed before a European public in the 1820s, when conservative governments gained power in European politics. A central question is how the Greek struggle for independence, narrated through the filter of dramaturgic genre conventions, became a prism for European self-understanding based on ideas of 'liberty', 'democracy', and 'humanity'? Of course, such values were not unique to the theatre, but were in broad circulation in the contemporary media, not least through daily newspapers and the political debate. However, my aim is to consider how theatrical fiction communicated via other aesthetic and affective channels, and in which ways the re-creation of events of the war on the theatrical stage might supply other answers and perspectives to the debate. My focus will be on the shifting relationships between the political discourse about Greece and the theatrical staging of the war, its agents, and its significance in the construction of an identity that understood itself as 'European'.

4. The Progress of the War

The Greek War of Independence was immediately precipitated by Alexandros Ypsilantis (1792-1828), the Greek nationalist military leader who, in February 1821, marched his military detachment into Moldavia and declared the Danubian provinces and Greece free countries, independent of Ottoman rule. The operation failed, but rumours of it gave rise to a wave of chaos and rebellion all over the country, instigating Greek militias' massacres in Turkish villages. According to British historian William St. Clair, twenty-thousand Turks were murdered within the first weeks of the war.⁹ This spiralled into retaliatory actions decreed by the Sultan's government in Constantinople, beginning with the execution of the Patriarch of the Greek Orthodox Church and continuing for more than six years, in ongoing battles between the Ottoman army and the Greek rebel forces. On the Greek side, a united strategy was intermittently impeded by internal conflicts in the revolutionary government. There were problems between the local *klepht* captains and their anarchist guerrilla troops, and there were quarrels between chief captains such as Kolokotrones, Odysseus, and Botsaris and the central war command under General Mavrokordatos, whose Italian military education did not always correspond to the style and ideas of the native warriors. As a consequence, Greek positions gradually weakened, while the Turkish army was continuously reinforced with a supply of Egyptian and African troops serving under the Sultan. In addition to this, the first years of the war were characterised by unstable alliances between the Greek rebels and the Albanian governor Ali Pasha, who, taking advantage of the events, sought to strengthen his position as ruler of Albania and Epirus, detaching the provinces from the reign of the Porte.

The war attracted the participation of young philhellenic men from all over Europe who wanted to volunteer as soldiers. In different phases and in varying numbers, they arrived from Germany, Italy, France, England, Sweden, Denmark, and Switzerland to the Ionian Islands, and proceeded from there to the camps in Kalamata, Nafplio, and Missolonghi. Organizing the volunteers caused problems because of the lack of a regular military leadership and because of insufficient resources, provisioning, and war equipment, and also because the differences between the Greek mountain and village militias and the foreign soldiers who were trained according to Western military standards of discipline were hard to overcome. A great many of the volunteering soldiers who set out for Greece were soon disillusioned and returned home after having spent only a short time in the country.¹⁰

---

9 William St. Clair, *That Greece Might Still Be Free. The Philhellenes in the War of Independence* (Cambridge: Open Book Publishers, 2008) 1. In the following account of the Greek war, the main references are to William St. Clair (2008) and Roderick Beaton, *Greece: Biography of a Modern Nation* (London: Penguin, 2019). For a discussion of the politics and attitudes of the European great powers in relation to the Greek war, see for instance Allan Cunningham, 'The Philhellenes, Canning and Greek Independence' *Middle Eastern Studies*, Vol. 14, No. 2 (May, 1978)151–181; Nina Maria Athanassoglou-Kallmy, *French Images from the Greek War of Independence, 1821–1830. Art and Politics Under the Restoration*, Chap. 1: Some Historical, Political, and Artistic Facts about the French Restoration and the Greek War of Independence (Yale: Yale University Press, 1989); Alexis Heraclides and Ada Dialla, *Humanitarian Intervention in the Long Nineteenth Century: Setting the Precedent*, Chap 6: Intervention in the Greek War of Independence 1821–1832 (Manchester: Manchester University Press, 2015). doi.org/10.11647/obp.0001, doi.org/10.1080/002632078087000373, doi.org/10.7208/Chicago/9780226673882.001.0001.

10 William St. Clair arrives at the total of 940 registered European volunteers participating in the

Despite the fact that the revolutionary government in Nafplio appealed to the Western powers for economic and military support, the British as well as the Russian and French governments remained passive in the conflict. For conservative governments throughout Europe the watchword 'liberty', when referring to the Greek struggle, contained a potential danger, even though the Greek rebellion was not directed towards national authorities, but against the colonial dominion of the Ottoman Empire. The Austrian and Prussian governments went so far as to issue a direct ban on philhellenic activities and to shut down committees organising volunteers for Greece. The French government, which had its own diplomatic interests involving the Sultan and furnished the Egyptian army with weapons and ships, remained passive until 1827.

Philhellenic engagement, which spread throughout Europe, was organised on a private basis and most often sponsored and led by spokesmen of the liberal opposition in the larger cities. It usually took the form of cultural activities, the liberal press playing an important part with daily publication of information and political analysis, and sometimes also including literary essays and responses to the events of the war. Similarly, various private associations, church associations, and learned societies promoted solidarity through concert performances and lectures, etc. The most important work was done by Greek Committees, such as the London Committee (established in 1823) and the Paris Committee (established in 1825). The activities of these Committees were mostly of a practical and financial character, raising money and procuring supplies in support of the Greek struggle, which tended to rely on large financial contributions from private donors.

It was the reports on the horrors of the war – and especially those from the massacres committed against the Greek population by the Ottoman army – which had the effect on public sentiment that eventually made itself felt in political circles. Nevertheless, a long time was spent in diplomatic interludes before Russia, England, and France eventually agreed to intervene. The massacre on the island of Chios in 1822, in which 25,000 of the male population of the island died, while 45,000, mostly women and children, were deported as slaves, sent shock waves across Europe.[11]

---

war. Of these, 313 died. He further estimates the realistic number of volunteers to be on a scale between 1100 and 1200 in total. German volunteers made up the obvious majority during the first years of the war (342 throughout the period), the French wave from 1825 and onwards reached a total of 196, the British contingent was comparatively smaller (96 for the whole period), Swedes totalled 9 and Danes totalled 8. See *That Greece Might Still Be Free* (2008) Appendix I: Remarks on numbers, 356. Historians do not entirely agree on the numbers. Other sources are W. Barth & M. Kehrig-Korn, *Die Philhellenenzeit von der Mitte des 18. Jahrhunderts bis zur Ermordung Kapodistrias' am 9. Oktober 1831* (Munich, 1960).

11 As noted by William St. Clair, it is at the same time important to observe that news about the war that reached Western Europe were communicated via pro-Greek channels. The news

However, it took the siege and the massacre at Missolonghi four years later (in 1826) to get negotiations underway in Europe. Reports from the starving town, which recounted the slaughter of 3,000 men as they attempted to evacuate the population through enemy lines, and of the imprisonment of 3-4,000 women and children, offered a terrifying example of the war's atrocities. Furthermore, the defeat at Missolonghi seemed to signal a turning point in the war, paving the way for Ottoman victory and for an Egyptian takeover of Greek territory. In the face of this threat, in October 1827, Russia, England, and France sent their joint navies to Peloponnese, backing up their demand for a ceasefire with military power. The result of the war was determined in a final sea battle in the Bay of Navarino in the southern Peloponnese where the French-British-Russian navy came to the rescue of the Greek military and marine and definitively defeated Ibrahim Pasha's Egyptian navy. Sultan Mahmoud II was forced to give up the war and to let the European governments start negotiations about the borders of a free and independent Greek state.

5. Genres: Tragedy and Melodrama

The military plays of the Napoleonic era, which would inspire many philhellenic productions of the 1820s, were largely modelled on the popular melodramatic formula, always playing on intrigue and suspense and always concluding with the celebration of a patriotic victory. Plays about the Greek War, however, operated on a broader scale. Next to melodrama we find tragedies or heroic dramas, depending on the sombreness of their subject or their degree of engagement with the heroic sufferings of the Greek rebels. Some national markers or dividing lines seem to appear in the material, indicating a greater weight of melodrama in the British material, while the majority of the French productions followed the style of tragedies composed in Classical verse style. As to the German productions, they often figure as 'Trauerspiel' [plays of sorrow]. Perusing the German material presented here, we do not find a single dramatic composition on the Greek subject labelled as a melodrama on the title page. These differences seem to coincide fairly well with general tendencies in the theatre productions of these countries during the 1820s and perhaps also with the differences between British, French, and German engagement in the Greek cause.

---

said nothing about the plunders and massacres committed against the Turkish population undertaken by the Greeks during their storms at Monemvasia, Navarino, and Tripolitza, which were of comparable dimension and atrocity, see William St. Clair, *That Greece Might Still be Free*, Chap. Two Kinds of War, 41-44.

On the title pages of the printed editions, the playwrights designated their plays according to pre-established genre categories. But the genres of the period were in constant change. This was, among other things, because those genres responded to changing theatre legislation, which in France as well as in England accorded the right to perform Classical genres only to the national theatres. These circumstances led to the creation of numerous cross-over types and to new genres that could be played on the smaller stages, and which would often absorb disparate genres into new types of dramatic performance. An example of this is the melodrama's combination of music and spoken theatre, a theatre style that grew in popularity at the time and which proved to have long-term viability. In connection with this, it is interesting to see the way in which the classical military show, popular in the early years of the Napoleonic wars, was rapidly developed and transformed into melodramatic plays, typically with a plot about love and family, enabling the audience to engage in the war drama, and giving them the opportunity to admire the grandiose re-enactment on stage of glorious battles.

What particularly distinguishes the philhellenic drama of the 1820s from earlier military pieces (apart from a different relation to the East) is that the philhellenic plays are about a contemporary war, the outcome of which is not yet known. Thus, what is represented on stage is the heroic bravery of the rebels, rather than victorious honour and glory. Driven by philhellenic zeal, some of the playwrights even conjure up the most horrific events of the war. The massacre at Missolonghi in 1826, for instance, appears to have been the event that made the biggest impact on the European theatre stages. In other words, the appeal of the Greek plays consisted of something different from the appeal of the older military plays. The latter would always take their departure in a battle already won, and the play would invite celebration of the national victory. The grand finale of the last act indicated a full stop and constituted the happy ending both to the war drama and to the plot's love intrigue.

In the portrayal of a war not yet concluded, the story cannot reach a conclusion that reflects real life, and the play will therefore have to appeal to the audience's feeling of solidarity with the fighting heroes at a time when history is still in the making. So, how does one draft this undetermined complex of events on stage, and according to which dramaturgic principles? Can the massacre at Missolonghi be represented by following the rules of tragedy? Can the disaster at Missolonghi be represented according to the framework of melodrama? We do find examples of both genres in the corpus of plays. We have the tragedy by Ozaneaux *Le Dernier Jour de Missolonghi,* and we also have Carmouche's melodrama *Parga, ou le Brûlot.* These pieces were first performed in 1828 and 1827, that is, a little more than a year after the massacre and around the time when the allied forces intervened in the war.

On the whole, documentary ambitions and references to the contemporaneous war make up a common denominator in the philhellenic drama of the 1820s. And, as we shall see, this common denominator also accounts for the dramaturgic problem pertinent to the greater part of the Greek plays. Because, as a category 'the unfinished' is non-dramatic, or is considered so in Classical dramaturgic theory. The formula of tragedy and the melodramatic composition both presuppose a plot built on a succession of completed events building up to a conclusion from which the whole of the play can be retroactively interpreted.

In tragedy, according to Aristotle's commentary in *Poetics*, the chain of events forming the plot is determined by a central conflict. Typically, this conflict is between the individual's personal ambition and desire in combination with his or her limited perspective and the larger powers that the character is up against, whether they be the law of the gods, fate, or an ethical norm. The critical element here can be connected with Aristotle's definition of *hamartia*, that is, the hero's lack of knowledge concerning the values against which he is offending. This lack of insight functions as the hero's flaw, which releases an inescapable chain of events, which in turn will lead to a tragic conclusion. As a rule, there is no possible mediation between the tragedy's opposing sets of values, and consequently the conflict will come to an end with the destruction of the main character. In Sophocles' tragedy *Oedipus Rex*, which is the model play that Aristotle used, Oedipus is ignorant of the fact that he himself is the source of the crime against the gods, which, as the ruler of Thebes, he is bent on punishing. It happens to be that he is, in fact, the murderer of his own father and has unwittingly become his mother's lover. During the plot, the complexities multiply until the moment of insight when Oedipus acknowledges the concealed connection (*anagnorisis*), after which a sudden change of fate comes about (*peripeteia*) pushing the plot to its conclusion, in which the hapless king Oedipus curses and blinds himself.[12]

As mentioned above, the other genre adopted in philhellenic plays is the melodrama, which had gained a dominant status in the theatre world by the 1820s. The breakthrough of the genre is often dated back to 1800, which was the time of the first performance of Guilbert Pixérécourt's *Coelina* at the Théâtre de l'Ambigu-Comique, in Paris. The play was reprised several times and became a model for popular imitations and for new productions everywhere in Europe. The novelty of the genre was the way in which it combined the dialogue of the theatre with a musical background. This was different from the style of the scattered songs performed in the vaudeville or the ballad opera, as it included music composed to function as a specific background score to the play, intensifying the atmosphere of the drama from beginning to end. Melodrama and tragedy share

---

12 See Christian Dahl, 'Ødipus vor samtidige: Christoph Menkes tragedieteori i perspektiv', *Peripeti*, No. 13, 05.2010, 21–31.

features with regard to composition as well as in the timing of the plot. In both genres, the hero will be situated in a conflict or entangled in an intrigue that drives the action forward towards the end, at which a crime or falsity is brought to light. But in melodrama, unlike in tragedy, we do not have a collision of equally strong values that eventually cause the destruction of the hero. On the contrary, melodrama has a clear-cut, simplified structure that separates villains from heroes. Moreover, the logic of its plot demands the final unmasking and punishment of the villains in order to secure a happy ending with the celebration of the hero's moral values, most often firmly anchored in the family, nation, and the church. The organization of the plot in melodrama is also different from the tight and inescapable chain of events that is typical of tragedy. The plot line of the melodrama involves unlikely coincidences and stark contrasts accompanied by shocking stage effects, and it is often burdened with secondary plots and loose ends. Melodrama is a theatre of the affect, addressed to the audiences of the boulevards. At the time, the genre would therefore often be rejected by theatre reviewers, who criticised the improbable plots. Modern theatre studies have discussed the appeal of the melodrama in the light of its historical context. The assumption is that the continuous background of upheaval and turmoil of war in Europe during the first decades of the nineteenth-century existed as a mental condition and therefore became a sounding board for audiences watching the melodrama in the theatre. With all of its suspense, danger, and shock effects, melodrama captured the mood of its time, not least in its appeal to the feelings of hope and consolation played out in the final act, in which temporary chaos is finally overcome and peace and order restored.[13] To put it in simple terms, melodrama is a genre that responds to the desire for order felt in the years following the Congress of Vienna (1815), after the savagery of the revolutionary era and the turmoil of the Napoleonic wars. As a genre, the logic of tragedy does not confirm an established order; rather it reflects upon the basic patterns of social life and the course of history from a philosophical perspective.

6. Missolonghi on the French Stage

In the French material, the plays about the Greek War tend to be in the tragic genre and take somewhat after the neoclassical tradition of Racine and Corneille.[14] The Greek events inherently possessed a pathos and a heroism that

---

13 See Jeffrey Cox, 'The Death of Tragedy; or, the Birth of Melodrama', in Tracy C. Davis & Peter Holland, *The Performing Century* (Basingstoke and NY: Palgrave Macmillan, 2007) 161–181. doi.org/10.1057/97802305894839.
14 For a discussion of French classicist tragedy in relation to Aristotle and the antique Greek

made them suitable for treatment in the classical diction of tragedy, with its highflown language and alexandrine couplets. Yet the combination of revolt and pathos on the public stage was inflammatory, as can be seen from the many problems such dramas had with censorship. Representative in this regard is the year 1825, when the fate of three philhellenic plays was decided: Lemercier's *Les Martyrs de Souli* and Fabre's *Irène ou l'Héroïne de Souli* were both stopped by the censors, while Michel Pichat's tragedy *Léonidas* only premiered at the Théâtre Français after three years of quarrelling with state censors. This presents us with a clear example of how the system of censorship operated, essentially precluding any content that referred directly to contemporary political issues, particularly when it came to representations of rebellion. The tragedies by Lemercier and Fabre were both heroizing portrayals of current episodes from the war, parading the authentic names of Greek rebel leaders and Ottoman generals in the *dramatis personae.* In Pichat's tragedy *Léonidas*, however, the story was set in a distant historical time, and featured a heroic figure from Classical Antiquity: Leonidas, king of Sparta, who, with a few men and at the risk of his life, defended the pass of Thermopylae against the invasion of the Persian king and his army. Thanks to its historical framing, the play passed through censorship. According to contemporary reviews, however, its tremendous success on the night of the first performance was not only because of the brilliance of the author's text, but also, perhaps especially, because of the aura lent to it by the famous and charismatic actor Talma, who starred in the leading role. Also significant was the presence in the theatre of the young sons of the famous Greek captains Canaris and Miaoulis, invited by the theatre's managers to attend the performance.[15] Pichat avoided any direct references to contemporary events on stage, but he was less reticent about this in his preface to the printed edition, in which he explicitly dedicated his play to the Greek rebels. In addition to this, the pro-Greek audience in the theatre hall would respond with enthusiasm to the prophetic lines in the monologue of Leonidas:

> … Leur gloire vengeresse
> Dans l'avenir encor ressuscite la Grèce.
> Oui, vaincus, opprimés dans les siècles lointains,
> Les Grecs ne seront pas déchus de leurs destins

---

tragedy see: John Lyons, *Phantoms of Chance: From Fortune to Randomness in Seventeenth-Century French Literature*, Chap 1 'Fortune, Mistress of Events: Corneille and the Poetics of Tragedy' (Edinburgh: Edinburgh University Press 2011) and Pascale LaFountain, *Theatres of Error: Problems of Performance in German and French Enlightenment Theatre*, Palgrave Studies in Theatre and Performance History (London: Palgrave Macmillan, 2018).

15 See Théodore Muret, *L'histoire par le théâtre 1789–1851*, Vol. 2 (Paris 1868) 276 and Nina Maria Athanassoglou-Kallmy, *French Images from the Greek War of Independence, 1821–1830. Art and Politics Under the Restoration* (Yale: Yale University Pres, 1989).

Tant que, de notre gloire entretenant leurs villes,
Vous resterez debout, rochers des Thermopyles.

[(Leonidas' and his soldiers') avenging glory
shall in the future restore Greece once more.
Yes, though defeated and oppressed in distant centuries,
the Greeks shall not be denied their destiny.
As long as you, the rocks of Thermopylae,
shall remain standing preserving their cities surrounded by our glory.][16]

Fig. 1: Louis Maleuvre: Costume for Talma in the role of Leonidas in the tragedy *Léonidas* by Michel Pichat. '... Rassure-toi, tu mourras' [... Be sure, you will die]. Engraving 1825. Source: La Bibliotèque Nationale de France.

---

16 Michel Pichat, *Léonidas*, tragédie en cinq actes (Paris 1825) Act 3, Scene VI, 45.

As in the plays just mentioned, *Le Dernier Jour de Missolonghi* by George Ozaneaux is a tragedy composed in rhymed couplets in the classical French style. And, as with Mercier's and Fabre's plays, it directly refers to an event of the Greek War that had recently shocked Europe and put the name of Missolonghi on everybody's lips. Its plot centres on the year-long Ottoman siege of the city of Missolonghi on the western coast of Epirus and the final massacre in April 1826 when Greek troops failed to evacuate the population, resulting in the citizens committing collective suicide by burning down their town.

One might expect a play with this kind of content to be banned by the censors and in fact, prior to its first performance at the Théâtre de l'Odéon in April 1828 it was withheld for ten months and was only licensed after an important political change had taken place: in October 1827, the French government took military action, and the French navy, in joint action with the allied forces, defeated the Ottomans in a decisive sea battle at the bay of Navarino. The predicament of Ozaneaux's play was changed by this event in two ways, which the author would later comment on in his literary reflections, *Erreurs poétiques* [Poetical errors].[17] First, French neutrality in the war had vanished all of a sudden, a circumstance that made a licensing of the play possible, although it was still to be performed in the censored version with the cuts and amendments imposed by the examiners. However, this political change also diminished the play's topicality, because Missolonghi was no longer on everybody's lips. In fact, public interest in the sufferings of the Greek people soon declined after the action of the allied forces, as this turned the fortunes of war in favour of the Greeks.

Furthermore, Ozaneaux's ambition to provide a documentary up-to-the-minute account of the war created a problem for his play, in terms of genre. In his *Erreurs poétiques* he refers to *Le Dernier Jour* as a *tragedy*, whereas on the title page of the printed version he puts the designation *heroic drama*, and there is a reason for the indeterminacy: the immediate events of the actual war could not easily be narrated in the form of a tragedy. They could not be presented as a logically ordered chain of events progressing forward to its conclusion, where some deeper truth would be revealed.

The characters of the play are historically authentic. They are the military commanders of Missolonghi: Captain Capsali with General Noti Botsari, the town's bishop, and a few fictive figures, among them a French officer, Gérard, who is fighting on the Greek side. The plot has no real conflict or line of suspense, but is rather a count-down on the spot to the inescapable catastrophe. However, the catastrophe is not unavoidable or inescapable in the sense indicated by the poetics of tragedy, where catastrophe is released by the fatal blindness of the hero. But it is so in the historical sense, because this is what actually happened in

---

17 George Ozaneaux, *Erreurs poétiques*, Tome 2 (Paris 1849), 3.

Missolonghi on 22 April 1826; this is what Ozaneaux wanted to document in his play, and this is what the audience expected to see performed on stage. The count-down starts in the first scene, where the Greek defence is seen in the citadel debating the hopeless situation. The exchange of words between Captain Capsali and the French officer has death in view, as when the Frenchman says:

> Qu'importe où le brave s'expose / Quand il a des lauriers, la gloire à conquérir! / Qu'importe où sa cendre repose / Quand l'immortalité devant lui va s'ouvrir!
>
> [What does it matter where the brave man exposes himself to danger / When he is to win the laurels and the glory! / What does it matter where his ashes are laid to rest / When immortality will open itself to him!][18]

Similarly, when Captain Capsali answers a question about whether starving under siege or dying in the middle of fighting is to be preferred he replies:

> Capsali: Consolez-vous, la céleste patrie / Aux éternels banquets nous verra tous demain. / Gérard: Et quoi! cher Capsali, nul espoir ne nous reste? Capsali: Tout espoir de secours est maintenant détruit.
>
> [Capsali: Take comfort, the heavenly fatherland / shall see us all tomorrow at the eternal feasts. / Gérard: But how, dear Capsali, is there no hope left for us? / Capsali: All hope of assistance has now been abandoned.][19]

Resignation, a patriotic spirit of self-sacrifice, and the preparation to die are the utterances exchanged, including variations on the strength of Christian faith and the curse of the Turks, all the way until the play's final tableau of destruction: a slaughtered civilian population, fighting soldiers, cries for help amidst blazing explosions.

At this point, questions about the significance of the dramatic conclusion need to be asked. In what way, for instance, does the ending of *Le Dernier Jour de Missolonghi* provide an interpretative context for the play as a whole? And how does Ozaneaux transform the factual event of a war not yet concluded into a fiction to be played on stage with a beginning and an end? We shall return to this problem of dramaturgic composition in Ozaneaux, after considering a parallel, though different structure of composition in the case of another contemporary play referring to the massacre at Missolonghi, that is, the melodrama *Parga ou le Brûlot*, written by Pierre-Frédéric-Adolphe Carmouche.

Carmouche, like Pichat, displaces the inflammatory topic of Missolonghi onto a parallel event in Greek history: the conquest of the city of Parga by the Ottomans, during the Venetian wars in 1672, and the exodus of the population from the city after they had set it on fire. This historical displacement is doubly intricate,

---

18 George Ozaneaux, *Le Dernier Jour de Missolonghi* (Paris 1828) Acte Premier, Scène Première, 4.
19 Ibid.

given that Carmouche, through hints of the plot, also associates the Parga catastrophe of 1672 with a more recent political event: the British handing over of Parga to the Ottomans in 1817, which was part of a strategic game about the Ionian Islands. What Carmouche gains by displacing the contemporary massacre at Missolonghi onto a distant historical event with similar features is, in the first place, to avoid censorship. In the second place, this distancing allows him more liberty to put fictive characters into action and to invest the historical frame of events with a melodramatic intrigue of his own invention. The Greek patriots or the Ottoman enemy in the cast list for this play could not be identified with real names and persons chronicled in history; they are made up types. Carmouche's ambition is not, like Ozaneaux's, to give a testimonial report of the moment of disaster. Rather, it is, through the allusion to Missolonghi, to bring together the suspense of the melodrama with a general compassion for the sufferings of the Greek people in the war. The plot has its criminal villains and moral heroes, and does not rely on a simple dichotomy of a fearful Ottoman enemy versus Greek patriots in distress, because among the Greek freedom fighters who defend their town, Carmouche places a vile traitor, Thelsistor, a Judas-figure who bargains away his native country to the enemy. In the attempt to avenge himself for disappointments concerning military leadership and his marriage to the captain's daughter, he betrays the Greeks' secret plan of defence and occasions the catastrophe of the play. In the last scene, when the Parganiotes, attacked by the Ottomans, flee the burning city, he is seen imploring the crowd to let him go with them. But he is left standing on the stage, caught by guilt and condemned to be forever cursed.

As a melodramatic finale, this ending is tricky. On the one hand, it seems wholly satisfying, because the villain is finished off and properly punished for his crime, setting a moral standard. On the other hand, it is not clear that the excitement and anxiety stirred up by the previous dramatic events can be convincingly resolved in the affirmation of a moral order, as required in melodrama. Unfortunately, I have found no information about the music composed for the play by Alexandre Piccini. It might have been interesting to consider the music in order to estimate the emotional pitch intended for the final tableau, particularly since the images of escape and expulsion, indicated in the stage direction for the last scene, are strong representations of catastrophe, even if the play invents a scapegoat to take the blame.[20] At the time when Carmouche wrote his play, the

---

20 The stage direction reads: 'accompanied by a magnificent music [une musique brillante] Turks with drawn scimitars appear in great numbers on the ramparts of Parga; some of them set the Greek temple on fire, the flames illumining this final tableau. THE END' (*my translation*). The magnificent music accompanying the closing scene of disaster, as indicated by Pichat, might be seen to underline the ambiguous message of the play as discussed above. I am grateful to Jens Hesselager for this observation.

likely course of the war was still entirely uncertain, but on opening night, at the Théâtre de Porte Saint-Martin in December 1827, the situation had changed as an effect of the intervention of the allied forces only one month before. All things considered, the ending of the play is ambiguous, seemingly belated in its relation to the historical moment, and vacillating between the restorative finale of the melodrama and the glance into the abyss of the tragedy.

To sum up, the undertaking of writing the war into the theatre seems to be a challenge to genre, and the more documentary the ambition of the author, the more problematic it is in relation to convention. As an example of this, we can follow how Ozaneaux's documentary motives were subject to criticism in his own time, not only by censorship for political reasons, but also by the liberal, pro-Greek theatre criticism for aesthetic reasons: a fact about which he makes sarcastic remarks in his *Erreurs poétiques*. He is clearly annoyed by the interventions of censorship, complaining of the 'mutilation' of his play, as he terms it, and infuriated by the delay of the premiere. In his view, the protraction of the process by the censors is what led to Carmouche's pre-empting the topic of catastrophe as a subject for drama, and to Carmouche's stealing public attention from his own play, so to speak. In his later printed edition of the *Missolonghi* play, he removed the censor's corrections from the text, including the censor's cancellation of some minor roles, such as that of the English officer and the priest, which were thought likely to cause offence in clerical and political circles. Completely absurd is his statement that he was compelled to erase all lines in the manuscript containing the word 'liberté!'. As he writes in 1849:

> as if I were a revolutionary, a republican, a dangerous madman with the sole goal of stirring up the youth by putting the Jacobin cap on the top of the banner of the cross ... I, a good and honest Christian, I, the learned professor of philosophy at Collège royal de Louis-le-Grand [21]

Ozaneaux defended himself against theatre reviews in a prologue, in which he had 'the author' (Ozaneaux) complain to 'a friend' about the criticism of the papers concerning the form of the play: 'Un style par trop lyrique' [A much too lyrical style] (*Courrier Français*); 'ma pièce n'en est pas une' [my play is not a play at all] (*Journal des Débats*); 'Point d'action surtout, point d'intrigue d'amour / Point de ces coups de scène ou l'on crie, ou l'on pleure' [Above all, no plot, no love intrigue / None of these *coups de scène*, where they scream and they cry]; 'la pièce est une conjugaison du verbe mourir' [the play is a declination of the verb to die] (*Le Courrier des Théâtres*).[22]

---

21 Georges Ozaneaux, *Erreurs poétiques*, Tome 2 (Paris 1849), 9 (my translation).
22 Ibid., 20, 22.

While Ozaneaux here evidently distances himself from the sensational '*coups de scenes*,' of melodrama, it is hard not to agree with *Journal des Débats* and *Courrier des Théâtres* that an intrigue is lacking, and that in this sense there is no play. And, in continuation of this criticism one might add that, strictly speaking, there is no conclusion either. It is the documentary intention that prevents the play from becoming a play: that is, from forming a dramatic composition where the threads of the action are gathered in the end. The conclusion of *Le Dernier Jour* is not based on the internal events of the drama, but drawn from the historical facts. In 1827, while the play was under review by the censors, the massacre was an episode in an open-ended and fluctuating history of war, of which the conclusion was still unknown – and, as such, was difficult to understand as anything but a example of the horrors of war. When the play was actually produced in 1828, however, it was already two years since the event had taken place, and the allied powers had affected a ceasefire during the closing phase of the war. So Ozaneaux was probably right in thinking that the readiness of audiences to engage with the horror and pathos of the Greek war on stage had decreased in a short time. From the perspective of Ozaneaux, it was a question of *bad timing.* From a different perspective, however, it may be perceived as the incompatibility of the documentary ambition of the playwright with an efficient dramaturgy for the play.

We must look to England, and to the domestic scene in London, to learn how it is possible to dramatize a war that is taking place simultaneously in a distant corner of Europe.

7. Greek Melodrama on the British Stage

It should be noted that pro-Greek theatre was also produced across the Atlantic. The American author Mordecai Manuel Noah had his melodrama *The Grecian Captive; or, The Fall of Athens* staged at the New York Theatre in 1822. In the preface to the book version of the play, Noah reflects on the theatrical representation of facts and fiction about the war. While the play has no basis in history, the cast list uses the real names of some famous agents in the war, such as Ali Pasha, the Turkish governor of Epirus, and the Greek-Russian officer prince Ypsilantis, who initiated the rebellion. Most strikingly, and indeed contra-factually, he has the Greeks winning the war with the help of the Americans only one year after its outbreak: that is, in 1822, the year the play was staged in New York. Thus, in the final speech of the last scene, he anticipates the course of history, when he has the victorious Greek combatants joining each other in homage to military triumph: 'Behold a glorious termination to all our painful struggles! Greece is free! .... Now to merit freedom by the establishment of just laws – a free and upright government – a liberal, tolerant, and benevolent spirit to all'.[23] In the preface of 1822, Noah casually defends his method with reference to the privilege of artistic licence:

> Several pieces have already been performed in England, relative to the present struggle in Greece, and events dramatized, which 'tis said, have never occurred. This privilege of imagination is the peculiar property of the dramatist, who is not bound to wait for the tardy movements of armies, or the cold progress of cabinet negotiations, he is only to know that war exists in Greece, the cradle of the Arts, where Homer sang, where Themistocles conquered, and his fancy and invention must supply the rest; therefore, if eventually the Greeks should not recover Athens, it will not be my fault, it was necessary to my play, and so I gave them possession of that interesting spot with a dash of my pen, being too far removed from the scene of action to take any part in fighting for it.[24]

This statement could be taken as the short formula for the British (and American) melodramatic productions about the Greek war of the 1820s. Thus, according to Noah, the problem of how to end the dramatic plot, *vis-a-vis* the uncertain ending of the contemporary war, appears to be no problem at all. All the author needs to do, we learn, is to cut events into shape so as to fit the dramatic form. Although none of the three plays discussed below positively ends either the plot or the war with Greek victory, the authors found other means to conclude their plots in a display of military victory and with a grand finale, i.e., in accordance with the pattern of melodrama. The plays in question are C. E. Walker's *The Revolt of the Greeks; or, The Maid of Athens* (1824), J. B. Buckstone's 1829 play of the same title, and William Barrymore's *The Suliote; or, the Greek Family* (1829). All three plays end with the *outbreak* of the Greek rebellion. The rebellion is presented as the abrupt inversion of power relations in a plot in which the Greek characters have for a long time suffered the persecution and injustices of the Ottoman authorities in the various guises of tax-collectors, police, soldiers, gaolers, and pashas. The entire melodramatic palette of disguise, incognito, prison, false promises, and dangerous rescues is staged, until the moment in the last scene, when the Greek rebels throw off their turbaned disguises and declare armed revolt against their Turkish oppressors.

Lord Byron's shadow hovers over the English plays, not only as an effect of his engagement in the war and his early death by fever in the military camp at Missolonghi in 1824 (two years in advance of the massacre), but also due to his influential engagements with Classical and contemporary Greece in *Childe Harold's Pilgrimage* (1812–1818) and the so-called 'Turkish Tales' (1813–1816). As early as 1818, two of his Turkish poems had been arranged together (by William Dimond) and produced as a melodrama at the Royal Theatre Drury Lane

---

23 Mordecai Manuel Noah, *The Grecian Captive; or, The Fall of Athens* (New York 1822), 48.
24 Ibid., III.

in London. Also, the curious repetition of the title *The Revolt of the Greeks; or, The Maid of Athens* in two separate plays (Walker's, of 1824, and Buckstone's, of 1829) reflects Byron's influence. The title reads as a reference to his popular poem from 1810, 'Maid of Athens, Ere We Part', several times set to music by composers of the era. In C. E. Walker's play the title functions only as a loose reference to the heroine of the play, whereas in Buckstone's case, the mythic personality of Byron figures as a leading character in the dramatic plot.[25]

Walker's play passes through censure with only a few remarks shortly before its opening night at Drury Lane in June 1824. In the correspondence between the censor Colman and Lord Chamberlain Montrose attached to the manuscript, Colman makes a brief note saying, that besides a couple of oaths and strong expressions, which have to be omitted, there is nothing to object to, 'unless, indeed, War between the Turcs *[sic]* & Greeks be, at this juncture, objectionable subjects altogether'.[26] Montrose answers that the subject of the play 'required to be considered with attention; but the manner of treating it makes the whole difference'. Throughout the manuscript, then, we can follow the substitutions made by Colman for loaded expressions such as 'tyrant' and 'despot' with the neutral term 'Pasha', or we find a complete deletion of lines where the Pasha is addressed in an abusive way: for example, 'the worst of thy fell race' or other similarly hostile references to the Turkish authorities. By contrast, lines expressing attitudes toward political issues, such as revolt or oppression, are not necessarily suppressed, as when, for instance, at one point in *The Revolt of the Greeks,* the Pasha comments on the strained political conflict between Greeks and Turks: 'I would, but dare not kill him [his Greek opponent] – such an act were too dangerous at this time & might enflame the already disaffected multitude to deeds of desperate notes.'[27] No direct abuse of the Turks, no offence to The Porte, could be pronounced from the legitimate British theatre stage, and it is clear that British censorship worked as a safeguard for the foreign policy pursued by the current government. It is thus striking to consider the comparative *laissez faire* of English censorship, compared to French practices one year later, in

---

25 Amy Muse has a discussion of the two plays in 'Byron and the Maids of Athens'. http://internationalassociationofbyronsocieties.org/files/proceedings/london_2013/muse.pdf. Among other things she indicates the ways in which Walker's play re-uses characters and plot elements from a popular novel by Sidney Owenson, *Ida of Athens* (1808), which also Byron knew.

26 Correspondence between the censors added to the manuscript of C. E. Walker's play *The Revolt of the Greeks; or, The Maid of Athens*, MS 42867 in Lord Chamberlain's Plays. Vol. III. May-July 1824. May 1824-Jul. 1824, se note 8.

27 C. E. Walker, *The Revolt of the Greeks; or, The Maid of Athens*, MS 42867 p. 83/19 in Lord Chamberlain's Plays. Vol. III. May-July 1824. May 1824-Jul. 1824. MS Lord Chamberlain's Plays, 1852–1858 Add MS 42867. British Library. Nineteenth Century Collections Online, http://tinyurl.galegroup.com/tinyurl/6gsE82. Accessed 26 June 2018.

1825, which suppressed each and every utterance of the word 'liberté' or any hint of revolt. It is 'the manner of treating it [that] makes the whole difference' (quote Montrose), and, in the English theatre of the time, a play could bear the title '*Revolt* of the Greeks', and its first scene could open in a cheerful song of the rebels:

> Sons of the Greeks arise! –
> The glorious hours gone forth! –
> Unworthy of such ties –
> Display who gave you birth.
>
> Chorus
> Sons of Greeks! – let us go
> In arms against the foe;
> Till this hated blood shall flow
> In a river past our feet.[28]

One of the other English philhellenic melodramas treated here, namely William Barrymore's *The Suliote; or, The Greek Family*, staged at Drury Lane on 24 October 1829, provides an interesting example of the role of censorship in English theatre at the time. No printed edition of the play has survived, but, as in the case of Walker, Barrymore's original manuscript is kept in the archives of the Lord Chamberlain's Office, to which it was submitted by the manager of Drury Lane Theatre one month before its first performance. Attached to the manuscript we find, once more, the correspondence between Colman and Montrose with a discussion of whether permission should be given to perform the play. On this occasion, the evaluation and exchange of views signal a heightened political concern, compared to the discussion about *The Maid of Athens* in 1824, which may seem surprising since British neutrality had long been suspended in 1829, and the war was now, broadly speaking, continuing at the level of negotiations. Censor Colman sums up his considerations about the play in relation to the political situation:

> The content of the above incidents may be classed among the common-place constructions of our numerous Melo-Dramas; but the Turks are exhibited in an odious point of view, and (to quote from the Author) as: "[unreadable] who pride themselves in cruelty,

---

28 Ibid., p. 75/3. I detected that the song of the rebels is a hidden quotation from Byron's translation of a popular Greek war song, written by the Greek writer and revolutionary Riga Velestinlis (1757–1798). Walker does not mention the source. Byron published the translation of the song in an appendix to *Childe Harold's Pilgrimage* (1812) with the prefatory remarks: 'Translation of the famous Greek War Song, written by Riga, who perished in the attempt to revolutionize Greece. The translation is as literal as the author could make it in verse, which is of the same measure with that of the original.' See Lord Byron, *The Complete Poetical Works*, ed. by Jerome J. McGann, Volume I (Oxford: The Clarendon Press 1980) 330–333, 452–453. doi.org/10.1093/actrade/9780198118909.book.1

who build their fame on brutal insult and esteem ferocity and lust as social virtues:" The question, therefore, is whether our old allies, the Turks, are to be exhibited (particularly at this momentous crisis of their political affairs) as the oppressors of the Greeks, and as an inhuman & detestable race.[29]

As Coleman's comments indicate the depiction of the Turks is starkly negative, and when the key figures barely escape the numerous threats and machinations arranged by the tyrants, heroes and villains are without exception painted in jarring contrasts. The Greek rebels and Demetrius, the rebel leader, are praised and idealized while the Ottoman Pasha and his henchmen are demonized to the same degree. The action of the play, which centres on a local fight between the rebels and the Turkish oppressors, concludes with the fall of the Pasha and the declaration of revolution. In the last tableau, before the final curtain, we see Demetrius stepping forward to address his guerrilla comrades with a call to victory in the fight for freedom:

> Now, gallant comrades, forward to our mountain home, there to remain till the wished for moment shall arrive which ends this fearful struggle. Then, with our little band, will we rush to the glorious strife, restored like warlike Sparta's daring sons of old, to perish or be free! ....
> Grand Chorus
> Arouse! Arouse! Arouse!
> When for our laws and nature land
> We have the embattled field,
> By freedom freed[?], a patriot band,
> No foe shall make us yield!
> Then let the haughty Tyrant boast
> And vaunt his fortune high
> Him and all his slavish host
> We'll conquer or we'll die!
> The end.[30]

Diplomatic considerations safeguarded by censorship concerning 'our old allies, the Turks', however, had grown more complicated by 1829. Constantinople had lost the war for Greece, and in the peace negotiations, the allies were engaged in securing their own positions in the region. In addition to this, Russia had declared war on the Ottoman Empire after a disagreement about territories around the Black Sea. In this conflict, the British sided with the Ottomans against their Russian ally, which may explain Colman's concern regarding the enemy image in the melodrama.

---

29 Lord Chamberlain's Plays. Vol. XXXIII. Sept.-Oct. 1829. Sep. 1829-Oct. 1829. MS Lord Chamberlain's Plays, 1852–1858 Add MS 42897, p.40, British Library. Nineteenth Century Collections Online, http://tinyurl.galegroup.com/tinyurl/6gsLD3. Accessed 26 June 2018.
30 Ibid., 444.

Fig. 2: Ludovico Lipparini: Lord Byron at the tomb of Markos Botsaris in Missolonghi (Chromolithography 1850). Source: The Engravings Collection of the National Historical Museum, Athens.

The printed edition of J. B. Buckstone's *Revolt of the Greeks* was also published in 1829, and to my knowledge, the play had no trouble with the censors. In fact, as Amy Muse comments, its content was more than anything 'a celebration of the British intervention, which established modern Greece'.[31] The greater part of the characters are British diplomats stationed in Greece, and even though the moment of action is dated to the war years, about 1823, the fight for freedom is not at the centre of the play, but appears rather as the background to a messy and tangled love intrigue. Madeleine, 'the maid of Athens' and the daughter of an English diplomat, loves the young rebel Demetrius (another rebellious Demetrius!), who in the course of the action grows aware of his mission to become the leader of a future free, Greek nation. The enemy image of the Ottoman administration is more humorous than threatening, and no Turks figure in the cast list. In fact, the villain's part is taken over by a power-crazy French officer. Appointed Governor by the Sultan, he abducts Madeleine for a life of oriental exuberance in Constantinople. However, the freedom loving young couple will have each other in the end, through the intercession of Lord Byron, who appears in the periphery of the action. He acts the part of a secret puppeteer, secretly pulling the strings

---

31 Amy Muse, 'Encountering Ali Pasha on the London Stage: No Friend to Freedom?' *Romanticism* 17.3 (Edinburgh University Press 2011), 346.

behind the revolutionary events and arranging a meeting with the famous Greek war leaders, Kapodistrias and Kolokotrones. In the last scene of the play, when all schemes and deceits have been brought to light, Byron initiates the young Demetrius in his future vocation as the leader of the liberated Greek nation. In 1829, when the play had its first performance, the public was no longer much concerned about 'the terrible Turk' nor about the Greek struggle and its victims, but – in accordance with the perspective of this play – rather focused on British influence in the Balkans as well as in the whole, now impaired, area of the Ottoman empire.

8. The Revolt of the Greeks; or, The Maid of Athens

Walker does not use authentic names from the war, as Buckstone, Noah, and Ozaneaux do. In other words, the documentary dimension is limited to the fact that, as Noah said, a war goes on between Greeks and Turks in Greece, and it is up to the author to supply the rest. However, Walker has another reference for his play, which is familiar to the audience: namely, Sidney Owenson's popular novel from 1808, *Ida of Athens*, from which some of the plot elements are borrowed. In the following, I shall look more closely at three aspects of Walker's melodrama: first, at the picture of the Turkish side of the war or 'the oriental other'; second, at the view of gender and gender roles – we have a woman protagonist, Ida Rosemeli, in the title role; and third, at the use of the harem motif, which associates the play with the popular contemporary genre of the oriental drama.

As the play opens, resistance to the Ottoman regime in Athens is growing. The patriarch of the Greeks, Archon Rosemeli, is imprisoned and his family banished from the town. In the second scene of the play, we see his daughter Ida escaping, exhausted and disguised in men's clothes, on her way to the rescue of her imprisoned father. She is helped by the fisherman Hassan and his wife Fetuah, and the remainder of the plot consists of Ida and Hassan's attempt at reaching the prison in the Pasha's fortress at the Acropolis. Here, they come across Lysander, Ida's lover, who acts under cover as a confidential janissary of the Pasha, but who is, in reality, a spy and Greek rebel leader. Ida defies many dangers, assisted by Hassan and Lysander, but her identity is revealed, and the Pasha takes her away to his harem. In the last tearful scene, the Pasha pressures her to yield to his lust or see her father executed. Disaster is averted at the last moment when Lysander's guerrillas burst into the fortress, disarm the Pasha and his guards, and initiate the Greek rebellion.

The picture of Turks and Greeks here is not black and white, as in most of the philhellenic dramas from the 1820s. In the cast list, we find the agents of the Ottoman regime, the Pasha of Athens, his guards in the fortress, and his police spy who carries out raids on the population. All of these, as in the other plays, are monsters exercising an arbitrary and sadistic power. But next to the agents of the regime we have the ordinary Turkish population, the fisherman Hassan and his wife, who act the main parts as helpers to Ida and the rebels. Interestingly, the tendency in all other plays to underline the inhumanity of the Turks is here partly reversed, so that the central motif of 'humanity' is realised in the parts of the Turkish fisherman and his wife. The scene in which Hassan takes the persecuted Ida under his wing demonstrates this by an almost too conspicuous illustration of the meaning of 'heart' and 'humanity' across the boundaries of race and religion. At first, Hassan doubts whether, as a Muslim, he can help a Greek: 'I'm a Mussulman & bound to shut my *heart* against all unbelievers.' But as Ida (disguised as a man) is fainting from exhaustion, he accuses himself:

> 'I have killed him – my *inhumanity* has murderd him – help – help....' But the heart wins: 'Fetuah: What must be done? – Husband! – Hassan: Wife! – we must – ay? Mus'nt we? – Fetuah: What? – Hassan: What says your *heart?* – Fetuah: Protect her – Hassan: At any risk. – There spoke the wife of my *bosom*, the friend of virtue and distress – there spoke – a woman'.[32]

These character sketches show traces of the slightly earlier bourgeois tragedy, as for instance in Lessing and Schiller, where an opposition between aristocracy and petite bourgeoisie is central, and where the common man is destroyed in the cynical power game of the nobles, often by the Prince's seduction of his innocent daughter (*Emilia Galotti, Kabale und Liebe*). Fisherman Hassan is the same type of hearty, everyday figure and an equivalent to the oppressed petit bourgeois of these plays. A theme of seduction is also present when the Pasha abducts Ida while she is in Hassan's care. Interestingly, the otherwise constant executioner-victim opposition of Ottomans versus the oppressed Greeks, which is ubiquitous in philhellenic dramas, gives way here to an opposition between the prince (the Pasha) and the man of the people (Hassan). It is the humanity and 'the heart' of this Turkish man of the people, along with the heroism of the rebels, that are at the centre of the play. The criticism in this play tends thus to be a bourgeois humanistic criticism of princely dominion rather than a political criticism of the Turkish-Ottoman regime. It may well be this 'way of treating the subject [that] makes the whole difference' to Lord Chamberlain Montrose and enables him to permit the performance of the play.

Moreover, there is a clear feminist trend in the play, derived from its source in Sidney Owenson's novel *Ida of Athens*. This trend is not indicated in a criticism of gender roles, but rather in an emphasis on the courage and resourcefulness of

---

32 C. E. Walker, *The Revolt of the Greeks; or, The Maid of Athens*, Act 1, Scene 2, in: Lord Chamberlain's Plays. Vol. III. May-July 1824. May 1824-Jul. 1824. MS Lord Chamberlain's Plays, 1852–1858 Add MS 42867 p. 76–75–78–79, (my italics).

women. Ida's cross-dressing and her project of rescuing her father from prison, despite all dangers, is praised by Hassan as being 'heroic'. Among the gallery of Turkish characters there is also Zobeïde, the Pasha's daughter who, after a vain attempt to seduce Lysander, takes her revenge by revealing his rebel identity to the Pasha. The figure of Zobeïde also has a parallel in the above-mentioned bourgeois tragedies, namely in the strong-willed noble 'Machtweib', who plays on her jealousy and pride, but who also demonstrates greatness in helping her bourgeois rival against her own interests. Zobeïde, too, overcomes her jealousy, and helps Ida and Lysander escape at the moment of danger. In this case, too, the play modifies the stereotypical picture of the Turkish enemy, while maintaining an element of suspense in the plot.

Most remarkable among the feminine parts, in relation to the prevailing representation of the oriental woman, is that of Fetuah. In the popular oriental melodrama of the period, women are represented either as languishing slave girls performing the task of inciting the sex drive of their masters (and at the same time titillating that of the audience), or, as closely covered wives obeying the commands of their domineering husbands (to whom the enlightened Western public can respond with a feeling of superiority). None of this is found in Fetuah. She is a loving and powerful wife, courageous and resolute at the right moment. And, as we have already observed, she is praised by her husband for exactly those qualities, as when he says: 'There spoke the wife of my *bosom*, the friend of virtue and distress – there spoke – a woman'. This is not a tyrannical Muslim husband. On the contrary, these are two equal spouses. I have not as yet been able to establish what the initials in C. E. Walker stand for, or what the author's gender was, but the type of feminism present in Owenson's novel has quite obviously been transferred to Walker's adaptation.

9. The Harem Scene

The harem scene is of central interest to a discussion of the uses of theatrical genres and effects in plays about the Greek War of Independence. As previously mentioned, the oriental melodrama is a vital part of the type of orientalism which spread across Europe as a result of European colonial politics and encounters with the foreign cultures of India, Persia, and the Arab countries. Several generations had enjoyed *The Arabian Nights' Entertainment*, and these tales continued to be published in new editions all over Europe and found their way to the theatres, where the content was recast in ballets, divertissements, and pantomimes, and where references to a mythical East were exploited in costumes and set pieces. *Aladdin* was first performed on an English stage in 1788, and *The Arabian Nights* was influential in historical melodramas about the

Eastern dynasties, and in military plays of the Napoleonic era, both of which adopted the codes and sceneries of the well-known fairy-tale Orient.[33]

Harem mysticism was an important component of this code. The oriental pantomime, the historical drama of the East, and the military colonial drama were all compositions featuring elements of chorus and dance and very often also an episode taking place in the harem of an Eastern ruler. The splendour and the draperies of the palace and the sensual dance performed by slave girls would often be staged as the trappings of an oriental court, and as a device to illustrate pomp and power, typically in an episode where the female protagonist was exposed to danger and her virtue threatened. Among the Greek plays considered here, the harem topic is pertinent to at least two English plays and to one American (Walker's, Buckstone's, and Noah's), even though the motif has more to do with orientalism and the theatre-Orient than with the Greek rebellion.

As seen through the eyes of the Western theatregoer, the harem was an institution connected to oriental despotism and sensuality. The oriental despot ruled a universe of unlimited pleasure and had an endless number of women at his disposal, ready to satisfy his desire. In that respect, the harem was simply a cultural qualification of the Ottoman ruler, and as such the harem scene could be seen as logically integrated in the picture of the Ottoman enemy displayed in the Greek plays, even if what was at stake in the Greek struggle was not the sexual power of the Ottoman ruler, but his political oppression of the Greek people.

We can observe, then, a discrepancy in the plays between a general dimension, inviting the audience to feel solidarity with the Greek struggle and the demands of 'liberty', 'independence', and 'humanity' as capital European virtues, and, on the other hand, a dimension of the theatre-Orient, inviting sexual curiosity and the enjoyment of forbidden desires. In reference to Walker's play it is interesting to note that the censors, Colman and Montrose, did not change so much as a comma in the extended rendition of the Pasha's menacing sexual approaches to Ida, all of which culminate in the final scene where she is on the point of surrendering, hoping to rescue her father. All moral values are put on the line, exploiting sex, coercion, and patricide as instances of the melodramatic gamut of affects, up to the moment when Lysander and his guerrillas rush onto the stage, overpowering the Pasha and declaring the Greek revolution a fact, as if sexual assault and not political oppression were the target of revolution. The fact that, in reality, sexual assault and political oppression may very well walk hand in hand is not the point here. What is still a problematic duplicity, however, is that on the one hand the play and the performance titillate the audience, while on the other hand,

---

33 Cf. Edward Ziter, *The Orient on the Victorian Stage* (2002) and Angela Pau, *The Orient of the Boulevards: Exoticism, Empire and Nineteenth-Century French Theatre* (1998).

this effect leads to the pro-Greek heroism of the final tableau. This is playing to the gallery, you might say. Nor does it have the true ring of philhellenism!

So, the play is pointing in all directions, which are tentatively brought together in the final outbreak of the Greek revolution. In the Turkish fisherman and his spouse, we have the ideal of humanity, transcending all borders of nation, religion, and gender; in the couple of Ida and Lysander, we have the patriotic rebellion against Ottoman dominion, and, at a third level, we have a fascination with oriental sensuality. One may ask if this is really a satisfactory finale in a melodrama?

10. Conclusion

Theatrical convention, theatre censorship, theatre as a business, and the Greek rebellion are not easily compatible phenomena. As we have seen, the limits of what could be said, the demands of the genre, and the expectations of the audience, were all determining factors in the narration of the war on stage. They were also decisive for the way in which the Western European audiences were invited to involve themselves in this narrative. The identification of the theatregoer with the Greek cause was frequently achieved by the playwrights' insertion of a flattering national perspective: in Ozaneaux, through the part of the French philhellenic officer Gérard; in Noah, through the part of the American soldier Burrows; in Buckstone, through the whole series of English diplomats, including Byron, in the cast list. In this way, a national point of view was established from which the Greek struggle was interpreted with regard both to East-West relations in general as well as to the influence of the nation in question in the new developing South-European region. All the way through plot and dialogues, the emphasis is on the indispensability of French / British / American assistance in the Greek combat, and, in consequence, the admiration of the war heroes, so important to the popularity of the plays, could also be claimed as a national heroism.

On a general level, philhellenic drama is crudely black and white with regard to the characterisation of the two parties in the war. The Greeks are the self-sacrificing and heroic figures in what is presented as a fight to save the European basis in Greek antique culture, lost through 400 years of Ottoman occupation. In this way, the philhellenic commitment also contains a vision of recapturing the lost ideal of a glorious common Western past.[34] An almost parodic illustration of

---

[34] As emphasized by William St. Clair, this philhellenic interpretation of the purpose of war was far from the purposes motivating the Greek war leaders. They did not have Antiquity in view, even though they used the reference in their propaganda. They wished to get rid of the Turks and to overtake their position as rulers of the country. See *That Greece Might Still Be Free*, 22.

that vision is found in the closing tableau of Noah's *The Grecian Captive; or, The Fall of Athens* (the play that ended with a contra-factual Greek victory in 1822), where a procession of victory is staged, presenting Homer and Themistocles wandering side by side with Washington and La Fayette:

> SCENE the last – a view of Athens and the Acropolis – music – enter Greek soldiers with spoils, Turkish captives – ALEXANDER in a car, black slaves – ACHMET, OSMIN, and NADIR in chains, ZELIA, KIMINSKI, ROBERTO, and DEMETRIUS – females &c. – *Banners are scattered throughout the procession bearing the names of Homer, Euripides, Pericles, Solon, Lycurgus, Themistocles, Aristides, Epaminondas, Phocion, Leonidas, Socrates, Ypsilanti, Washington, Kosciusco, Bolivar, and La Fayette.* Kiminski: Behold a glorious termination to all our painful struggles! Greece is free![35]

Accordingly, the Ottomans are portrayed darkly both in melodrama and in tragedy, as indicated by censor Colman who, in reference to Barrymore's *The Suliote; or, The Greek Family*, raised the question of 'whether our old allies, the Turks, are to be exhibited … as the oppressors of the Greeks, and as an inhuman & detestable race.' It should be noted that the censors, at least in England, kept their calm and prevented the theatre scene and public feeling from being swept away by a blind, racial crusade against the Turks, even if their motives were tactical in nature.

'Liberty' and 'humanity' are the ideal values fought for by the Greeks in the philhellenic drama. Accordingly, 'liberty' and 'humanity' are set as ideals to be realised at the end of the plot, as was also the case in most of the English melodramas. Alternatively, the same values may be indirectly demonstrated through their renunciation, as in the French tragedies, where nothing but hope can be projected onto the future. In both cases, the Ottomans are perceived as the antitypes of 'liberty' and 'humanity': that is, as representing 'oppression' and 'cruelty', albeit with a margin for variations.

Walker's and Noah's melodramas, *The Revolt of the Greeks* and *The Grecian Captive*, are also useful to the analysis of how *genre* filters the images of each party in the war, as well as that of West and its relationship with the East. In both plays, the main conflict between the Greek freedom fighters and a Turkish Pasha culminates in a nearly identical harem scene, where the Pasha forces the captured Greek heroine into surrender in order to spare her father's life. While suspense is intensified to the extreme in both cases, the difference lies in the ways the two playwrights choose to resolve the problem of the melodramatic finale. Both of them are writing their plays at a time when the Greek War of Independence was still out of control and far from any conclusion.

---

35 Mordecai Manuel Noah, *The Grecian Captive; or, The Fall of Athens* (New York 1822), 48.

As has been shown, Noah solves the problem by putting an end to the war on stage. Greek and American soldiers enter the palace, disarm the pasha, and declare victory and Greece a free country. The rest, before the final curtain, is the jubilant procession, already quoted above, and the closing lines addressed to the audience, proclaiming the basic Western values to be 'virtue, law and liberty ... the only true basis of a happy republic'. And, in order to dispel any doubt that the West has won the war, the Greek hero of the play expresses his admiration for the American President Washington, 'that patriot and soldier, who gave freedom and glory to the Western world'.[36]

Walker works harder to manage the finale according to the melodramatic codex. In a similarly ominous harem scene, with the Pasha as a murderous rapist, he too resolves the tension, not by staging the end of the war, but by staging the outbreak of revolution. Western values are triumphant here, as well, but it takes a bit more effort to put the pieces of the puzzle in place, because the revolt is not accomplished, and the play does not reduce events to a binary opposition. This is one of the few examples among the Greek dramas from the period, where the Ottomans/Turks figuring in the cast list are not simply tyrants. Hassan and Fetuah epitomise the type of 'humanity' that is a central ideological value in the fight for independence (at least according to the coverage in the Western media).[37] Similarly, Zobeïde epitomises a 'high' character. This picture of the relations between East and West and between heroes and villains is much more complex than – and thus inconsistent with – the genre's demand for an unambiguous finale.

The extent to which Walker grapples with this problem is evident from the many corrections and erasures in the final scene of the manuscript. Bombshells are fired from Greek vessels, the fortress of the Pasha catches fire, Hassan lands his fishing boat and enters the scene. But gone is the line in the manuscript, in which he was meant to declare: 'Victory! – Victory! Though I'm a Mussulman, Humanity and Freedom for ever!' Even for the purpose of an efficient finale, the harmonising of differences implicit in this line would be too problematic for an English audience. Hassan is, therefore, a silent figure in the closing revolutionary tableau. The playwright's wish to draw a powerful image of the Turkish enemy in the shape of the Pasha, *and* at the same time to undermine that image by Europeanising the Turkish man of the people, does not hold up in a melodramatic finale.

However, where the Greek subject matter and the genre are seen to conflict with each other, we can detect threads of discussions leading to issues reaching far beyond the period of the Greek war, such as the building of a European self-

---

36 Ibid., 47.
37 See note 29.

understanding in the period and the relation between East and West in the processes of cultural identification.

The focus of this study is the popular theatre and the aim is to explore significant patterns of cultural attitudes and identification that do not necessarily find an exact mirror image in the political debate, yet an examination of the plays may have the potential to widen our concept of the historical situation. Walker's liberal proposal of the universal value of 'humanity' across the borders dividing East and West does not become a problem until the moment when he is to conclude his play on one note, and hesitates to include Hassan as a Muslim ('though I'm a Mussulman') in a universal humanity. The Eurocentric bias of so-called universal values has been widely discussed in European history. In Walker's melodrama, it is sharpened by the demands of the genre.

The public appeal of the Greek plays was carried by the strong wave of sympathy that the Greek War inspired in other European populations in the 1820s, and the plays themselves contributed to justifying this sympathy and to forming a picture of the inner and outer borders of Europe. As seen from a greater political perspective, Greece had shifted its position from being part of the Ottoman East to recapturing its place in the European Western world, while still retaining its identity as the exotic East of Europe. So, there was more than one East, but only one West. When the war was over, in 1830, Greek dramas disappeared from theatre repertoires and were replaced by other plays about other wars and other disasters, also entirely forgotten today. But a debate about the history of Europe, European identity, and about how to define the borders between East and West had entered the scene with the philhellenic drama.

Natalya Khokholova
(North Eastern Federal University, RF)

Gossiping and Ageing Princesses in Odoevsky's Societal Tales

Abstract
There have been numerous and extensive discussions of the role of 'слухи' [gossip] in nineteenth-century Russian literature; usually gossip was viewed as a formative force behind plot dynamics, and as the launching point for grotesque narrative effects. This article attempts to frame different perceptions of gossip, treating it in its specific relation to the subject of ageing and as a contributive factor to the development of the Russian realist tradition. This paper proposes a new approach to the reading of gossip by examining how it functions in the nineteenth-century Russian genre of the 'society tale'. It emerges there as a witch's spell, in which ageing heroines choose gossip as their defense mechanism in response to physiological and psychological changes within and around them.

Keywords
Gossip, Russian romanticism, Gothic, Ageing Bodies, Women, Witches

There have been extensive discussions of the motif of gossip in nineteenth-century Russian literature. Gossip as an embedded discourse within a discourse was viewed as a formative force behind plot developments, and as the lever for grotesque narrative effects. But also, gossip was recognized as a stylistic device to add the folk appeal to the refined and modeled after French sensationalist novellas, nineteenth-century Russian samples of prose writing, and thus representing a liberating power that overcomes social norms and hierarchies. In specific reference to Gogol's works, for example, Stephen Hutchings notes 'gossip is democratizing in the sense that it has popular folk appeal'.[1] While acknowledging the democratizing power of gossip, this study develops a different perception of gossip by examining it in its specific relation to the subject of ageing. Ageing and gossiping appear to be inseparable traits of the main antagonists and protagonists of so-called society tales in the canonical works of

---

[1] Stephen C. Hutchings, *Russian Modernism: The Transfiguration of the Everyday* (Cambridge: Cambridge University Press, 1997), 59.

nineteenth-century Russian literature. In many cases, ageing and gossiping appear to reinforce each other cyclically; the gossip of a spinster, for instance, might ruin the marriage prospects of its young victim, thus making her a spinster who deploys her own gossip in revenge.

In its semiotic association with ageing and ageing women, gossip may furthermore be seen to exemplify the notion of the physiological sketch, whereby certain societal dynamics are exposed, which in turn might explain the importance of gossip for the formation of the society tale genre. To uncover the function of gossip in its relation to the certain space and around certain people, I use Yuri Lotman's perception the way certain material objects and physical space in the life of nineteenth-century Russian nobility influence formation of rituals and discourses. In his work *Universe of the Mind: A Semiotic Theory of Culture*, Lotman discusses the way material things like 'bread' or 'sword', and certain uttered words and phrases, at once claim their presence and resonate certain associations. The author notes the ways that these material symbols, as elements of everyday life, demand maintenance of certain rituals in the lives of nobles, and the way the material and the setting influences the discourse within and about everyday life.[2] In this sense, gossip should be understood as a contributing factor in establishing realist prose as a nineteenth-century Russian literary tradition.

In the society tale genre, gossip is considered to be somewhat paradoxically as a witch's spell, at least by the ageing heroines, who choose gossip as their defense mechanism against physiological and psychological changes within and about them. In this connection, Prince Vladimir Odoevsky's (1803–1869) society tales, 'Княжна Мими' [Princess Mimi] (1834) and 'Княжна Зизи' [Princess Zizi] (1838) will be analyzed as critical examples of how the portrayal of women developed in nineteenth-century Russia.[3] The heroines of these tales voice their anxieties about changes in and about their lives by producing gossip and/or becoming the subjects of gossip themselves.

This analysis will first compare the society tale to the fairytale in terms of plot structure, and consider the assigned and pre-assigned functions of main characters as proposed in Vladimir Propp's formulaic reading of folk tale narratives.[4]

---

[2] I. M. Lotman, Ann Shukan, and Umberto Eco, *Universe of the Mind: A Semiotic Theory of Culture* (London: I. B. Tauris, 2001), 88–130.

[3] V. F. Odoevskiĭ, *Poslednii Kvartet Betkhovena: Povesti, Rasskazy, Ocherki, Odoevskiĭ v Zhizni* (Moskva: Moskovskiĭ rabochiĭ, 1987), 45–181. The texts in English, edited and translated by Neil Cornwell, are to follow the fragments in Russian [Princess Mimi] [Princess Zizi]. I use the translations in V. F. Odoevskiĭ, *Two Princesses*, ed. Neil Cornwell (London: Hesperus, 2010), 8–142.

[4] V. I. Propp, *The Russian Folktale*, ed. and trans. Sibelan Forrester (Detroit: Wayne State University Press, 2012), 5–37.

A definition of gossip, perceived as similar in its function to magic spells and curses will then be developed, providing grounds for a discussion of how the malicious language of gossipers influences the structural and semantic fields of the narrative. This is followed by a close reading of gossip as both a weapon and the means of sustaining a reputable status in society. Finally, this article will discuss the ways gossip disrupts the rigid structure of the society tale and allows for the intrusion of the gothic, of a covert presence of the supernatural in settings of closed, suffocating space, and in moments of emotional distress.

Although society tales feature predictable romantic tropes such as the expectation of and disillusionment with love, they are nevertheless groundbreaking in the sense that they practice a form of critical observation that represents an artistic rebellion against the traditional dynastic system of values in nineteenth-century Russian society. These forms of fiction are undoubtedly sarcastic parodies on high society, but they also contain an element of the uncanny, which evokes in the reader an inadvertent understanding of the presence of the Kristevan *abject:* a repulsiveness which serves as a reminder of a possible horrifying event or of an entity lurking in the gray areas of the social margin.[5] While the imagination is prepared to accept the abject as a possibility, however, it is also admonished to check this threat against existing reality. Mary Douglas initially identified this similar sense of remote, yet as possible, type of danger in her cultural-anthropological study on social taboos in primitive cultures.[6]

According to one of Prince Odoevsky's biographers-contemporaries, Pavel Sakulin, the desire to match fiction against existing realities was the author's intent.[7] Odoevsky's gothic stories 'Princess Mimi' and 'Princess Zizi' lack the marvelous or fantastic elements common to fairy tales, but the tangible presence of the uncanny that envelops both the events and the characters in these stories keeps readers in a continuously vulnerable state of apprehension. I use the term '*marvelous*' in reference to Tzvetan Todorov's progressive definition of the fantastic; the '*uncanny*' refers to the sense of hesitation and emotional distress that Sigmund Freud associated with of the experience of an oddity that triggers receptive memory and thereby recalls past traumatic events.[8]

---

5 Megan Becker-Leckrone, *Julia Kristeva and Literary Theory* (Basingstoke: Palgrave Macmillan, 2005), 33–39.
6 Mary Douglas, *Purity and Danger: An Analysis of Concepts of Pollution and Taboo* (London: Routledge, 2015), 5–112.
7 P. N. Sakulin, *Iz Istorii Russkogo Idealizma* (Moskow: Izdanie M. I. S. Shabashnikovvyh, 1913), vol.1, part 2: 75–302.
8 Tzvetan Todorov, *The Fantastic: A Structural Approach to a Literary Genre Tzvetan Todorov. Translated from the French by Richard Howard* (Cleveland: Press of Case Western Reserve University, 1973), 24–107.

The presence of the uncanny persists in the reader's imagination, from lingering fragments of personal letters to whispers shared in a kitchen space filled with *Schadenfreude* that could dangerously allow to reveal a terrifying beauty secret about the mistress's ugly and ageing rival. This state of oscillation between the familiar and the unfamiliar, the beautiful and the ugly, the imagined and the real is a signature trait of Odoevsky's writing. Due to this feature, Sakulin regards Odoevsky's works as contributions to the formation of *social psychologism* in the Russian literary tradition.[9]

Odoevsky himself explains the occurrence of the strange and marvelous in his later works as an intrusion of the uncanny (of the abject), as a rare moment of opportunity to glimpse the sublime realm of the mad:

> Приотворилась дверь в царство духов; чудесное вторглось в реальную жизнь, и всё покрылось глубокой мистической тайной, от которого трепещет душа чуткого человека, нездешнее заглянуло в очи человека, и он приобщился великаго безумия избранных.
>
> [It has been a crack around the door into the real world from the kingdom of spirits. And everything of a sudden is permeated by mystery, from which trembles the soul of a sensitive person. The uncanny has looked into the eyes of a human who has joined the privileged circle of the mad.][10]

This excerpt reveals Odoevsky's perception of madness as a condition of artistic creative exaltation, attainable only for the select few, comparable thus to Kantian perceptions of the sublime. In *Critique of The Power of Judgment*, Kant states sublime is ultimate truth because it surpasses human power to judge and perceive and is even 'violent to our imagination'.[11] Romantics to contest the rational postulates of the previous era, in which they perceived mechanisms dangerous and oppressive for the human race, marshaled this celebration of the senses as an integral part of human nature. This creative exhilaration found in Odoevsky's works is also present in the fiction of Alexander Pushkin and Nikolai Gogol in which events are supernatural and unrealistic, but are nonetheless perceived in quite realist terms.

Society tales and fairy tales have much in common as genres, because both, to a certain degree, communicate didactic messages to their readers, as Vladimir Propp, Maria Tatar, and Jack Zipes have noted. Mikhail Bakhtin's theory of genre memory, as well as Sakulin's critical reading of Odoevsky's works, would further help to understand my claim that ageing, gossiping characters and their stories

---

9 P. N. Sakulin, *Iz Istorii Russkogo Idealizma* (Moskow: Izdanie M. I. S. Shabashnikovvyh, 1913), vol.1, part 2: 90. Unless otherwise noted, all translations are my own.
10 Ibid., 75–118.
11 Immanuel Kant and Paul Guyer, *Critique of the Power of Judgment* (Cambridge: Cambridge University Press, 2008), 173–228.

are responsible for reclaiming gothic-fantastic tropes in nineteenth-century Russian prose.

In this connection, it is useful to consult Odoevsky's own perception of romanticism, which he identifies by the co-existence of [two worlds] ('двоемирие') [dvoemirie].[12] The duality to which he refers can be explained through Katharina Hansen Löve's compartmental distinction between actual physical reality and the imagined or otherworldly. She identifies romantic fiction by the presence of some form of conflict between the protagonist and her milieu, and by the idealization of the historical past. She also notes that along with descriptions of contemporary high society in romantic fiction there is always a parallel acknowledgement of the world of the fantastic and supernatural, and/or an admiration of exotic cultures.[13]

Also relevant is Vissarion Belinsky's tracing of the first occurrence of the physiological sketch. He saw this event in the genre progression in the prose writing of nineteenth-century Russian literature as means of providing 'a realistic, accurate portrayal of Russian life that would appeal to a broad audience'.[14] Belinsky and Odoevsky both viewed Gogol as an exemplar of style for Russian writers to follow. Overall, the Russian physiological sketch is, 'surveyed and classified in an almost scientific manner the lives of street merchants, prostitutes, hack journalists, and, most commonly, petty clerks …'. With regard to realism, I associate it with the view that 'the beautiful is life' and that 'art is in every meaningful sense inferior to a reality subject to rational comprehension'.[15]

For the purposes of this analysis, it is important to draw a distinction between the notion of 'gossip' and that of 'rumor'. In Russian, I therefore refer to actions and information identified as instances of gossip with the term '*сплетни*' [spletni] [gossip], rather than the term '*слухи*' [slukhi] [hearsay]. Spletni, which derives from the productive verb '*плести*' [pliesti] [to weave], carries the implication of plotting, thereby suggesting a false and fictive narrative within the fictional narrative. According to Ozhegov's dictionary, the Russian '*сплетн*' [spletni] [gossip] is originally fabricated information, designed to ruin someone's reputation.[16] Meyer Spacks also introduces gossip as a model of social speculation, which stems from the Latin *specula* (lookout, watchtower), a derivative of *specere* (to see, to look).[17]

---

12 Neil Cornwell, *The Literary Fantastic: From Gothic to Postmodernism* (New York: Harvester Wheatsheaf, 1992), 151.
13 Katharina Hansen-Löwe, *The Evolution of Space in Russian Literature: A Spatial Reading of 19th and 20th Century Narrative Literature* (Amsterdam: Rodopi, 1994), 38–56.
14 Kenneth A. Lantz, *The Dostoevsky Encyclopedia* (Westport: Greenwood Press, 2014), 318.
15 Richard Freeborn, *Trends of Development in the Russian Nineteenth Century Realistic Novel* (1830–1880) (Cambridge: Cambridge University Press, 2000), 259.
16 S. I. Ozhegov and N.Iu. Shvedova, *Tolkovyĭ Slovar' Russkogo Iazyka: 80,000 Slov I Frazeologicheskikh Vyrazheniĭ* (Moskow: Temp, 2010), 745.
17 Patricia Meyer Spacks, *Gossip* (Chicago: University of Chicago Press, 1986), 171.

Tales of Honor and of the Hidden Horror

It seems clear that the uttered word is potent in both fairy tales and society tales. In fairy tales, spells and/or curses command transformative powers able to amend and influence protagonists' destinies. As Tatar specifies, spells and curses possess 'the force of naming a condition to change reality'.[18] In society tales, gossip changes the plot-progression's trajectory; gossip has the power to overcome social moral values and even to subdue and manipulate the wills of people: it also has the ability to bring drastic changes to, and influence the destinies of others. Gossip and witches' spells – regardless of the negative connotation of ruining people's lives – serve in tales both of honor and of gory horror as political tools, which in a peculiar way deliver experiences and truths about reality. They give power and voice to the voiceless abject: ageing women.

Of course, gossip is by no means a noble type of weapon to wield against the pomposity of patriarchy or the dysfunctional artificiality of the Russian *beau monde*. Princesses Mimi and Zizi are far from being role models; in fact, they represent physical and mental deformity. But Odoevsky endows them with these grotesque qualities precisely in order to use them as mirroring reflections of the realities he observes, depicts, and renders for his audience. There is a sense in which Odoevsky's female characters are conduits through which he imparts these frustrations in writing. Before he narrates the problems of an empty, repetitious life, he observes what is around him in his real life. It is important to note that Odoevsky himself continuously tried to separate himself from the mundane formalities of life. The circumstances of his birth and a – noted in his biography – near-death experience when he was a newly born infant perhaps contributed to Odoevsky's quality of shamanic, perceptual clarity on the social diseases of his time.

Odoevsky's biographers report that he was born sickly and was nursed to life by being wrapped in a ram's skin to be reborn, a fact that is often taken to explain his fascination for the metaphysical and supernatural.[19] Beyond his extensive writings on German intellectuals and artists, he practiced music and chemistry and was interested in metaphysics. As a progressive thinker, Odoevsky often criticized Russian nobility for its vacuous life of rituals and formalities, and its mindless mimicry of French Aristocratic customs. His own, rather troubled, aristocratic origins might have influenced these views.[20] Remarkable also was his

---

18 Maria Tatar, 'Why Fairy Tales Matter: The Performative and the Transformative', *Western Folklore* 69.1 (2010): 55–64.

19 Neil Cornwell, *The Life, Times and Milieu of V. F. Odoyevsky: 1804–1869* (London: Athlone Press, 1986), 11–48.

20 Sakulin, *Iz Istorii Russkogo Idealizma* (Moskow: Izdanie M. I. S. Shabashnikovvyh, 1913), vol.1, part 2:185–182.

Fig. 1: Demoiselle d'honneur, A Ball in St. Petersburg, 1842. British Library.

willingness to bemoan the state of women, declaring that they had no function or rights in Russian society. In his diary, he goes so far as to compare a noble woman to a slave:

> Петербуржская дама есть самое ужасное произведение природы! ... разряженная она появляется в великосветских салонах и говорит избитыя слова ... Девушкой она – рабыня условностей и приличий. В своё время, по примеру других выходит за муж – без истинной любви к своему мужу. Жизнь ея течет по шаблону, без серьезных интересов. Под старость у ней не остается других воспоминаний, «кроме какого- нибудь туалета на придворном бале, каких нибудь имен и проч. и т.п.» Нового поколения она не понимает, и молодежь тяготится ею. Наконец, она умирает.

> [The Petersburg woman is the worst creation in nature! ... Dolled up, she appears in high places, where she mingles and utters her formulaic phrases .... As a young maiden – she is a slave to convention and propriety. Seizing her moment, she follows the examples of others and gets married – having no genuine feelings for her man. Her life follows a

pattern; she does not have any personal interests to preoccupy her. When she gets old, she has no other memories than her outfits and few flashy names. She does not understand the young generation; the youth do not like her. Finally, she dies ....][21]

This observation may be taken as foundational for both 'Princess Mimi' and 'Princess Zizi' and, also, importantly reflects Post-Enlightenment ideology, according to which woman is a slave to her own nature. But in the Russian context there is another layer to this ideology: a construction that frames woman as 'an abominable creation of nature' and as 'a slave to social norms'. In order to address this issue artistically, Odoevsky appropriates fairy tale storytelling, in which things are simplified to the dynamic of the captive and the jailer, and women are granted the ability to speak.

Odoevsky's tales have an educational value different from the early society tales of his predecessors and contemporaries, because they do not preach the Neo-Classicist canon; they operate rather like fairy tales on a primordial educational level. Jack Zipes posits the genre of the fairytale as having originated within an oral storytelling tradition and having been created and cultivated by adults to educate forthcoming generations. As he explains, 'the literary fairy tale in Europe is a type of literary discourse about mores, values, and manners so that children and adults would become civilized according to the social code of that time'.[22] Society tales, at first, were written with the didactic goal of conveying the values and ideas of Neo-Classicism, with the creative interpretive reflection of historical realities. For example, the society tales by Prince Odoevsky, Ivan Panaev, and Evdokiya Rostopchina convey political and cultural frustrations relevant in early nineteenth-century Russia, such as the suppression of the Decembrist revolt (1825), family and gender politics, economic reforms, and the lingering and domineering presence of a pseudo-romanticist mood in Russian art and intellectual thought of that time.

Although fairy tales represent the narratives of oral folklore traditions, society tales initially represented the influence of journalistic essays containing reports on the dynamics of high Russian society. Nevertheless, the two genres share similarities, such as the recognition of educational value, narrative structure, and a belief in the democratizing power of the intentionally uttered word.

The rigidity in plot structure shared by romantically-inclined fairy tales and society tales furthermore concurs with the formulaic reading of fairy tales of Vladimir Propp, who formulated thirty-one possible patterns of fairy tale plot-

---

21 Ibid., 93–98.
22 Jack Zipes *Fairy Tales and the Art of Subversion: The Classical Genre for Children and the Process of Civilization* (London: Routledge, 2006), 1–8.

development, and explained the predictable behavioral patterns of villains, which are responsible for narrative progress.[23]

For example, the five basic phases that characterize the behavioral modes of both the hero and the villain match plot points in the given society tale. The initial motor of a fairy tale plot is the villain, whose role is to disturb, to cause some form of misfortune, damage, or harm. The villain(s) may be a dragon, a devil, bandits, a witch, a stepmother, or an envious sibling. The villain identifies their victim, collects information on them, and then assumes a disguise. For example, a witch might pretend to be a 'sweet old lady' and imitate a mother's voice. As a result, the victim submits to the deception and unwittingly helps the enemy. The hero or the victim succumbs to all of the villain's persuasions; for example, takes the ring, goes to steam-bath, takes a swim, etc. In the end, the deceitful ploy is always accepted and fulfilled. It is usually a special form of deceitful proposal, and its corresponding acceptance is represented by the deceitful agreement. And, as expected, the villain expels someone (the hero, the victim), murders them, or threatens cannibalism. And always this gruesome end emerges from the exploitation of the lack of experience: in a bride, or a friend, or a human being generally. The hero is unmarried and sets out to find a bride, along with the requisite rationalized forms: money, the means, etc.[24]

The behavioral model of the villain posited by Propp matches what we see in the stories of Princess Mimi and Zizi, with the slight difference that Mimi and Zizi are simultaneously the protagonists and the villains. As flashbacks in the stories testify, these two heroines begin their first steps in the fictional world of refined manners and glitter as unseasoned naïfs, similarly to the characters in fairy tales. The demands of social norms and time turn them, not into frogs or white ducks, but into old gossiping spinsters, who become unmarried, miserable, ageing women because gossip and societal scrutiny ruin their prospects for marriage.

In addition, the structure of narrative progression in society tales, as well as in fairy tales, is of a predictable, trap-like circular motion. This type of structure in society tales also serves as further evidence of the presence of the gothic in this genre of Russian literature, since one of the main defining attributes of the gothic genre is a devotion of the narrative to one setting, to one physical place: usually, a castle, an old house, a garden, or a small town. For example, the *topos* for the society tale genre ('*светская повесть*' [*svetskaia povest*] [society tale]) is presented within the constrained setting of public life, such as drawing rooms, society spa-town, ballrooms, and theatres. The main characters are unable to

---

23 Jack Zipes, *The Russian folktale by Vladimir Yakovlevich Propp* (Detroit: Wayne State University Press, 2012), 5–37.
24 Ibid., 1–35.

escape their social milieu; even though they may travel, public scrutiny follows them throughout.[25]

Princess Mimi begins her journey as a frequent presence in ballrooms and at salons, with the purpose of finding a handsome match. Mimi becomes jaded, when an apparently promising, and prospective suitor is distracted by the Baroness. He ends up marrying the Baroness, and abandoning Mimi. As time goes by, Mimi feels the harassment attendant upon those who remain unmarried, and in response she turns into a mean old spinster with a plan to take revenge over the Baroness and the rest of the successful females around her. For example, after coming to the definitive realization that she failed to gain a respectable position in society through marriage, Princess Mimi literally embodies the malicious scrutiny of others, and begins her mission of being a moral judge within her social circle:

> вся обратилась в злобное, завистливое наблюдение за другими начала говорить о всеобщем развращении нравов
>
> [*vsiya obratilas' v zlobnoe, zavistlivoe nabludenie za drugimi, nachala govorit' o vseobschem razvraschenii nravov*].
>
> ... [She] applied herself totally to the malicious, envious observation of other people.... She started talking of the universal depravity of morals.[26]

Firstly, she uses gossip to incite a duel between the Baroness' husband and Grantisky, the houseguest of the Dauerthals. Eliza Dauerthal (the Baroness) is heartbroken and eventually dies. Gossip is the cause of the death of Baroness Dauerthal (Mimi's rival), who has been a target of gossip throughout the entire course of the tale. Mimi, and Mimi's interlocutors have accused the Baroness of having an affair with her husband's brother's acquaintance. In fact, the young man was involved with his former lover, Princess Rifeiskaia, and stayed as a family friend at the Baroness' house. According to Mimi, the reputation of the Baroness is already 'finished': '... Её репутация сделана'[... *Yeïe reputatsia sdelana*], [the Baroness is already a fallen, lost woman].[27] In the drawing room, her mother's guests provide the Princess with a report about the Baroness's behavior at the ball:

> Вы долго вчера оставались на бале? – спросила княжна Мими у одного молодого человека.
> Скажите ж, чем кончилась комедия?
> Княжне Биби наконец удалось прикрепить свою гребёнку...
> Ох! не то ...

---

25 *The Society Tale in Russian Literature: From Odoevskii to Tolstoi*, ed. Neil Cornwell, (Amsterdam: Rodopi, 1998), 16–77.
26 Одоевский, 'Княжна Мими' [*Kniazhna Mimi*], 103.
27 Ibid., 117.

О! Всё не то … вы, стало быть, ничего не заметили?
А, вы говорите про баронессу? …
О нет! Я и не думала об ней … Да почему вы об ней заговорили? Разве о чем нибудь говорят?
– … не сходила с доски.
Она совсем не бережёт себя. С её здоровьем…
О! Княжна, вы совсем не об её здоровье говорите. Теперь всё понимаю.[28]

[Tell me, then, in what way did the commedia end?'
'Well, Princess Bibi did finally manage to get her comb to fasten ….
'No! That's not …'
'Oh, are you talking about the Baroness?'
'Oh, no!' I wasn't even thinking about her …. But why are you talking about her?'
'Are people talking?'
'Well, that's the social world! I assure you I had no one in particular in mind. But apropos the Baroness: did she dance a lot after I had gone?'
'Oh, Princess! It's not her health you're talking about, at all. Now I understand it all ….'][29]

Princess Mimi, by acting like a concerned party, (expressing her concern about the baroness's health) and acting as if she knows more than others, receives the desired results. One of the guests finally gives up and admits:

– Ах, бога ради, перестаньте! Я вам говорю, что я об ней и не думала. Я так боюсь этих всех пересудов, сплетней.[30]

['Oh, for goodness' sake, that's enough! I tell you that I was not even thinking about her. I so loathe all of this tale-telling and scandal mongering.][31]

This exclamation demonstrates that Mimi has manipulated the others to gossip about the Baroness against their will.

Consequently, the conversation, which starts as a casual chat about yesterday's socializing at the ball, turns into gossip about the Baroness. Although, at first glance, these reports about the Baroness's behavior at the ball, and her other public appearances, lack any scandalous details, Princess Mimi in the end achieves her goal.

Princess Zizi (Zinaida), the protagonist of her own story, also begins her life attending social events, as the second in line, after her older sister, to be considered for courtship. Unfortunately, Zizi falls in love with her sister's suitor (Gorodkov). Consequently, she embarks on a path of misery and of self-abnegation, while simultaneously being controlled by her authoritative mother. Eventually, Zizi buries her mother and, later, her sister, who has been driven mad

---

28 Ibid., 118.
29 Odoevskiĭ, *Two Princesses*, 24.
30 Одоевский, 'Княжна Мими' [*Kniazhna Mimi*], 118.
31 Odoevskiĭ, *Two Princesses*, 24.

and sick by her scheming husband, Gorodkov. At last, Zizi is alone with her niece, who is under her care, fighting for her good name and for financial standing, both of which have been corrupted and tarnished by Gorodkov. Eventually, Gorodkov (her evil brother-in-law) is run over by a horse and dies. In the end, a decent young man approaches Zinaida with a marriage proposal, but it turns out that it is too late for her. She is forty years old. The last scene contains an eerie surprise; Princess Zizi takes off her mask in order to prove that she has aged. Here, the reader finally realizes that throughout the entire story 'the strange' Zinaida was wearing a mask, and her character can no longer be pitied as a victim or a captive, but rather as her own saboteur, mesmerizer, and jailer.

In these stories, the characters begin their lives in the relentless spotlight of high society, catering to its expectations and norms. The outlines of these two stories show that both heroines are at once captives and jailers, without an opportunity to escape their preordained settings.[32] For example, Sally Dalton-Brown in her in-depth reading of the story notes that Princess Mimi is not a mediator of social norms and morals, as she would like to believe, but a powerful jailer.

The lesson the society tale heroine learns, therefore, is not merely one of disillusionment or suspicion. She learns the true nature of her state – one of her captivity. Women such as Mimi or the Countess are indeed not merely keepers of social morals, as Mimi likes to think she is; they are, paradoxically, powerful jailers. But with time they develop the ability to transform themselves, and then their circumstances, by using and deflecting gossip.

Deadly Passions and Prosthetic Fashions

Neither *Княжна Мария* [*Kniazhna Maria*] 'Princess Mimi' nor *Княжна Зинаида* [*Kniazhna Zinaida*] 'Princess Zizi' possesses the pleasant attributes of the likable empathy-invoking heroine. Princess Mimi is an old spinster, envious and unhappy, who, in the end, sabotages another woman's reputation, leading to the woman's untimely death and a ruined opportunity to rekindle her long-desired romance. Odoevsky in a weighted manner describes the pleasure Princess Mimi derives from her sociopathic behavior, which is driven by a desire to reclaim her position in society. 'Mimi' appears to be a conversational name. In Russian fiction, when a heroine is given a fashionably Anglicized name, such as 'Princess Zizi', the readers eventually learn that her 'real' name is Zinaida.

Mimi, however, remains 'Mimi' throughout the entire story. The name refers to the concept of mimicry, which in turn refers to the Princess's survival skills in

---

32 *Society Tale*, 26.

Fig. 2: Carl Bloch, The Gossiping Wives, 1880. Statens Museum for Kunst. public domain.

society. For example, in response to the speculative gossip derived from public assessments of Mimi's age and appearance, Mimi disguises the outward manifestations of her aging by applying raw ground beef patties to her cheeks, plucking her grey hair and pouring herself into tight corsets. The story opens with Princess Mimi plotting a campaign of gossip against Baroness Dauerthal after socializing and talking with Baroness Dauerthal at the ball:

> Скажите, с кем вы теперь танцевали? – сказала княжна Мими, остановив за руку одну даму, которая, окончив мазурку, проходила мимо княжны.
> Он когда-то служил с моим братом! Я забыла его фамилию, – отвечала баронесса Дауэрталь мимоходом и, усталая, бросилась на своё место.
>
> [Skazhite, s kem vy teper' tantsevali? – skazala knyazhna Mimi, ostanoviv za ruku odnu damu, kotoraia, okonchiv mazurku, prohodila mimo knyazhny.

> *On kogda-to sluzhil s moim bratom! Ia zabyla ego familiiu,* – otvechala baroness Dauerthal mimohodomo i, ustalaia, brosilas' na svoyo mesto].
>
> ['Tell me, with whom were you dancing just now?' said Princess Mimi, stopping a certain lady with her arm who, having just concluded the mazurka, was walking past the Princess.
> 'Oh, he served with my brother once! I've forgotten his name,' replied Baroness Dauerthal as she passed and, tired out, hurried back to her seat.][33]

And it ends with Princess Mimi socializing and talking, this time not with, but about Baroness Dauerthal, because the latter is dead:

> Для княжны Мими была составлена партия, – она уже отказалась от танцев. Молодой человек подошёл к зелёному столу.
> Сегодня поутру наконец кончились страдания баронессы Дауэрталь! – сказал он. – Здешние дамы могут похвалиться, что они очень искусно её убили до смерти.[34]
>
> [*Dlya knyazhny Mimi byla sostavlena partiya,* – ona uzhe otkazalas' ot tantsev. Molodoy chelovek podoshol k zelonomu stolu.
> Segodnya poutru nakonets konchilis' stradaniya baronessy Dauertal'! – skazal on. – Zdeshniye damy mogut pokhvalit'sya, chto oni ochen' iskusno yeyo ubili do smerti.]
>
> [A card coterie had been assembled for Princess Mimi – she had already refused any dancing. A young man came up to the green table.
> 'This morning, the sufferings of Baroness Dauerthal finally came to an end!' he said. 'The ladies here will be able to pride themselves on their having so skillfully done her to death'.][35]

In the first conversation, Mimi retrieves information from her victim that she later spins into gossip. In the second conversation, we observe Mimi receiving the outcome of gossip: the news of the Baroness's death. Interestingly, the beginning and the end of the story involve the same cast of characters, and the use of gossip in both conversations indicates a circular structure and a sense of exposure of the theatrical stage. Princess Mimi receives the news of the Baroness's death with disinterest. While dealing her cards, Mimi casually pronounces her verdict in response to the news without interrupting her game: 'killing is done not by people, but by lawless passions'.[36]

Zinaida enters the plot as a victim of her brother-in-law, Gorodkov. He is the cause and the source of slanderous society talk about her. The gossip that targets Princess Zizi ruins her reputation and turns her into a pariah. At first, it appears that Zinaida is a classic romantic heroine, a sensitive maiden raised on sentimental novels. She is a fan of Zhukovsky and Pushkin; and, similar to the

---

33 Odoevskiï, *Two Princesses*, 56.
34 Одоевский, 'Княжна Мими' [*Kniazhna Mimi*], 115.
35 Odoevskiï, *Two Princesses*, 66.
36 Ibid., 67.

heroines (Lizas) of Karamzin and Pushkin, she struggles with the matriarch of her house, her own mother, who is in charge of decision-making in Zizi's life.

However, upon closer scrutiny, Princess Zizi reveals sociopathic tendencies. In the intimate letters to her confidante, Maria, Zinaida shares her jealousy of her sister, Lidiya, whom the antagonist Gorodkov has married, and that this overpowering jealousy makes her want to shred her sister to pieces: '... я ревную, я готова растерзать Лидию ....' [ia revnuiu, ia gotova rasterzat' Lidiiu], [... I am jealous, I am ready to shred Lidiya to pieces ....][37] But for Zizi, unlike for other heroines of early nineteenth-century Russian fiction, marriage is not her first priority. Zinaida stands for an unconventional type among female characters in nineteenth-century Russian literature. Initially, she bears a similarity to Tatiana in *Onegin* and falls in love with her future brother-in-law, Mr. Gorodkov, the first relatively good-looking young and articulate male she encounters. When he marries her sister, Lydia, however, Zinaida does not let her feelings towards him dissipate. Furthermore, when she meets the present protagonist, a romantically inclined and inexperienced young man, she engages in an unkind game of mixed messages with him. The apogee of Zinaida's transformation is the final scene, when she lures Radetsky into her masquerade, enchants him with her masked good looks, appears in front of him and ignores him. When they finally speak, she removes her mask, shows her face and declares that she is forty years old and cannot marry him. When Zizi takes off her mask and refuses the youth's marriage proposal, she is not showing her advanced years, but, as Lewis Bagby notes, '... she reveals the face of romance as outworn, old, past'.[38]

Drawing on this last line of interpretive reading by Lewis Bagby, one may conclude that Odoevsky, by focusing on ageing and apparently childless spinsters, is trying to warn his readers about the end of the romantic epoch and the traditional ways of life. Moreover, the society tale genre was often distinguished by the progressive device of featuring female characters with the agency of voice; be it for the sake of gossip, personal concerns, or expressing disagreement with social norms. As Elizabeth Shepard observes, in Lermontov's novel *The Hero of Our Time*, which is partially constituted of society tales, surprisingly also features a female protagonist who 'is realized as the hero'.[39] Here, the unattractive abject controls the plot's promulgations and thereby presents the means of articulation that remove romantic attributes from the story.

In this sense, as powerful jailers and matriarchs, Mimi and Zizi may be read as descendants of the Old Countess in Pushkin's society tale, 'The Queen of

---

37 Одоевский, 'Княжна Мими' [*Kniazhna Mimi*], 135.
38 Lewis Bagby, 'V. F. Odoevskij's "Knjažna Zizi",'. *Russian Literature* 17.3 (1985): 221–242.
39 *Society Tale*, 112.

Spades'.⁴⁰ The old Countess is herself based on the real-life prototype of Countess Natalya Golitsyna, who supposedly mixed with esoteric society and fully enjoyed the mythologized status of her name not only after, but also during her life. She becomes a gravitational center of the narrative, such that young Hermann is drawn to her, believing that he might unlock the secret combination of cards by becoming her lover. His obsession brings him directly to her bedroom, where he witnesses the old Countess' nightly ritual of undressing:

> Графиня стала раздеваться перед зеркалом. Откололи с нее чепец, украшенный розами; сняли напудренный парик с ее седой и плотно остриженной головы. Булавки дождем сыпались около нее. Желтое платье, шитое серебром, упало к ее распухлым ногам. Германн был свидетелем отвратительных таинств ее туалета; наконец графиня осталась в спальной кофте и ночном чепце: в этом наряде, более свойственном ее старости, она казалась менее ужасна и безобразна. Как и все старые люди вообще, графиня страдала бессонницею. Раздевшись, она села у окна в вольтеровы кресла и отослала горничных. Свечи вынесли, комната опять осветилась одною лампадою. Графиня сидела вся желтая, шевеля отвислыми губами, качаясь направо и налево. В мутных глазах ее изображалось совершенное отсутствие мысли; смотря на нее, можно было бы подумать, что качание страшной старухи происходило не от ее воли, но по действию скрытого гальванизма.⁴¹

[*Grafinya stala razdevat'sya pered zerkalom. Otkololi s neye chepets, ukrashennyy rozami; snyali napudrennyy parik s yeye sedoy i plotno ostrizhennoy golovy. Bulavki dozhdem sypalis' okolo neye. Zheltoye plat'ye, shitoye serebrom, upalo k yeye raspukhlym nogam. Germann byl svidetelem otvratitel'nykh tainstv yeye tualeta; nakonets grafinya ostalas' v spal'noy kofte i nochnom cheptse: v etom naryade, boleye svoystvennom yeye starosti, ona kazalas' meneye uzhasna i bezobrazna. Kak i vse staryye lyudi voobshche, grafinya stradala bessonnitseyu. Razdevshis', ona sela u okna v vol'terovy kresla i otoslala gornichnykh. Svechi vynesli, komnata opyat' osvetilas' odnoyu lampadoyu. Grafinya sidela vsya zheltaya, shevelya otvislymi gubami, kachayas' napravo i nalevo. V mutnykh glazakh yeye izobrazhalos' sovershennoye otsutstviye mysli; smotrya na neye, mozhno bylo by podumat', chto kachaniye strashnoy starukhi proiskhodilo ne ot yeye voli, no po deystviyu skrytogo gal'vanizma*].

[The countess began to undress before her looking glass. Her rose-bedecked cap was taken off, and then her powdered wig was removed from her white and closely cut hair. Hairpins fell in showers around her. Her yellow satin dress, brocaded with silver, fell at her swollen feet. Hermann was a witness to the repugnant mysteries of her toilette; at last the Countess was in her nightcap and dressing gown, and in this costume, more suitable to her age, she appeared less hideous and deformed. Like all old people in general, the Countess suffered from sleeplessness. Having undressed, she seated herself at the window in a Voltaire armchair and dismissed her maids. The candles were taken away,

---

40 Pushkin, Aleksandr S., and D. D. Blagoĭ, *Polnoe Sobranie Sochineniĭ* (Moskva: Khudozh. lit-ra, 1959), 248–249; and Pushkin, Aleksandr Sergeevich, and Paul Debreczeny. *The Collected Stories* (New York: Knopf, 1999), 211–233.

41 *Polnoe Sobranie Sochineniĭ*, ed. A. S. Puahkin, and D. D. Blagoĭ (Moskow: Khudozh. lit-ra, 1959), 248–249.

and once more the room was left with only one lamp burning. The Countess sat there looking quite yellow, mumbling with her flaccid lips and swaying to and fro. Her dull eyes expressed a complete vacancy of mind, and, looking at her, one would have thought that the rocking of her body was not a voluntary action of her own, but was produced by the action of some concealed galvanic mechanism.]^{42}

In this passage, the exposed decaying body of the Countess, who was known in her prime as the Venus of Moscow, represents a horrifying performance. Her private chamber becomes a stage for what is repulsive, but also attractive. It has the plot line of an old fairy tale of attraction and seduction, with a cannibalistic dénouement.

Lyubov Golburt's close reading of this passage explains the significance of the scene and the articles of fashion in catalogues. She states that Pushkin employs 'the temporality of fashion' to highlight 'the main tensions of modern life: its discomfort with history, commercialization, narrative, and the body'.[43] Golburt claims that by means of fetishistic fashion Pushkin achieves the intimacy of both a lover (from the past) and a murderer (of the present time) with the old Countess, similarly to the way a modern reader strives to achieve a relation to history. According to Golburt, when Hermann peeks in on the dressing ritual, he experiences a revelation that causes his madness: 'Hermann's is a kind of elegiac sensibility, gone awry feigning indifference and practicality, but miscalculating the danger of the encounter with the past which can strike back and drive one to madness ...'.[44] This observation demonstrates a split between the rational and irrational in these stories of societal observation. These qualities co-exist, but also come with the caveat that only a keyhole-sized opening exists for those who are ready to peep inside. This gap divides and at the same time co-joins the two traditions, which allows for psychologism to dictate its terms.

The Gothic Gossip and Boundaries of Genre

Gossip appears to be a nuisance to readers, but it is the force that drives the plot and opens avenues for genre development. Genre boundaries here become fluid due to gossip and the theme of ageing, which infuse the narratives with the senses of shame and death. It is under these conditions that the gothic may infiltrate and infect the narrative fabric of these tales with physiological effects.

---

42 *The Collected Stories, ed.* Aleksandr Sergeevich Pushkin and Paul Debreczeny (New York: Knopf, 1999), 211–233.
43 Lyubov Yefimovna Golburt, 'The Vanishing Point: The Eighteenth Century and the Russian Historical Imagination'. *Dissertation Abstracts International, Section A: The Humanities and Social Sciences* 67.9 (2007): 142.
44 Ibid., 68.

While P.N. Sakulin, in his biography of Odoevsky, states that Odoevsky considered it his duty to dispense with 'outdated' forms of classicism and *'pseudo-romanticism*' in Russian literature, one could conclude that Odoevsky uses gossip to provide a deeper psychological portrayal of women and makes definitions of gender and genre bendable.

The dynamics of socializing between characters in 'Princess Mimi' weigh solely on the material value of the prospective match. The social weight and value of women fluctuate rapidly from 'yesterday to now'. For example, the little flirt who yesterday sought Mimi's protection was now herself already speaking in the tones of a 'protectoress' because of her appropriated status as a well-married woman. In the meantime, readers also receive gossipy hints from the narrator that Princess Mimi's value has declined with time, as a result of unsuccessful courtship and visible signs of ageing, whereby she becomes a target of gossip in the forms of smirks and whispers, eroding her value to the level of cast-off furniture:

> Её положение сделалось нестерпимо: всё вокруг неё вышло или выходило замуж... Мими оставалась одна, без голоса, без подборы ... Хозяйка встречала её с холодной учтивостью, смотрела на неё, как на лишнюю мебель ....][45]

> [Ieio polozhenie sdelalos' nesterpimo: vsio dokrug neie vyshlo ili vyhodilo zamuzh... Mimi ostavalas' odna, bez golosa, bez podbory... Hozyaika vstrechala ieio s holodnoi uchtivostiu, smotrela na neie, kak na lishniuiu mebel'....]

> [Her situation had become unendurable. *Everyone* in her circle had already married, or were getting married ... only Princess Mimi remained on her own, without any such voice or prop ....][46]

On the one hand, the comparison of Mimi to superannuated furniture, and the usage of the definitive pronoun 'всё' [*vs'ie*] [in its entirety] in reference to other females, accentuates the author's critical observation of high society, and yet, the author brings awareness to the material in a seemingly romantic narrative. The tension engendered by representing material reality within the framework of a society tale becomes transparent in the juxtaposition of the concept of material values in society against women treated as worthless objects.

Regardless of the unattractive and even pitiful representation of his leading female characters, Odoevsky succeeds in raising the woman question by granting the power of discourse to the abject. In Odoevsky's tales, in tales of magic and terror, the abject lower class seizes power. Both forms of fiction aim to show ways of overcoming oppression and change society through the transformative power of language. As Bruno Bettelheim states in *The Uses of En-*

---

[45] Одоевский, 'Княжна Мими' [*Kniazhna Mimi*], 107.
[46] Odoevsky, 'Princess Mimi', 7.

chantment, 'Evil is not without its attractions' and 'a usurper succeeds for a time' and for a special purpose.[47]

As with the folk tales of the European tradition, nineteenth-century Russian literature never views female ageing favorably. This seems to be the fear of perishability and death. As the selected narratives reveal, the marketability of brides is in their economic value as well as in their nice, fresh faces. Youthful looks appear in tales by nineteenth-century Russian writers in terms of aesthetic appreciation; beyond references to the physiological there is no association to the possible fertility of the female match. In fact, society tales rarely provide closure in the form of a happy end of marital bliss; Natasha Rostova of Tolstoy's *War and Peace* (1869) is the exception. Ageing appears to be the cause of grief for female characters themselves, and the ageing body evokes horror and disgust in onlookers, while vanity seems to drive the continuous struggle for a respectable place in society and for ageing heroines in the narratives of Odoevsky. Similar to the evil queen in the Grimms' 'Snow White', Odoevsky's heroines use a cannibalistic mode of gossip to destroy their more attractive and younger rivals' reputations.[48] They use the circular setting of the places of socializing as a magic mirror or observatory to trigger their vanities, to spot the target and destroy it with the words of wishful thinking.

For Rapunzel and for Snow White, physical attributes represent not only salvation from the cursed physical space, but also the means of social advancement. Mimi and Zizi, as well as Pushkin's old Countess, are captives of their social milieu, from which there is no escape, and they thus become jailers themselves. Their bodies, also under their control, are crammed into corsets and covered with wigs and expensive fabric. They are ugly and grotesque and dangerous; they are the ultimate abject. The narratives themselves were considered filled with superfluous details and lacking in coherency.

Mimi and Zizi, however aged and barren, bear out the author's views on the decline of the nobility and romanticism; they and their gossip reveal the underside of the set traditions. With their ugly physiologisms, they believe the prim proprieties of their age: its failed Decembrist revolt and its backward views towards women and marriage. By trivial account of artificial high society and by revealing the truths hidden behind marble columns, these narratives expose the two Petersburgs, and thus begin the formation of the Natural school in nineteenth-century Russian literature:

---

[47] Bruno Bettelheim, *The Uses of Enchantment* (New York: Vintage Books, 1989), 9. doi: 10987654321.

[48] Jacob Grimm and Wilhelm Grimm, *Brothers Grimm Fairy Tales: An Illustrated Classic*, ed. Arthur Rackham, (San Diego, CA: Canterbury Classics, 2017), 171–185.

В философии и науке заметно стремление романтическому идеализму противопоставить строгий реализм. Народность и натурализм становятся лозунгами эпохи. Общий порыв к национальному самосознанию, прошедший через очистительное горнило романтизма, выразился в создании художественного реализма, в частности реальной повести и социального романа

[*V filosofii i nauke zametno stremleniye romanticheskomu idealizmu protivopostavit' strogiy realizm. Narodnost' i naturalizm stanovyatsya lozungami epokhi. Obshchiy poryv k natsional'nomu samosoznaniyu, proshedshiy cherez ochistitel'noye gornilo romantizma, vyrazilsya v sozdanii khudozhestvennogo realizma, v chastnosti real'noy povesti i sotsial'nogo romana.*]

[In philosophy and in science there is a definite inclination towards juxtaposing romantic idealism with strict realism. Nationhood and naturalism become the maxims of the epoch. There is a general striving for national consciousness which, forged in the hearth of romanticism, is expressed in the creation of artistic realism and, especially, in the realist tale and social novel].[49]

In 'Princess Mimi' and 'Princess Zizi', gossip functions as a prevailing form of discourse, because it simultaneously shapes and betrays the reader's expectations, thus fueling the curiosity to read further. It forces the reader to pay attention to the details of interactions, and to details such as time, décor, and habits of the physical space of socializing. After all, gossip is language, and, according to Bakhtin, 'language in the novel not only represents, but itself serves as an object of representation. The word in the novel is always self-critical'.[50] Therefore, it not only has the power to manipulate the characters involved in gossiping, but actually manipulates the perception of cultural and socio-economic codes and of the settings, in which gossip was first conceived. With the evolution of literary traditions from romantic to Realist, gossip emerges as a form of journalistic 'discourse' to influence the story. Thus, this wordiness floods the narrative and makes the narrative fabric of society tales more porous and accelerates time. It is by these means that the importance of pragmatics and insignificance enters the romantic genre. For example, Pavel Sakulin, Zinaida Gippius, and, later, Neil Cornwell point out that Odoevsky derived special pleasure from intruding upon the imagination of prim and proper society by offering tales of mysticism on the one hand, and of a caustic social critique on the other.

---

49 Sakulin, *Iz Istorii Russkogo Idealizma*, vol. 1, part 2, 3–11.
50 M. M. Bakhtin, *The Dialogic Imagination: Four Essays* (Austin: University of Texas Press, 2017), 219.

Troy Wellington Smith
(University of California, Berkeley)

Romantic Latecomers: P. L. Møller on Pushkin, Kierkegaard, and Flaubert

Abstract
This essay examines the Danish critic P. L. Møller's evaluations of Alexander Pushkin, Søren Kierkegaard, and Gustave Flaubert, three authors responding to a common problem of belatedness in respect to international and domestic romanticisms. Whereas Pushkin's historical consciousness and verse provided suitable forms for his contemporary content and allowed him to transcend his position as a post-Byronic romantic epigone, the supposedly formless realisms of Kierkegaard and Flaubert – in Møller's estimation – were inadequate solutions to their late moment. Although I conclude by suggesting that a formal structure can easily be found in the respective works of Kierkegaard and Flaubert, Møller's critical studies nonetheless offer a window into the aesthetics of late Scandinavian romanticism as they are about to be eclipsed by those of realism.

Keywords
Eugene Onegin, *Stadier paa Livets Vei*, *Madame Bovary*, Byronism, Form, Realism

As Kierkegaard scholarship became a global industry in the twentieth century, a narrative of the *Corsair* affair began to circulate as a morality play of sorts. In the role of Vice was Peder Ludvig Møller, the lascivious aesthete rumored to have been the model for the titular character of 'Forførerens Dagbog' [The seducer's diary], a novella within the first part of Kierkegaard's *Enten – Eller* [Either/Or]. Møller had written an *ad hominem* review of Kierkegaard's *Stadier paa Livets Vei* [Stages on Life's Way] in the 1846 volume of *Gæa*, his 'æsthetisk Aarbog' [aesthetic yearbook], that pathologized the author's chaste relationship with his (i. e., Kierkegaard's) ex-fiancée, Regine Olsen. Kierkegaard responded with an article in which he publicized Møller's *sub rosa* editorship of the dubious *Corsaren* [The corsair] thereby calling down on himself the wrath of the gutter press. The resulting caricatures, which appeared in *Corsaren* over a number of months, are now as famous as nearly any representation that we have of Kierkegaard, and they made the once-respected philosopher a laughingstock in the streets of Copenhagen. Møller, his hopes of a university chair dashed, went abroad, and into a hand-to-mouth existence. The other secret editor of *Corsaren*, Meïr Goldschmidt, soon decided to sell the paper and concentrate on writing literature, as Kierkegaard had once suggested to him. By voluntarily undergoing this social martyrdom, Kierkegaard not only rid Copenhagen of *Corsaren*; he also rigorously chastened himself for the writing of his religious authorship. That, in any case, is the popular account of the *Corsair* affair.

Yet the theory that the villainous Johannes the Seducer is based on Møller, first advanced by Frithiof Brandt in his *Den unge Søren Kierkegaard* [The young Søren Kierkegaard], depends upon Kierkegaard having read an unpublished manuscript of Møller's, a cycle of erotic poems.[1] But 'there are', according to K. Brian Söderquist, 'so few similarities between the manuscript in question and 'The Seducer's Diary', and the circumstances are so speculative, that it is difficult to move beyond the sphere of possibility and conclude that Møller's poetic work influenced Kierkegaard at all'.[2] As for the notion that the *Corsair* affair sent Møller slinking off into exile, he did not actually leave Denmark until two years after his collision with Kierkegaard, and it was on a governmental scholarship.[3] And if Møller did have expectations for the Chair in Aesthetics at the University of Copenhagen, his aspirations were, according to Paul V. Rubow, wholly unrealistic, and therefore the *Corsair* affair would hardly have had an impact on his career in this respect.[4] Furthermore, Goldschmidt's claim that he decided to sell *Corsaren* after receiving a withering glance from Kierkegaard in the street is probably a bit of self-mythologizing. This encounter took place immediately after Kierkegaard's *Afsluttende uvidenskabelig Efterskrift* [Concluding Unscientific Postscript] was published on 27 February 1846, but Goldschmidt did not actually part with *Corsaren* until October of that same year.[5] Finally, the fact that the usually reflective Kierkegaard published his provocative salvo against Møller on 27 December 1845, just one week after the appearance of *Gæa*, would strongly suggest that his reaction was an impassioned one, and not part of some philanthropic project of self-sacrifice.

---

1 Frithiof Brandt, *Den unge Kierkegaard. En række nye Bidrag* (Copenhagen: Levin, 1929), 202–243.
2 K. Brian Söderquist, 'Peder Ludvig Møller: "If He Had Been a Somewhat More Significant Person" ...', in *Kierkegaard and His Danish Contemporaries, Tome III: Literature, Drama and Aesthetics*, ed. Jon Stewart (Farnham: Ashgate, 2009), 249.
3 Hans Hertel, 'P. L. Møller and Romanticism in Danish Literature', in *Kierkegaard and His Contemporaries: The Culture of Golden Age Denmark*, ed. Jon Stewart (Berlin: De Gruyter, 2003), 359.
4 Paul V. Rubow, *Goldschmidt og Nemesis*, Det Kongelige Danske Videnskabernes Selskab Historisk-filosofiske Meddelelser 42.5 (Copenhagen: Munksgaard, 1968), 118.
5 Johnny Kondrup, 'Meïr Goldschmidt: The Cross-Eyed Hunchback', in *Kierkegaard and His Danish Contemporaries, Tome III: Literature, Drama and Aesthetics*, ed. Jon Stewart (Farnham: Ashgate, 2009), 132.

With all of that said, this venue is not the proper one to enumerate all of the ambiguities, biases, and untruths in the folkloric narrative sketched in the first paragraph above. To do so would mean writing the 'fully documented history of the *Corsair* affair' that W. H. Auden called for over fifty years ago.[6] Instead, by using Møller as a case study, my purpose in this essay is to delineate the aesthetics of late Scandinavian romanticism on the cusp of realism. Møller's 'Et Besøg i Sorø' [A Visit in Sorø], the review of *Stadier* that triggered the *Corsair* affair, will be at the figurative – if not the literal – center of this investigation. Rather than being a libelous attack on Kierkegaard, as it is often imagined, Møller's essay is in fact a critical judgement of the philosopher's response to their common problem: that of historical belatedness. Bookending 'Et Besøg i Sorø' are Møller's writings on two other authors who follow in the wake of the first waves of European romanticism, namely Alexander Pushkin and Gustave Flaubert. Møller's work on these canonical figures will be consulted in order to locate his criticisms of Kierkegaard within the larger framework of late romantic aesthetics. Like Kierkegaard himself, Pushkin and Flaubert are also responding to the difficulties of writing in the *Spät-* or *Nachromantik* [late- or post-romantic] periods, even if their answers to this challenge appear to be widely divergent. Pushkin receives Møller's praise for his formalism, for being 'en umiddelbar Discipel af Byron' [an immediate disciple of Byron].[7] Yet, while looking backwards to George Gordon, Lord Byron for inspiration, Pushkin's Janus-like epigonism simultaneously faces forwards to the present, as it is of its own contemporary moment, just as Byronism itself was. In accordance with Møller's iteration of late Scandinavian romanticism, Pushkin is commended for giving form to raw material, both through his historical consciousness and his application of verse. Kierkegaard and Flaubert, on the other hand, are censured for the supposed formlessness of their prose. More precisely, Møller derides Flaubert for his realism, for pursuing 'en Art physiologisk Sandhed' [a sort of physiological truth] in (presumably) *Madame Bovary*, a critique which Møller had aimed at Kierkegaard in his review of *Stadier paa Livets Vei* some 15 years earlier.[8]

Kierkegaard and Møller were born only one year apart, in 1813 and 1814, respectively, and they therefore came of age during what – at the time – could only be considered a late moment in Danish literary history. Romanticism, of course, had come to Denmark relatively early, with the lectures of Henrik Stef-

---

6 W. H. Auden, 'A Knight of Doleful Countenance', *New Yorker*, May 25 (1968), 141.
7 P. L. Møller, 'Skildringer af Frankrigs Poesi. Brudstykker af et academisk Prisskrift', in *Gæa. Æsthetisk Aarbog*, ed. P. L. Møller (Copenhagen: published by the editor, 1845), 309. All translations, unless otherwise noted, are my own.
8 [P. L.] M[øller], 'Fransk Litteratur', in *Nordisk Conversations-Lexicon,* vol. 3 (Copenhagen: Forlagsbureauet, 1860), 161. Although this article is signed with only one initial, I am assuming that it is Møller's on the authority of Hans Hertel. Hertel, 'Møller', 371.

fens and the publication of Adam Oehlenschläger's *Digte* [Poems] in 1802.[9] Fresh from Jena, the Norwegian Steffens had arrived in Copenhagen with the gospel of Schelling and Friedrich Schlegel, and his lectures were eagerly attended by the first generation of Danish romantics, which included Oehlenschläger. Although Danish romanticism was far from a purely autochthonous phenomenon, Oehlenschläger strove to locate a native romanticism in the Danish soil with his poem 'Guldhornene' [The Gold Horns], in which a peasant lad and maiden unearth two Iron Age drinking horns. Around the time that Kierkegaard and Møller entered the University of Copenhagen, the aging national romantics were being edged aside by the younger dramaturge and critic Johan Ludvig Heiberg, who, in his 1833 essay *Om Philosophiens Betydning for den nuværende Tid* [On the Significance of Philosophy for the Present Age], shifted the dominant philosophical paradigm from Schlegel and Schelling to Goethe and Hegel.[10] That Hegel and Goethe had both died a year or two before Heiberg published *Om Philosophiens Betydning* is quite telling. Instead of looking ahead, at home, to the rising generation that would include Kierkegaard and Hans Christian Andersen, Heiberg turns back to two German authors – albeit titanic ones – who had already come to the end of their productivity. Kierkegaard and Møller, then, were doubly, perhaps triply, late. Not only were they twice removed from Jena romanticism; they also found themselves on the wrong side of the *Goethezeit* [the age of Goethe].

Turning now to Møller's essay on Pushkin, which was first published in the journal *Brage og Idun* [Brage and Idun] in 1839 and later revised for the 1847 collection *Kritiske Skizzer fra Aarene 1840-47* [Critical sketches from the years 1840-47], one finds high praise for the Russian poet, in spite of his belatedness in respect to German and Danish romanticism. Møller would refer to Pushkin in his later treatise on French poetry as 'an immediate disciple of Byron', but this designation was not intended to be disparaging, even if it might seem to suggest an unreflective appropriation of the British baron. To follow Byron, in Møller's critical opinion, meant above all to cast one's poetry in a recognizably modern form. As he wrote in an 1840 review of Heiberg's comedy *Syvsoverdag* [Seven Sleepers' Day], 'Heiberg er ikke nogen modern Digter. Skjøndt samtidig med Byron, er han tilsyneladende ikke bleven berørt af ham eller hans Skole' [Heiberg is no modern poet. Although contemporary with Byron, he has apparently not

---

9 Although the title page is dated 1803, *Digte* was published during the Christmas season of 1802.
10 '*Göthe* og *Hegel* ere upaatvivlelig de to største Mænd, som den nyere Tid har frembragt' [*Goethe* and *Hegel* are undoubtedly the two greatest men that the modern age has produced]. Johan Ludvig Heiberg, Om Philosophiens Betydning for den nuværende Tid, in *Prosaiske Skrifter,* vol. 1 (Copenhagen: Reitzel, 1861), 417.

been touched by him or his school].¹¹ While Møller concedes that Scott's historical novels did awaken an interest in France for that nation's *'romantiske Middelalder'* [romantic Middle Ages], which in turn comprised *'eet af Hovedmomenterne i den nye franske Poesi'* [*one* of the main moments in modern French poetry], Byron is 'den gjærende og misfornøiede Tids ægteste Søn' [the truest son of the restless and dissatisfied age].¹² Byron's poetry is, 'som enhver sand Poesi, en virkelig Blomst af sin Tid, saa god og slet som denne selv, og en aandig Organverden, hvori alle denne *egoistiske* Tids Tvivl og Savn, Fortrin og Feil, vare samlede' [like every true poetry, a real flower of its age, as good and as bad as this age itself, and a spiritual world of organs, in which all of this *egoistic* age's doubts and wants, virtues and faults, were gathered].¹³

Fig. 1: A.S. Pushkin, Portrait of Eugene Onegin, 1830. Complete Works of Pushkin, Vol.3, 1909.

By historicizing, Møller eases the sense of belatedness that had seized his generation. If 'every true poetry' is a reflection of its age, then the successors of Byron, such as Pushkin, are not tasked with depicting Byron's revolutionary period, but their own. Their originality, then, will be assured by the uniqueness of their historical moment, if only they are true to it. Thus does Luba Golburt define

---

11 P. L. Møller, 'J. L. Heiberg. *Syvsoverdag*', in *Kritiske Skizzer fra Aarene 1840–1847,* vol. 1 (Copenhagen: Philipsen, 1847), 132.
12 Møller, 'Frankrigs Poesi', 309.
13 Ibid.

'Pushkin as interpreter rather than imitator of Byron'; the titular character of *Eugene Onegin* is 'a post-Byronic gloss on the forms of personhood propagated through Byronism, forms so tragically inhabited by the heroes of Pushkin's southern narrative poems, but thoroughly interrogated in *Eugene Onegin*'.[14] That is to say, Pushkin writes of his age: not the point at which Byronism was emerging, but slightly later, when it had become ossified and institutionalized, and was therefore ripe for critique. In *Eugene Onegin*, the Byronic posture is but one of the many contemporary Petersburg fashions trumpeted by the narrator in chapter 1, among them Bolívar hats, Bréguet watches, and roast beef.[15] By making his hero a reader of Byron, Pushkin, according to Golburt, 'implicitly claims a different purpose for his work: not to contribute yet another Byronic portrait to a well-populated gallery, but rather to explore the consequences of modelling one's life upon literature'.[16] Following Jerome McGann's definition of the Byronic hero, Golburt argues that, in *Eugene Onegin*, Byron's 'poetic environment ... comes into conflict with the socio-historical as well as poetic conditions of a world where Byronic personhood is no longer the mark of an autonomous rebel, but rather of a weak individual's susceptibility to fashion'.[17] There is, then, a marked contrast between Byron's age and Pushkin's, not least in respect to the Byronic hero. *Eugene Onegin* could therefore be said to be something of a thought experiment, one that imagines the results of living out a particular character type's *modus operandi*, not in the Mediterranean amidst the romantic ferment of the Napoleonic Wars (as with the original Byronic hero, the eponymous protagonist of *Childe Harold*), but on the Baltic, in a Petersburg seized by an increasingly oppressive political regime over the course of the 1820s. Adhering to these contemporary conditions, Pushkin endows his *Eugene Onegin* with a freshness sorely lacking in ahistorical, banal imitations of Byron.

It is fitting, then, that Møller stresses the historical particularity of most – if not all – poetry in the first section of his Pushkin essay. Rare is the work 'hvor Kunstens Idé i særdeles höj Grad er bleven realisereret, hvor der kan tales om Fuldenthed for alle Tider. Tværtimod bære de fleste, selv meget navnkundige, Digterværker et eller andet Præg af Tidsalderens Brøst' [where the idea of art has been realized to an especially high degree, where there can be talk of perfection for all ages. On the contrary, most poetic works, even very famous ones, bear one

---

14 Luba Golburt, 'Alexander Pushkin as a Romantic', in *The Oxford Handbook of European Romanticism*, ed. Paul Hamilton (Oxford: Oxford University Press, 2016), 522, doi: 10.1093/oxfordhb/9780199696383.013.27.
15 Alexander Pushkin, *Eugene Onegin: A Novel in Verse*, trans. James E. Fallen (Oxford: Oxford University Press, 1995), 10–11.
16 Golburt, 'Pushkin', 522.
17 Ibid., 523.

or another stamp of the defects of the age].[18] Furthermore, one will find that 'de mest fuldendte Kunstværker' [the most perfect artworks] exert 'en höjere moralsk Kraft hos den Tidsalder, der frembragte dem, end hos en anden' [a higher moral force with the ages that produced them than with another].[19] From this same historicist vantage point, Møller, in section 2, describes the genesis of contemporary Russian poetry as the convergence of several cultural vectors. Until relatively recently, Russia had been under the tutelage of France, which provided 'det formelle Prinsip i Litteraturen' [the formal principle in the literature].[20] Only now is there a poetry which 'kunde kaldes russisk' [could be called Russian] thanks to 'en ... fremgaaende Folkeliv' [an ... emerging folk-life].[21] For Møller, the Herderian *Volksgeist* [national spirit] does not exist in a vacuum; on the contrary, one spirit combines with others when it comes into contact with them through the play of historical forces. Not only is Russian culture inherently synthetic – Møller describes it as 'græsk-orientalske' [Greek-Oriental]; its poetry has just been 'paaviftet af en nordlig Romantiks Aande' [fanned by a breath of northern romanticism].[22] While the other Slavic countries and Hungary received impulses from Germany, namely from Goethe and Schiller (although neither is, strictly speaking, a romantic), Pushkin took his 'næsten udelukkende fra *Byron*, der med sin nordiske Kraft, Følelsens Fylde, med Tvivlens Sønderrivelse og Lidenskabens sydlige Glød, stærkt maatte gribe Puschkins beslægtede Natur' [nearly exclusively from *Byron*, who, with his Nordic power, abundance of feeling, and with the tearing-asunder of doubt and the southern glow of passion, must have strongly seized Pushkin's kindred nature].[23] One should note that here Byron's power is not described as 'northern', as romanticism was above, but as 'Nordic', which is almost equivalent to 'Scandinavian'. Møller was not the only Scandinavian critic who attempted to appropriate Byron during this period. In his 1845 dissertation *Om Lord Byron* [On Lord Byron], the Icelander Grímur Thomsen sought to demonstrate that the English were a Nordic people: 'Til Norden regne vi nu sædvanligviis ogsaa *England*, ligesom jo tillige Englændernes Herkomst, hvad enten vi tænke paa Saxer eller Normanner, er nordisk' [We usually also count *England* among the North, just as the Englishmen's extraction, whether we think of Saxons or Normans, is Nordic].[24] But if Byron was born a Norseman, he died a southerner, spending the last years of his rather short life in Italy and Greece. Møller no doubt alludes to this biographical arc when he refers to Byron's

---

18 P. L. Møller, 'Digterskildringer', *Brage og Idun* 1, no. 1 (1839): 232.
19 Ibid., 233.
20 Ibid., 239.
21 Ibid., 238.
22 Ibid., 239.
23 Ibid., 239–240.
24 Grímur Thorgrímsson Thomsen, *Om Lord Byron* (Copenhagen: Høst, 1845), 12.

'southern glow of passion'. If Pushkin's culture is 'Greek' - or, rather, 'Greek-Oriental' - he shares a territory with the philhellenic Byron; and, while in the nineteenth century Russians were considered 'Oriental', they had traditionally been conceived of as Northerners, which perhaps explains why Møller's Pushkin was 'seized' by the 'Nordic power' of Byron, as if by a 'kindred nature'.[25] If Byron is a southern northerner, then Pushkin is a northern southerner, not only because of his national culture's Greek roots (presumably through the Orthodox Church), but also by dint of the African ancestry that Møller traces in his physiognomy.[26] With their very selves split between the cardinal points of the compass, both Byron and Pushkin embody the *Zerrissenheit* [inner conflict] that would come to define Danish *Romantisme* in the 1830s and 1840s. As an acolyte of Charles Augustin Sainte-Beuve, Møller claims that what he calls (in the 1847 edition of the Pushkin essay) 'den psychologisk-biografiske Kritik' [the psycho-biographical criticism] is of interest because the lives of great poets, such as Byron and Pushkin, manifest the historical particularity of their age - in their case, they echo its dissonances.[27]

'Det kan ikke noksom indskærpes' [It cannot be emphasized enough], writes Møller in the revised Pushkin article, 'at det virkelig Aandsfyldige, det Poetiske, det Evige i Menneskeaanden, hvor det end findes, altid har det mest absolute historiske Værd, og bør interessere Menneskeaanden stærkest' [that the truly spirited, the poetic, the eternal in the human spirit, wherever it is found, always has the most absolute historic worth, and ought to most strongly interest the human spirit].[28] 'Den poetiske Interesse' [The poetic interest], he continues, 'saavel som den sande historiske, er kosmopolitisk, og i høieste Forstand *liberal*' [as well as the truly historical, is cosmopolitan, and in the highest sense *liberal*].[29] Here Møller distinguishes between the materialistic ends of liberalism, which he abhorred, and the spiritual values of this political philosophy, which he admired. Niels Egebak claims that Møller rejected materialism 'og den naturalistiske litteratur' [and the naturalistic literature] because within it 'han kun kunne se småborgerlighedens triumf' [he could only see the triumph of the *petite bourgeoisie*].[30] With that said, Møller by no means fell into the opposite camp with J. L. Heiberg's Danish Hegelians. In fact, according to Hans Hertel, 'Møller, in his

---

25 I am indebted to Luba Golburt for the constructive feedback I received on an early draft of this essay, and I thank her especially for her insight into how western Europeans' perceptions of the Russian people evolved over the course of history.
26 Møller, 'Digterskildringer', 240.
27 P. L. Møller, 'Alexander Puschkin', in *Kritiske Skizzer fra Aarene 1840-1847*, vol. 2 (Copenhagen: Philipsen, 1847), 4.
28 Ibid., 21.
29 Ibid.
30 Niels Egebak, *Mellem Heiberg og Brandes. P. L. Møllers plads i dansk kritiks historie* (Aarhus: Modtryk, 1992), 120.

fierce anti-Hegelianism, thought that he found "sterile dialectics" and "system building" in Kierkegaard's work and overlooked its polemics against the dialectics of Hegel'.[31] Møller, writes Egebak, was convinced that 'det var Fichtes og Schellings ånd, der skulle genfødes, derfor kunne han fable om sin romantiske muse med foden på jorden og brystet i himlen' [it was Fichte's and Schelling's spirit, which ought to be reborn, and therefore he could fantasize about his romantic muse with her foot on the earth and her breast in heaven].[32] In his preference for Fichte and Schelling over Hegel, Møller sides with Steffens, Oehlenschläger, and the first generation of Danish romantics over against Heiberg and his Hegelian coterie. It is worth noting here that *Gæa*, the 'aesthetic yearbook' in which Møller's 'Et Besøg i Sorø' was published, was given its title as a rebuff to Heiberg, who had dubbed his own yearbook *Urania*.[33] Perhaps this suggestion that one school of German idealism is more otherworldly than the other will seem like an all-too-fine distinction, but, regardless of whether Møller's assessment of Hegel vis-à-vis Schelling is correct, he has in any case shown a marked preference for a literature in which idealism and materialism – or form and content – are held in a dialectical tension; and, even if (as we shall see) form is ultimately privileged as the *sine qua non* of Møller's aesthetics, he appears to have found a theoretical underpinning for this critical position in Steffens' Schelling, and not in Heiberg's Hegel.[34]

Møller studied medicine at the University of Copenhagen, and it is therefore unsurprising that he would model his 'psycho-biographical criticism' on the work of Sainte-Beuve.[35] The French critic had described his practice as follows: '[J]'analyse, j'herborise, je suis un naturaliste des esprits' [I analyze, I botanize, I am a naturalist of the spirit], and he even called his method 'un cours de physiologie morale' [a course in moral physiology].[36] In spite of his enthusiasm for Sainte-Beuve, the science of physiology would not always be a metaphor for impeccable art in the eyes of Møller. In an article on French literature published in the *Nordisk Conversations-Lexicon* [Nordic encyclopedia] in 1860, Møller writes:

> I den nyeste Tid har Realismen baade paa Theatret og i Romanen antaget en extrem Skikkelse, idet den ikke blot med koldblodig Nysgjerrighed søger en Art physiologisk Sandhed (den yngre Dumas, Barrière, Flaubert) eller et klingende Spil med Formen

---

31 Hertel, 'Møller', 358.
32 Egebak, *Møllers plads*, 92.
33 '[E]arth versus space'. Hertel, 'Møller', 357.
34 Yet, according to Michael O'Neill Burns, Hegel (like Schelling) does not neglect the interplay of matter and spirit in favor of a substance monism. Michael O'Neill Burns, *Kierkegaard and the Matter of Philosophy: A Fractured Dialectic* (London: Rowan & Littlefield, 2015), 31–32.
35 Hertel, 'Møller', 357, 367–369.
36 Quoted in Egebak, *Møllers plads*, 19–20.

(Banville), men stræber efter en photographisk Sandhed i tilfældige, materielle Yderligheder, der ikke længer er Realisme men Materialisme.

[Most recently, realism has both in theater and in the novel taken on an extreme figure, as it not merely with cold-blooded curiosity seeks a sort of physiological truth (the younger Dumas, Barrière, Flaubert) or a jingling play with form (Banville), but strives after a photographic truth in accidental, material extremes, which no longer is realism but materialism.][37]

One would assume that Møller is referring here to Flaubert's *Madame Bovary*, since it was the only complete major work that Flaubert had published by 1860, although fragments of *La Tentation de Saint Antoine* [The Temptation of Saint Anthony] had appeared in the journal *Artiste* in December 1856 and January 1857. Flaubert, according to Møller, does not practice sheer photographic materialism, but he is not far off, as Møller describes Flaubert's project as one of physiology. This science is not, note well, the 'moral physiology' of Sainte-Beuve, but neither can it be restricted to a literal physiology, even if Flaubert had studied medical textbooks in order to depict Emma's death by poisoning.[38] Rather, to extend this metaphor a little further, Sainte-Beuve's 'course in moral physiology' might well be described as one in pathology, insofar as the moralist passes judgement on the behavior of an individual or the mores of a society, just as the pathologist assesses the function of an organ or a body by a normative standard.

So, when Møller accuses Flaubert of hankering after 'a sort of physiological truth', he is actually echoing a charge that had been leveled against the novelist during the obscenity trial of *Madame Bovary:* that Flaubert had described immorality without rendering a verdict against it. Imperial Counsel Ernest Pinard writes in his brief:

Quel est le titre du roman? *Madame Bovary.* C'est un titre qui ne dit rien par lui-même. Il en a un second entre parenthèses: *Mœurs de province.* C'est encore là un titre qui n'explique pas la pensée de l'auteur, mais qui la fait pressentir. L'auteur n'a pas voulu suivre tel ou tel système philosophique vrai ou faux, il a voulu faire des tableaux de genre, et vous allez voir quels tableaux!!!

[What is the title of the novel: *Madame Bovary.* It is a title that signifies nothing by itself. There is a second one between parentheses: *Provincial Life.* This is yet another title that does not explain the thoughts of the author but intimates them. The author did not mean to follow such or such true or false philosophical method, he meant to compose genre paintings, and you shall see what kind of paintings!!!][39]

---

37 M[øller], 'Fransk Litteratur', 161.
38 Bernard Doering, 'Madame Bovary and Flaubert's Romanticism', *College Literature* 8. 1 (1981): 3.
39 Ernest Pinard, 'Ministère public contre M. Gustave Flaubert. Réquisitoire', in *Madame Bovary* (Paris: Garnier-Flammarion, 1966), 369–370. Translated by Bregtje Hartendorf-Wallach as

Fig. 2: Eugène Giraud, Gustave Flaubert, c.1856. Palace of Versailles.

'La couleur générale de l'auteur ... c'est la couleur lascive' [The overall color of the author ... is lascivious], as is, Pinard suggests, 'la physionomie générale de Mme Bovary' [the general physiognomy of Mrs. Bovary].[40] What is worse, 'Les peintures lascives ont généralement plus d'influence que les froids raisonnements' [Lascivious paintings generally have more influence than cold reasoning].[41] This 'cold reasoning' is conspicuously absent, and '*Madame Bovary*, envisagé au point de vue philosophique, n'est point moral' [*Madame Bovary*, considered from a philosophical point of view, is not in the least moral].[42] Pinard searches the novel for a character who could serve as its moral center, and who would thus have been capable of judging Madame Bovary, but he finds no one.[43] When Møller reproaches Flaubert's 'cold-blooded' pursuit of 'a sort of physiological truth', he is reiterating Pinard's accusations of 'lascivious paintings'; in his depiction of French provincial life, Flaubert neither pathologizes nor

---

'The Ministry of Justice against Gustave Flaubert: Brief', in *Madame Bovary*, ed. Margaret Cohen (New York: Norton, 2005), 315.
40 Pinard, 'Réquisitoire', 373, 375. Trans. by Hartendorf-Wallach, 319, 321.
41 Ibid., 386. Ibid., 333.
42 Ibid., 386. Ibid., 333.
43 Ibid., 387–388. Ibid., 334–335.

prescribes. The novelist, with great *sangfroid*, and even greater imaginative power, fictionalizes a newspaper article he had read about a country doctor's wife who had poisoned herself after running up a number of adulteries and debts – without, allegedly, morally condemning her.

In the concluding paragraph of his brief, Pinard not only anticipates Møller's complaint against *Madame Bovary*; he also asserts the late romantic tenet of form's ultimate necessity, just as Møller had in his review of *Stadier paa Livets Vei*:

> Cette morale stigmatise la littérature réaliste, non pas parce qu'elle peint les passions: la haine, la vengeance, l'amour; le monde ne vit que là-dessus, et l'art doit les peindre; mais quand elle les peint sans frein, sans mesure. L'art sans règle n'est plus l'art; c'est comme une femme qui quitterait tout vêtement. Imposer à l'art l'unique règle de la décence publique, ce n'est pas l'asservir, mais l'honorer. On ne grandit qu'avec une règle.
>
> [This morality stigmatizes realist literature not because it paints the passions: hatred, vengeance, and love – the world lives for nothing else, and art must paint them – but when it paints them in a fashion that is uncontrolled and lacks moderation. Art without rules is no longer art; it is like a woman who would take off all her clothes. To impose upon art the unique rule of public decency is not to subordinate it but to honor it. One grows greater only in accordance with a rule.][44]

In other words, a work of art is not to depict 'the passions' as they naturally appear; to do so would mean to let content overrun art itself in a wanton confusion. Rather than presenting the reader with this sprawling tangle, the novelist must espalier his material by the means of form; or, to employ another metaphor, a novel's subject matter should always be glimpsed through the gauzy veil of the ideal – and never with the cold-blooded precision of the physiologist's microscope.

In the aesthetics of late Scandinavian romanticism, verse was the surest formal superstructure for mastering content. The 1839 edition of Møller's Pushkin essay complains that the past age's 'prosaiske Vantro' [prosaic unbelief] has had a 'fordærvelig Virkning paa vore Digtere' [ruinous effect on our poets].[45] In contemporary French literature, there are 'saa faa Værker af ren ideal og blivende Værdi' [so few works of pure ideal and enduring value], and in German letters, as well, there is a 'gribende Sammenblanding ... af Poesiens rene Former med alle Arter af det prosaiske Foredrag, hvorfor saa stor en Masse af disse Litteraturer ser ud som lutter Bastarder' [grasping confusion ... of poetry's pure forms with all sorts of prosaic execution, for which reason so very many of these literatures look like sheer mongrels].[46] Møller laments that, in the present age,

---

44 Ibid., 388. Ibid., 335.
45 Møller, 'Digterskildringer', 234.
46 Ibid., 235–236.

'Vers læses, som bekjendt, ikke; de mere materielle Romaner og Noveller skaffe deres Forfattere oftest kun knapt Brød og liden Ære' [Verse is, as is known, not read; the more material novels and short stories most frequently provide their authors with only a bit of bread and little honor].[47] The critic concludes the introductory section of this essay by invoking Pushkin:

> Kunde man undre sig meget, hvis en mægtig Aand, der af alle Egenskaber mindst manglede Kraftens, Varmens og Ærgjærrighedens Flammeglød, under en vexlende Skjæbne sandsynlig ofte stillet mellem matte, aandløse Omgivelser, uretfærdige af Mangel paa Forstand, misundelige af Egenkjærlighed, – i mörke, utrøstede, ikke forstaaede Timer søgte ligesom over en Grundvold af Frygt og Had at rejse Sjeniets Trofæer, *tvinge Materien til at ydmyge sig for Aanden?* –
>
> [Could one really wonder if a powerful spirit, who of all qualities least lacked the flameglow of force, warmth, and ambition, under a varying fate was often enough positioned among dull, spiritless circumstances, unjust from lack of understanding, envious from selfishness – in dark, inconsolable, not-understood hours, if he sought to raise the trophies of genius via a foundation of fear and hate, *to compel matter to humble itself before the spirit?*][48]

The genius, according to Møller, does not allow existence in its immediacy to dictate his poetry, but instead reflects and reshapes this material through the formal categories and by the power of the intellect or spirit – the word *Aanden*, of course, can mean both. Content, in other words, must ultimately be subject to form, and versification, as Møller's earlier remarks suggest, is the best safeguard against a lapse into the prosy amorphousness of raw content.

To repeat, Pinard would later allege that Flaubert, in his quest for realism, failed to rein in his material and ran roughshod over every formal rule of decorum. When Møller, in his parenthetical reference to Flaubert in the *Nordisk Conversations-Lexicon* article, accuses the novelist of seeking only 'a sort of physiological truth', he is, whether consciously or not, tracing the main thrust of Pinard's brief. For instance, a physiologist might draw a typical or normal heart, but she does not describe the heart's Platonic Form. Likewise, in imagining the fictional dorp of Yonville, Flaubert depicts life in provincial France as no better than it is, not as it should be. This turn away from the ideal towards the real would be what Møller means by the pursuit of 'physiological truth'. In 'Et Besøg i Sorø', the critic aims essentially this same charge of physiology against Kierkegaard in a reading of the '"Skyldig?" – "Ikke-Skylidig?"' ['Guilty?'/'Not guilty?'] section of *Stadier paa Livets Vei*. This anatomization of society or of oneself is, for Møller, a violation of the canons of late Scandinavian romanticism and an unsatisfactory solution to the mutual dilemma of belatedness that he shares with Pushkin,

---

47 Ibid., 237–238.
48 Ibid., 238; emphasis mine.

Kierkegaard, and Flaubert. While Pushkin earned Møller's commendation for compelling the material of his particular milieu to subject itself to the spirit of form (in, for example, *Eugene Onegin*, as a novel-in-verse about contemporary Russian life), Kierkegaard and Flaubert are rebuked for forsaking the ideal for a physiological empiricism. As I will note, however, in the conclusion of this essay, Møller's criticisms, no matter how well intended, overlook the role that ideal forms play in *Stadier*, as well as in *Madame Bovary*.

'"Skyldig?" – "Ikke-Skyldig?"' is 'En Lidelseshistorie' [A story of suffering], as it is subtitled, but this novel-within-a-novel is further subtitled 'Psychologisk Experiment' [Psychological experiment].[49] As we shall see, Møller takes this suffering to be an immediate outpouring of Kierkegaard's own, overlooking the degree to which the text is an imaginary construction indebted to traditional literary forms. The diarist narrator, who is referred to in the frame narrative as Quidam, recounts in the morning entries his broken engagement to a certain Quaedam, and then agonizes over his sense of responsibility to her in the passages recorded at midnight. *Stadier paa Livets Vei* was published under the editorial pseudonym Hilarius Bogbinder [Bookbinder], with Kierkegaard's name appearing nowhere on the title page or elsewhere, but it was already an open secret by this time that he was responsible for the profuse, polyonymous authorship. The parallel, then, between the broken engagement of Kierkegaard and Regine Olsen, and that of Quidam and Quaedam, would have been obvious to the Copenhagen literati, such as Møller.

'Et Besøg i Sorø' is a review in the form of an autobiographical narrative, in which Møller calls on the novelist Carsten Hauch, who is in residence with the other eminences of Danish letters at Sorø Academy. Hauch asks Møller and the others in attendance whether they 'har ... læst det sidste Volumen af Philosophen med de mange Navne, "Hilarius Bogbinder" troer jeg, han denne Gang kalder sig ....' [have ... read the last volume by the philosopher with the many names, 'Hilarius Bookbinder' I think he calls himself this time ....].[50] 'Han har vist ikke havt nogen varmere Beundrer, end mig' [He has certainly not had any warmer admirer than me], Møller replies, 'men saa har jeg ogsaa desto større Ærgrelse af den golde og fordærvelige Brug, han undertiden gjør af sine udmærkede Evner, og som især culminerer i den sidste Artikel af "Stadier paa Livets Vei"' [but then I have also all the greater annoyance at the barren and ruinous use he sometimes makes of his fine powers, which particularly culminates in the last article of *Stadier paa Livets Vei*], i.e., '"Skyldig?" – "Ikke-

---

49 Søren Kierkegaard, *Stadier paa Livets Vei*, in *Søren Kierkegaards Skrifter*, ed. Niels Jørgen Cappelørn et al., vol. 6 (Copenhagen: Søren Kierkegaard Forskningscenteret, 2014), 173, http://sks.dk/SLV/txt.xml.

50 P. L. Møller, 'Et Besøg i Sorø', in *Gæa. Æsthetisk Aarbog*, ed. P. L. Møller (Copenhagen: published by the editor, 1846), 172.

Skylidig?'".[51] In order to understand what is 'barren and ruinous' in *Stadier*, it will be worthwhile to quote at length Møller's analysis of the first work of Kierkegaard's authorship proper, i. e., *Enten – Eller*, where he expresses his preference for part one, the papers of the aesthete, over part two, the letters of the ethicist:

> I den første mærker man *Mesteren, som behersker sit Stof,* og man træffer derfor næsten altid *en rigtig, ofte en fortrinlig Form,* som kun af og til forstyrres ved en skeptisk Dissonants af de Dæmoner, han i senere Skrifter har søgt at betvinge. I anden Deel seer man derimod Begynderen, den søgende og vordende Personlighed, hvis Foredrag stadig "stripper ud i Mangekanten", fordi han *ikke meddeler et beseiret og organiseret Stof,* men kun udvikler sit ethiske Jeg – skrivende. Som æsthetisk Praktiker og Experimentor kan han siges at have fuldendt sin Udvikling, som moralsk Personlighed er han endnu en Mulighed; derfor er anden Deel, trods det Interessante i Dialektikens Anvendelse paa det sociale Liv, trods alle Glimt af Skjønhed og Aand i det Enkelte, *mindre et Litteraturværk, end en Materialsamling.*

> [In the first, one notices *the master who commands his material,* and therefore one almost always encounters *a correct, often excellent form,* which only now and again is disturbed by a skeptical dissonance by the demons he has sought to control in later writings. In the second part, one sees, on the other hand, the beginner, that seeking and future personality, whose delivery is constantly 'polygonizing' because he *does not communicate a conquered and organized material,* but only develops his ethical ego – writing. As aesthetic practitioner and experimenter he can be said to have completed his development; as a moral personality he is still a possibility. Therefore, the second part, despite the interestingness in the dialectic's application to social life, despite all the flash and beauty and spirit in the individual, is *less a work of literature than a collection of material.*][52]

Enten – Eller is a work of prose, but Møller does not find part 1 to be prosaic, as he did much of contemporary literature in the 1839 Pushkin article. To be prosaic, for Møller, is to be formless, but in part 1 Kierkegaard usually finds a felicitous form to match his chosen content.

In a subtle manner, this passage speaks to Møller and Kierkegaard's common plight as late Scandinavian romantics. As we saw in Møller's writings on Pushkin, the Russian poet was able to overcome his belatedness by not only writing of his post-Byronic, Russian moment, but also by finding a suitable form for this content. This form is the piquant Onegin stanza, which Møller does not mention explicitly in the postscript to the 1847 revision of the article, probably because he read Robert Lippert's 1840 German translation of this 'Roman paa Vers' [novel in verse], which would appear to employ a different prosody than the original does.[53] Whatever this particular verse form was would not have been as important to

---

51 Ibid., 173.
52 Ibid.; emphasis mine.
53 Møller, 'Puschkin', 28.

Møller as the fact that this novel is versified in the first place, since the prose novel risks becoming 'physiological' or 'material', as was evident in Møller's criticisms of *Madame Bovary* and contemporary literature in general. Like Pushkin, Kierkegaard also wrote as a late romantic, but he was able to give his content the proper form – at least, according to Møller, in some cases – without writing a line of verse. One of Hauch's guests (who, given his familiarity with Pushkin, undoubtedly serves as a mouthpiece for Møller himself) claims that Kierkegaard's *Frygt og Bæven* [Fear and Trembling] '[s]om lyrisk Digt indtager ... en høi Plads i den nyere Litteratur, og kan stilles i Række med Byron, Puschkin og "die ungöttliche Comedie" [The ungodly comedy]' [as a lyrical poem assumes ... a high place in modern literature, and can be ranked with Byron, Pushkin, and *Die ungöttliche Comedie*].[54] Published under the pseudonym Johannes de Silentio in 1843, *Frygt og Bæven* is subtitled *Dialektisk Lyrik* [Dialectical Lyric], which to some extent would explain Møller's classification of this prose work 'as a lyrical poem', but the text also has the subjectivity and compactness of the lyric, which Møller no doubt appreciated, given his late romantic formalism.

While both 'Forførerens Dagbog' and '"Skyldig?" – "Ikke-Skyldig?"' are diary novels, Møller celebrates the former, yet claims that Kierkegaard is grasping after a suitable form for his content in the latter, just as he was said to be doing in the epistolary novel composing the second part of *Enten – Eller*.[55] Here the content resists every assayed form, remaining as a series of autobiographical sketches or a 'collection of material'. The same anonymous guest, who, again, is most likely echoing Møller's sentiments, points out that the polyonymous philosopher 'begaaer den samme Feil, som man har bebreidet Digteren Andersen, at han lader hele sin indre Livsudvikling foregaae for Alles Øine' [commits the same mistake for which they have reproached the poet Andersen, that he allows the whole of his inner life development to take place before the eyes of all].[56] The irony here, of course, is that 'they' is none other than Kierkegaard himself, who, in his authorial debut of 1838, entitled *Af en endnu Levendes Papirer* [From the Papers of One Still Living], took Andersen to task for too closely identifying with the protagonist of his novel *Kun en Spillemand* [Only a Fiddler], which had ap-

---

54 Møller, 'Sorø', 174.
55 'Som hans høieste Fortjeneste, hvor han virkelig har bragt Videnskaben et nyt og uskatterligt Udbytte, anseer jeg dog de Grundlinier, han i "Forførerens Dagbog" har draget til en Philosophi af *Kvindeligheden*, et Stof der, saa rigt og tiltrækkende det end er, neppe tidligere har været bearbeidet' [As for his highest service, where he really has brought science a new and invaluable profit, of which I perceive only the foundations, he has in 'Forførerens Dagbog' drawn towards a philosophy of *womanliness*, a subject which, as rich and attractive as it is, had previously hardly been worked on]. Ibid., 175.
56 Ibid., 173–174.

peared the year before. In *Af en endnu Levendes Papirer*, Kierkegaard writes in a footnote:

> Andersens første Potens maa snarere sammenlignes med de Blomster, hvor Han og Hun sidde paa een Stengel, hvilket som Gjennemgangsstadium er yderst nødvendigt, men ikke egner sig til Productioner i Roman- og Novelle-Faget, der kræve en dybere Eenhed og følgelig ogsaa forudsætte en stærkere Kløftelse.
>
> [Andersen's first potency must sooner be compared with the flowers where male and female sit on a single stalk, which as a transitional stage is extremely necessary, but is not suitable for productions in the craft of novels and short stories, which demand a deeper unity and consequently also presuppose a stronger divide].[57]

Andersen's 'egentlige poetiske Frembringelse ... ikke er andet end en fyldig, i en friere Verden sig indskabende og i denne sig rørende, reproducerende 2den Potens af det i første Potens allerede paa mangfoldig Maade poetisk Oplevede' [poetic production proper ... is none other than a copious second potency which, forming itself in a freer world and moving about in it, reproduces from what it has already poetically experienced in multiple ways in the first potency].[58] Without delving too far into Kierkegaard's botanical metaphor – or his torturous early prose – one can conclude that this passage, like many others in the book, reiterates Kierkegaard's basic argument: that Andersen has failed to sufficiently separate his personal experiences from his fiction.

Møller next charges Kierkegaard with the same lapse in judgement of which he (i.e., Kierkegaard) had accused Andersen, and, quite significantly, Møller employs his own metaphor from reproductive physiology:

> Men da jeg tog hans sidste store Bog "Stadier paa Livets Vei" i Hænderne, var det næsten med en uhyggelig Følelse. En saa overdreven, ja saa unaturlig Produktivitet kan maaske være sund for Forf., men for Litteraturen og Læseren – aldrig. Produktionen synes at være bleven ham en physisk Trang, eller han benytter den som et Medikament, ligesom man i visse Sygdomme bruger Aareladning, Kopsætning, Dampbad, Vomitiv eller deslige. Naar et sundt Menneske udhviler ved Søvnen, synes han at udhvile ved at lade Pennen løbe, istedenfor at spise og drikke mætter han sig ved at skrive, istedetfor at den ordinære Menneskenatur reproduceres ved et Foster om Aaret, synes han at have en Fiskenatur og at lægge Rogn.
>
> [But when I took up his last book, *Stadier paa Livets Vei*, it was nearly with an uncanny feeling. One such exaggerated, yes, such an unnatural productivity can perhaps be healthy for the author, but for literature and the reader – never. Production seems to have become a physical need for him, or he uses it as a medicine, just as one with certain

---

57 Søren Kierkegaard, *Af en endnu Levendes Papirer*, in *Søren Kierkegaards Skrifter*, ed. Niels Jørgen Cappelørn et al., vol. 1 (Copenhagen: Søren Kierkegaard Forskningscenteret, 2014), 39, http://sks.dk/LP/txt.xml.
58 Ibid., 38.

illnesses uses bloodletting, cupping, steam-baths, emetics, and the like. While a healthy person rests by sleeping, it seems that he rests by letting his pen run; instead of eating and drinking, he nourishes himself by writing; instead of the ordinary human nature, which reproduces itself with a fetus each year, he seems to have a fish-nature and spawns.][59]

Since Kierkegaard, by some accounts, broke his engagement to Regine Olsen in order to pursue his vocation as the author of a school of pseudonyms, this last remark would have cut painfully close to the bone. Møller published a fairy tale and three poems by Andersen in this same volume of *Gæa*, and thus the editor appears to be avenging his contributor in the passage of the review quoted above; if Andersen and his poetic production could be compared to a hermaphroditic flower, then Kierkegaard and his pseudonymous authorship are like a fish and its roe.

Møller begins by reading '"Skyldig?" – "Ikke-Skylidig?"', which, as he notes apprehensively, 'udfylder de sidste 242 tættrykte Sider' [fills the last 242 closely printed pages] of *Stadier paa Livets Vei*.[60] As we saw in the critic's remarks on the second part of *Enten – Eller*, the problem here, too, is a lack of form: 'Han bekymrer sig ikke om Læseren; thi han skriver for sin Magelighed, ikke om et klassisk Forfatternavn, *thi han skriver formløst*' [He does not care about the reader, for he writes for his comfort; he does not care about a classic name as an author, *for he writes formlessly*].[61] Yet what is most interesting is that this formlessness, as one finds later in Møller's dismissal of Flaubert, is described as a sort of physiology. Although the science of physiology undoubtedly describes given forms, this practice – for Møller, anyway – is not comparable to 'compell[ing] the matter to humble itself before the spirit', as Pushkin had done, most notably in his *Eugene Onegin*.

As was said, '"Skyldig?" – "Ikke-Skylidig?"' has close parallels to the intertwined biographies of Kierkegaard and Regine Olsen. In fact, Kierkegaard even went so far as to print the letter with which he broke with her in this fictional diary.[62] Like Pushkin, who sought to overcome his belatedness by giving form to the raw material of his contemporary moment in a versified novel, Kierkegaard avoided aping Goethe or the German romantics by refracting his unique experience through a series of pseudonyms, allegories, and parables. Møller, however, sees through – or simply ignores – the sometimes-thin veil of literary artifice, and assumes that Kierkegaard is straightforwardly Quidam's referent, and Regine is Quaedam's. Kierkegaard was no doubt incensed by Møller's allegation that

---

59 Møller, 'Sorø', 175–176.
60 Ibid., 176.
61 Ibid.; emphasis mine.
62 Kierkegaard, *Stadier*, 307.

'det kvindelige Væsen, som lægges paa den experimentale Pinebænk, bliver naturligvis i Bogen ogsaa til Dialektik og fordunster; men i Livet maatte hun nødvendigvis blive gal eller gaae i Peblingesøen' [the female being, who is laid on the experimental rack, naturally becomes dialectic in the book and evaporates, but in real life she must by necessity go mad or drown herself in Peblinge Lake].[63] Indeed, Regine had taken the split so badly that Kierkegaard had feared for her life, and the fact that the rakish Møller sided with her out of a sort of chivalrous unctuousness would have touched Kierkegaard on the raw.

Like Flaubert, Kierkegaard – according to Møller – resorts to a sort of literary physiology in overcoming his late moment. But whereas Flaubert performed a vivisection on the collective body of provincial France, Kierkegaard operates microscopically on himself and, claims Møller, on Regine, as well – all without her consent. That Møller finds this procedure to be an unsatisfactory and unethical response to belatedness should be unsurprising, given that he would prefer the formal mastery of a Pushkin to the 'physiological truth' of a Flaubert. Apostrophizing Kierkegaard, the critic declaims:

> Vil Du betragte Livet som en Dissectionsstue og Dig selv som Cadaver, saa lad gaae, sønderflæng Dig selv saameget Du vil; saalænge Du ikke gjør Andre Fortræd, vil Politiet ikke forstyrre Din Virksomhed. Men at indspinde et andet Væsen i sit Edderkopvæv, dissekere det i levende Live, eller pine Sjælen draabevis ud af det, i Kraft af Experimentet, det har man dog ikke endnu Lov til, uden ved Insecter, og har ikke allerede Tanken herom noget Rædselfuldt, noget Oprørende for den sunde Menneskenatur?

> [If you want to consider life as an anatomical theater, and yourself as a cadaver, then go ahead, tear yourself to pieces as much as you want; as long as you do not do another harm, the police will not disturb your activity. But to spin another being into one's spiderweb, to dissect it alive or to torture the soul out of it drop by drop by means of an experiment, that, however, one still does not have permission to do, except with insects, and hasn't already the thought of that something horrifying, something outrageous, for the healthy human nature?][64]

Rather than giving form to content, as Pushkin did, Kierkegaard dedicates himself to recording his sorrows and speculating on those of his ex-fiancée. In other words, instead of providing this material with an ideal structure, Kierkegaard, Møller alleges, traffics in a crude psychological realism that 'allows the whole of his inner life development to take place before the eyes of all'. 'Her er' [Here are], writes Møller, 'Gjentagelser, Selvudhuling, glimrende Geniglimt og Tilløb til Vanvid' [repetitions, the scooping out of the self, brilliant flashes of genius, and signs of madness].[65]

---

63 Møller, 'Sorø', 177.
64 Ibid., 177–178.
65 Ibid., 176.

Kierkegaard's reply to Møller's narrative review, entitled 'En omreisende Æsthetikers Virksomhed, og hvorledes han dog kom til betale Gjæstebudet' [The Activity of a Traveling Esthetician and How He Still Happened to Pay for the Dinner], appeared in the liberal newspaper *Fædrelandet* [The fatherland] on 27 December 1845. It would precipitate the *Corsair* affair, and thus had lasting consequences for Kierkegaard, if not for Møller, as well. As a coda to this essay, I will turn to a footnote in Kierkegaard's open letter, as it would indicate that Møller overlooked the formal qualities of '"Skyldig?" – "Ikke-Skylidig?"'. In fact, it could also be argued that Møller, in his campaign against realism, failed to notice the subtle formalism of *Madame Bovary* 15 years later.[66] Neither Kierkegaard nor Flaubert resorted to 'physiology', if by 'physiology' one means an unsophisticated psychological or social realism that pays no heed to literary form.

But before consulting the footnote in question, it is worth noting that this letter to Møller is not signed by Kierkegaard himself, but by Frater Taciturnus, one of the pseudonyms in *Stadier paa Livets Vei*. In the first section of '"Skyldig?" – "Ikke-Skylidig?"', the silent brother writes of how he found Quidam's diary locked within a box wrapped in oilcloth that he had pulled up from the bottom of Søborg Lake in northern Zealand. Of course, the frame narrative of the found manuscript is a well-worn novelistic topos (one that Kierkegaard had already employed multiple times in *Enten – Eller*), and later Frater Taciturnus even admits in the 'Skrivelse til Læseren' [Letter to the reader] that he has in fact 'manet frem' [conjured up] Quidam as a fictional character.[67] Furthermore, the subtitle, 'En *Lidelses*historie', invokes, with its German cognate, the title of Goethe's epistolary novel *Die* Leiden *des jungen Werthers* [The Sufferings of Young Werther], as Carl Roos seems to suggest in his monograph *Kierkegaard og Goethe* [Kierkegaard and Goethe].[68] Additionally, as was mentioned above, the sub-subtitle of '"Skyldig?" – "Ikke-Skylidig?"' is 'Psychologisk Experiment'. Both of these subtitles indicate an adherence to certain formal parameters. Whereas the first subtitle, with its Goethean echo, is strictly literary, the second adopts a more scientific register, but not, note well, that of empirical psychology. Contrary to Møller's article, Kierkegaard is decidedly not anatomizing himself in order to collect immediate psychological data. Like Werther, Quidam, the experimental subject, is an imaginary creation. And the fact that the frater's frame narrative surrounding Quidam is framed still further by that of the editorial pseudonym Hilarius Bogbinder – who, at the encouragement of his children's teacher, de-

---

66 'The continual and often too obvious presence of irony in *Madame Bovary* not only violates the first canon of Realism, namely that the author must observe and choose but never conclude; it also violates the second because the irony invariably turns to moral commentary'. Doering, 'Flaubert's Romanticism', 6.
67 Kierkegaard, *Stadier*, 369.
68 Carl Roos, *Kierkegaard og Goethe* (Copenhagen: Gads, 1955), 44.

cided to publish the papers that a deceased 'Literatus' had left behind to be bound, including "'Skyldig?" – "Ikke-Skylidig?"' – would once and for all refute the claim that Kierkegaard was unoccupied with literary form in the composition of *Stadier*.[69]

As Møller admits, he began reading *Stadier paa Livets Vej* with "'Skyldig?" – "Ikke-Skylidig?"', which would explain why he failed to notice that it was couched within two other narratives. In *Fædrelandet*, Frater Taciturnus rebukes the critic for his careless reading of the novel:

> En Experimentator siger: for ret at blive opmærksom paa det Afgjørende i de religieuse Existens-Kategorier, da Religieusitet saa ofte forvexles med Allehaande og med Dvaskhed, vil jeg experimentere en Figur, der existerer i en sidste og yderste Approximation til Afsindighed men i Retning af Religieusitet .... Nu kommer Indvendingen af Hr. P. L. Møller: "det er næsten Afsindighed, det er Tilløb til Vanvid". Svar: ja ganske vist, deri laa jo netop Opgavens Vanskelighed .... Efter Bordet angriber han Experimentet, han sigter det for næsten Afsindighed, men see, det var netop det, Experimentet ogsaa sigtede efter ....
>
> [An experimenter says: in order to properly become attentive to the decisive in the religious existence-categories, when the religious so often is mixed up with allspice and with lethargy, I will experiment on a figure that exists in the last and most extreme approximation of madness but in the direction of the religious .... Now comes the objection of Mr. P. L. Møller: 'It is nearly insanity; it is signs of madness'. Answer: Yes, quite certainly; that is exactly where the difficulty of the task lay .... After dinner, he attacks the experiment, he charges it with nearly insanity, but see, that was exactly what the experiment also aimed for ....][70]

Here Møller is not only reminded of the formal moment of pseudonymity; he is alerted to it by one of the pseudonyms themselves! The diarist Quidam is thrice removed from Kierkegaard, being separated from him by Frater Taciturnus and Hilarius Bogbinder in the book's puzzle-like structure. Seeing only the affinities between Kierkegaard and Quidam, Møller read *Stadier* as a straightforward *roman à clef*, as though the content of the author's personal experience had not been filtered through a series of frame narratives.

Undoubtedly, Møller's review is a misprision of Kierkegaard's novel, but it is far from being pure invective. As is evident from his remarks on the first part of *Enten – Eller* and *Frygt og Bæven*, Møller held Kierkegaard's poetical powers in high esteem. 'Et Besøg i Sorø', then, is not a hatchet job, but an appeal from a young generation's greatest critic to its foremost prose stylist. If one will write

---

69 Kierkegaard, *Stadier*, 11–14.
70 Søren Kierkegaard, 'En omreisende Æsthetikers Virksomhed, og hvorledes han dog kom til at betale Gjæstebudet', in *Søren Kierkegaards Skrifter*, ed. Niels Jørgen Cappelørn et al., vol. 14 (Copenhagen: Søren Kierkegaard Forskningscenteret, 2014), 79, http://sks.dk/AeV/txt.xml.

prose, it should display, like the 'lyric' *Frygt og Bæven*, the same formal mastery found in the verse of Byron and Pushkin, and not the recalcitrant matter of 'physiology'. A desperate turn towards formless realism, which Møller would later identify with Flaubert (however unjustly), is not a viable solution for the late romantic, who should strive instead – in the spirit of Schelling – for a dialectic of the material and the ideal.[71] Whether the aesthetics of late Scandinavian romanticism were Schellingian (as with Møller) or Hegelian (as with Heiberg), they were in any case idealist, and Kierkegaard, with his formalism, is no exception in this regard, even if his nested narratives were completely lost on Møller. In spite of the short-sightedness and effrontery of his review, Møller in fact has a constructive admonition for Kierkegaard, although for many later critics this message has been – like the conciliatory words at the end of Kierkegaard's notorious book on Andersen – written 'med sympathetisk Blæk' [with invisible ink].[72]

---

[71] Flaubert's famous quip, 'Madame Bovary, c'est moi' [Madame Bovary, that's me], appears as a fissure in the monolithic realism so often ascribed to the novel by critics such as Møller. Bernard Doering writes, 'In the face of all the other characters, Flaubert is incapable of maintaining his impersonal aesthetic distance because of his violent anger. In the case of Emma he cannot keep himself from intruding; but this time it is because of an overwhelming tenderness. As a Realist Flaubert maintained that the novelist must enter into the person of his creation, not draw that person to himself. Flaubert's sympathy for Emma as an embodiment of his own aspirations, struggles, and illusions, and his hatred of the false and exaggerated aspects of Romanticism in her that he wished to condemn, prevented him from making up his mind about her'. Doering, 'Flaubert's Romanticism', 9–10.

[72] Kierkegaard, *Levendes Papirer*, 57.

Reviews

C. J. L. Almqvist, Murnis: Idyllion. Samlade verk, serie III: Otryckta verk

Ed. by Petra Söderlund
Stockholm: Svenska Vitterhetssamfundet, 2018
Xxviii + 140 pp., $14 (130 SEK)

Imagine a heavenly region shaped as a vulva, add a script explaining that the ruby-red fissure dividing the shiny white pieces of land is the valley of God, and there you have an emblem of man's relationship to God – at least as it was envisioned by the Swedish romantic writer C. J. L. Almqvist (1793–1866) when he wrote the tale *Murnis* in 1819. Inspired by Emanuel Swedenborg among others, Almqvist imagined that the afterlife offered a variety of habitats for the righteous, depending on their hearts and minds. Murnis is the realm for those whose lives have centred on the desire for their one true love, as part of their desire to love and serve God. The human body serves as a master trope, and a system of correspondences is explained to the newcomers: Christ served as God's genitals in relation to the human world, into which he entered, planted his seed, died, and withdrew into divine existence. Hence the shape of a vagina. But the Murnis landscape is also changeable, according to the mood, and the level of insight, and need of the moment. So, the reader is told, the fissure might resemble a ruby river but is actually a line of angels with a ruby temperament as well as a deep, blessed valley leading to other countries and habitats – and the whole realm is certain to look quite different from the viewpoint of other angels.

In the years around 1819, Almqvist's thinking and writing circled around the relations between love, sexual desire, religion, and poetry. Most of his writings remained unpublished in these years, however, including his most radical experiment with literary depiction of a pure, Christian eroticism, *Murnis*. Transcripts circulated among his friends and admirers at the time, but the work remained unpublished except for Almqvist's own revised and censured version in 1845, *De Dödas Sagor* [Tales of the Dead], and, again in 1850, as part of *Törnrosens bok* [The Book of the Wild Rose] (1833–1851). Almqvist's original manuscript has been lost, while two contemporary transcripts survived, and in 1960 Erik Gamby published an edition from one of these, a copy by an anonymous hand.

Now, 200 years later, the work has been made available to readers in a new critical edition based on the other, hitherto unpublished manuscript. The editor,

Petra Söderlund, who is currently the main editor of Almqvist's collected works, has chosen a transcript made by one of Almqvist's close admirers, Gustaf Hazelius, as copy text. The compelling argument is that this manuscript is known to have reached the primary readers in Almqvist's own time. Further, Söderlund argues that the Hazelius-manuscript appears to be a more accurate rendering of the lost autograph than the one used by Gamby, and adds that all research, with the exception of a 1937 study by Henry Olsson, has in fact been based on an 'unsatisfactory transcript' (p. 126, all translations are mine). Naturally, this is a scoop for a critical edition, and there is reason to be grateful for this opportunity to re-read – as well as to acknowledge the instability of the text in the company of solid textual criticism. Both manuscripts are described in bibliographical detail in the comments and a list of variants is included. At a closer look, however, the differences turn out to be less substantial and therefore less likely to lead to fundamental revisions of the overall picture of *Murnis* and its author.

Fig.1: Francesco Albani, Hermaphroditus and Salmacis. Louvre Museum.

The subtitle is 'Idyllion', and Almqvist also called *Murnis* an erotic epic poem in his letters. It relates different lovers' transition from an early medieval world, governed by both pure and perverse desires, to the glittering, educating, and changeable world of Murnis. In heaven, nakedness is a sign of innocence, and the sexual union between loving pairs is described as a divine service. In the introduction, Söderlund perhaps stresses the centrality of the child a bit too much (XII–XIII). After all, it is not childlike bodies that are presented as the ideal in *Murnis* but sexually mature, strong, and beautiful young bodies. Even the boys playing and fighting in the heavenly gold-castle for children's education have arms with bulging sinews (p. 88). A slightly more varied palette of masculinities and femininities is displayed among the adult characters, but the basic system is patriarchal, complementary, and monogamous: all angels must mature according to their sex and pair up in order to become whole. It would take some more years before Almqvist created the most famous androgynous and/or transsexual character in Swedish literature in *Drottningens juvelsmycke* [The Queen's Tiara] (1835), published as volume 6 in the series, and more forcefully championed women's rights in *Det går an* [It Can be Done] (1839), published as volume 22 in the series.

The narrative thread binding the gallery of lovers in *Murnis* together is the separation, trials, sacrifices, and reunion of the main characters Albion and Nuna. Furthermore, all the stories are enclosed in an elusive, lyrical frame, which suggests that the whole tale is sung by Nuna in the shape of the bird Philomela, or produced in cooperation between a painter/poet and Nuna/Philomela, or that the tale somehow produces itself. The voices speak directly to a listener (you) and to a group of listeners, addressed as 'brothers'. This complex, ironic frame, which is somewhat downplayed in the introduction, contributes highly to the overall impression that *Murnis* is not just an interesting otherworldly vision and didactic experiment, but at the same time a fascinating piece of self-reflective romantic poetry, akin to a work like *Heinrich von Ofterdingen* (1802).

As Söderlund explains, Almqvist did offer *Murnis* to the leading romanticist of the time, P. D. A. Atterbom, to be published in his annual poetical calendar. The first three chapters which Almqvist sent him would not give Atterbom or the publisher V. F. Palmblad any obvious reason to refuse it, so they must have had an idea of the totality of the work. It is easy to agree with Söderlund's assessment that the refusal meant that an important piece of Almqvist's thinking was obscured and that 'Swedish romanticism was deprived of a work which was more bold, revolutionary, and experimental than any other work published by any other Swedish romantic' (IX). One additional factor in this equation is not just the risk of scandal, as pointed out in the introduction (X), but also the utopian core of Almqvist's project, or *his* refusal to be realistic in relation to existing laws and limits of the press. He forced Atterbom and Palmblad to be pragmatic stand-ins for him, so to speak, and made no other move to have his work published in its original version.

Whereas early Almqvist research often dismissed or downplayed *Murnis* with gestures of embarrassment, Petra Söderlund's introduction rightly presents it as a centrepiece in the philosophical, theological, aesthetic, and pedagogical puzzle, which is Almqvist's oeuvre around 1819. The introduction relies on the extensive Swedish Almqvist-research and offers an overview of the relevant contributions, which are briefly summarised. In the commentary, historical facts, such as the dating of plume-decorated helmets, or the unlikeliness of a certain kind of trees growing in that particular geographical area, are perhaps somewhat superfluous in a tale such as *Murnis*, but they do help the reader understand the degree to which Almqvist constructs his fantasy carelessly against (worldly) realistic claims.

In one instance, however, the zealous dating risks barring more metaphorical readings, such as when 'så kom ett hagel' [a hailstorm came] (p. 28) is translated into 'de blev beskjutna' [they were shot at], (p. 136) followed by a remark that it is anachronistic to introduce small shots in an early medieval context. A more likely reading is a metaphorical 'hail' or 'hailstorm':

> Just när vi blifvit vigde till deras män i Kyrkan, så kom ett hagel från hafvet. Det var hedniske män, långväga ifrån. De föllo in, och röfvade våra hustrur.
>
> [Just as we had become wed in the church to be their husbands, a hailstorm came from the sea. It was pagan men, from far away. They fell upon us [or: attacked], and abducted our wives].

I would also argue that *Philomela* is not just another word for nightingale (p. 135) and that a short comment on the Ovidian myth and the traditions of using Philomela in poetry could have been added. It would furthermore have been helpful, if the word-explanations were clearly marked when a word is Almqvist's neologism and therefore open to different interpretations.

To be sure, it is always a precarious task to calibrate the inclusion and exclusion of information, and where to draw the line between explanation and interpretation. My objections to certain details should not overshadow the fact that Söderlund's solicitous edition has provided researchers and other fans of Almqvist with a solid ground for new interactions with one of his most fascinating and challenging works. It is gratifying and reassuring to see that the important project of producing a thorough, critical edition of Almqvist's collected works is in fact proceeding, even though it lacks central funding.

Gunilla Hermansson
University of Gothenburg, Sweden

The Reception of William Blake in Europe

Ed. by Morton Paley and Sibylle Erle
London: Bloomsbury Academic, 2019
768 pp., £225

The Reception of William Blake in Europe, the latest volume in Bloomsbury's comprehensive series on the European reception of canonical British and Irish writers, is intended to broaden the scholarly picture of Blake's "afterlife" – a term which, as series editor Elinor Shaffer points out, is all too often and with all too little justification treated as synonymous with an author's legacy in his or her native country (xii). The resulting collection of twenty-six essays, edited by Morton Paley and Sibylle Erle, is as robust, rich, and varied as the territory it covers; the fact that, even at 700 pages, there is evidently far more that could be said feels less like a fault than a testament to the importance of the book itself: through this gap gleams the future research for which the volume will undoubtedly prove an invaluable resource.

Blake's reputation as a universal poet probably rests at least partially on the degree to which he resists categorization. The difficulty of fitting Blake into even the traditions with which he shares significant attributes – romantic, Neoplatonist, Hermetic, Gnostic, Christian – paradoxically makes it easier to claim him for traditions where the connection is more tenuous: Blake is a foreigner wherever he goes, which means that he is equally at home everywhere. The fact that the reception of Blake in most European countries only begins in earnest during the early twentieth century adds an additional distancing factor in the form of time: unlike the other major British romantics, Blake was already a historical figure by the time he was introduced to the rest of the continent. Thus, we learn that Blake has been enlisted in various national contexts as a "direct precursor to Soviet ideology" (519); as a "dissenting voice against Communist ideology" (470); as a representative of a Celtic-European sensibility rebelling against Anglo-French dominion (276); as a Catholic (159); as a radical Protestant (560); as an early representative of Jungian depth psychology (207); as an early surrealist (186); as an early anticipator of the theory of relativity (221); as a Nietzschean materialist rebelling against Hegelianism (131); and as a Christian antidote to Nietzscheanism (142). In many cases, such readings reveal new and surprising

Fig. 1: William Blake, Europe. A Prophecy, Plate 1, Frontispiece, 1794. Yale Center for British Art, Paul Mellon Collection.

qualities inherent in the works themselves, but more often it is the acts of creative appropriation that are of special interest – the "hybrid" Blakes, and the unique traces that those have left in each literary tradition.

Most of the twenty-six chapters are devoted to Blake's reception in a particular country or region, with roughly equal attention given to each part of the continent. The one curious exception is the almost complete omission of the Baltic states, which receive only a few lines in the introduction, even though it is stated that "in Latvia the reception of Blake was of special importance" and that there are "many translators of Blake into Estonian" (12–13) – however, in all other areas, the distribution seems judicious and fair. Finally, the book concludes with two thematic chapters, the first of which traces Blake's influence in music, while the second is devoted to the history of exhibitions of Blake's art throughout Europe.

Of the mainland European countries, it is only in Germany that reception begins during Blake's lifetime, thanks largely to the contributions of Henry Crabb Robinson, whose 24-page article in the journal *Vaterländisches Museum* (published in 1811) sets the tone for the subsequent reception of his countryman. In the chapter dealing with Blake's reception in Germany and Austria, Susanne Schmid sets out to disprove the prevailing notion that Blake's work went largely unnoticed until the publication of Alexander Gilchrist's *The Life of Blake* in 1863; instead, she argues, many German readers would already have known about his work through early mediators like Robinson, who emphasized his paintings and illustrations over his poetic output, and Allan Cunningham, whose account of Blake in *The Lives of Most Eminent British Painters, Sculptors and Architects* (1830–1833) was influential in popularizing the legend of "mad Blake". Schmid does a thorough job mapping the trajectory of influence from the earliest responses, which were often the product of social contacts (the writer points out the irony of Blake, "certainly no man of fashion," first entering the public consciousness through inadvertent networking; 230), through early mentions in academic journals and articles, to the more complex phase of reception which begins in the late nineteenth century.

In France, the first responses to Blake emerge a few years after his death, but the process of reception continues fitfully until the late nineteenth century, when the Symbolists arrive to claim him as one of their own. However, in the majority of European countries, Blake remains virtually unknown until the turn of the century, when a surge of interest in his work is prompted by the publication of Edwin John Ellis's and William Butler Yeats's *The Works of William Blake* (1893). Ellis and Yeats successfully introduce the idea of Blake as a gifted mythmaker and system-builder, as opposed to an uncouth eccentric, by reinterpreting works which had previously been written off as rough and unbalanced as deliberately crafted expressions of a coherent Gnostic doctrine. In other countries, reception begins with the more familiar entry-points offered by Blake's interaction with their own arts and literature; thus, we find that Blake's reception in Switzerland often centers on his personal connection to Henry Fuseli and Johann Caspar Lavater (299), that Italy first comes to know him through his illustrations to Dante (125–126), and that his influence in the Netherlands begins with his illustrations for Dutch-born John Gabriel Stedman's *Narrative of a Five Years' Expedition Against the Revolted Negroes of Surinam* (386).

As important as these chronologies are for understanding the international reception of Blake's work, it is in the cases where this process is complicated through the authority of a particular critic or cultural figure that the book attains its greatest analytical depth. In the chapter dealing with Blake's influence in Denmark and Norway, Robert Rix explains how the Danish religious historian Vilhelm Grønbech's reading of Blake, wherein the poems are read as an expression of the psychological damage of cultural fragmentation and the mind's attendant need to regain psychic wholeness, was instrumental in shaping the poet's reception in Denmark, to the extent that Blake is still often read within the context of religious studies (420–422). Similarly, the understanding of Blake in Switzerland has been heavily filtered through his resonances with Jung, resulting in a mystical-archetypal development, which Angela Esterhammer describes as having exerted a "remarkable tenacity over Swiss-German Blake scholarship" all throughout the twentieth century (300–302). In other countries, Blake's influence is best measured through his influence on other poets and literary figures; this is the case in Greece, where, Maria Schoina writes, it is the poets Odysseas Elytis and Zisimos Lorentzatos who open up the country's relationship with Blake through the creative ways in which they borrow from, and engage with, his work (635–638). Given the staggering scope of material that needs to be dealt with in a book of this format, it is perhaps unavoidable that breadth will occasionally have to be prioritized over depth, and it is certainly the case that many chapters, such as those focusing on France, Germany, and Russia, could easily have been expanded into book-length studies. However, this must be considered a necessary compromise stemming from the format itself, and it certainly does not detract from what is clearly a highly comprehensive work. In sum, *The Reception of William Blake in Europe* performs an important task in expanding Blake's afterlife to better encompass its true reach and complexity, and in doing so, opens up foundations for new research that will surely be built upon in many years to come.

John Öwre
Lund University, Sweden

Fantasiens morgonrodnad.
En studie i Clas Livijns romaner

By Ljubica Miocevic
Lund: Ellerströms, 2017
Eureka, Ellerströms Akademiska, vol. 63
461 pp., SEK 255

Kjell Espmark, retired professor of literature at Stockholm University and a member of the Swedish Academy, suggests in the introduction to the academy's edition of Clas Livijn's novel *Spader Dame* (1825) that Livijn is the most 'curious *minor classic*' in Swedish literature. To be sure, when it comes to the quantity of research and criticism, Livijn cannot be compared to such key writers of the romantic era as C. J. L. Almqvist and Erik Johan Stagnelius. On the other hand, Livijn's texts are reprinted from time to time, and although book-length studies are rare – the latest was published a century ago – his work is still read and commented on. Typical of a minor classic, Livijn's fame relies almost exclusively on one work, the above-mentioned novel *Spader Dame*, whereas his other three novels, *Lifbergs Leverne* (1810), *Axel Sigfridsson* (1817), and *Riddar Sanct Jöran* (printed in parts 1830 but never published in full), have been out of print since the 1850s.

On the other hand, there is nothing classical, in the narrower sense of the word, about Livijn's work. Neither his own age, nor posterity has attempted to follow suit. The novels are as romantic as they get, drawing on the well-known romantic repertoire of irony, self-reflection, and medial *metalepsis*. Furthermore, there is no typical Livijnian style, and he seemed to have abhorred repetition, which is perhaps what makes his work such a hyper-romantic experience. His texts are unique, resisting all forms of simple summarization and comprehensive accounts.

Consequently, the four main chapters (4–7) in Ljubica Miocevic's study of Livijn's novels, *Fantasiens morgonrodnad. En studie i Clas Livijns romaner*, can, to some extent, be read as four separate studies. Chronologically ordered, each chapter is devoted to one novel, from Livijn's first and unfinished 'comic novel' *Lifbergs Leverne* to the likewise unfinished 'qvodlibet' *Riddar Sanct Jöran*. Whereas the analysis of *Lifbergs Leverne* focuses on the romantic practice of collective writing, the chapter on *Axel Sigfridsson* emphasises the novel's relation to the genre of the Bildungsroman. *Spader Dame* is read within the context of romantic irony and against the backdrop of several religious intertexts. The chapter on *Riddar Sanct Jöran*, finally, provides an intermedial and intertextual interpretation. These individual readings are preceded by three chapters, which give the necessary background to the analyses of the novels. They outline, among other things, the romantic theory of the novel, the use of satire, and the practice of collective writing.

Miocevic's book is a well-researched, well-argued, and empirically well-founded study. The argument is both convincing and easy to follow. Consulting available manuscripts, the author reconstructs in great detail the writing process, the publication, and reception of the novels. Nothing is left to chance, and Miocevic's conclusions are rooted both in Livijn's texts, published as well as unpublished, and in vast amounts of scholarly work on Swedish and European romanticism. To the reader – well versed in romantic criticism – who is presumably the intended readership of the book, the majority of the themes (romantic irony, the novel as progressive universal poetry, etc.) are most likely familiar, and in this sense, the book does not alter in any significant degree the long-established image of European, particularly German, romanticism as self-reflective and theoretically advanced. Thus, Miocevic's most important contribution pertains to the understanding of Livijn's work rather than to romanticism in general.

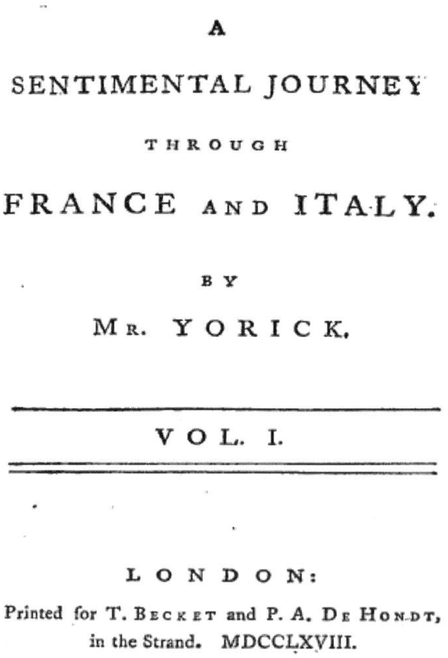

A

SENTIMENTAL JOURNEY

THROUGH

FRANCE AND ITALY.

BY

MR. YORICK.

VOL. I.

LONDON:

Printed for T. BECKET and P. A. DE HONDT, in the Strand. MDCCLXVIII.

Fig.1: Laurence Sterne, "Sentimental Journey", Vol.1, Title Page, London: T. Becket and P. A. De Hondt, 1768.

However, there is one important exception to this rule, which will hopefully have repercussions on romantic studies in general. Throughout the book, Miocevic refrains from grounding her argument in the typical romantic-idealistic triumvirate, namely, Kant, Fichte, and Schelling. As a matter of fact, these three are more or less absent, and Kant is not even mentioned. Instead she highlights the influence from British seventeenth- and early eighteenth-century literature, Samuel Butler and Alexander Pope, among others. Together with Laurence Sterne, whose *Sentimental Journey* had a great impact on the German romantics, these satirical writers are a virtual goldmine for Miocevic, as she traces the comic theme in Livijn's novels. In point of fact, these intertexts deserve an even more thorough investigation including other writers of the romantic generation as well – a project for the future perhaps.

Unlike many other studies in this particular field of research, Miocevic's book is not very theoretically driven, and there are a number of theoretical considerations that would have provided the study with points of departure for more elaborate interpretations. Genette's theories of intertextuality and genre, or the vibrant contemporary discourses on intermediality, are just a few areas from which the book's argument would have benefited. There are in fact a few theoretical concepts that are introduced by the author in the introduction, Lotman's concept of intersemiosis and Kristeva's of intertextuality, for instance, but they are rarely put to practice in the concrete analyses. In a way, the book is refreshingly empirical, as the line of argument is based on common sense rather than on theoretical speculations. On the other hand, Miocevic repeatedly refers to such theoretical concepts as intertextuality and intermediality, but leaves the reader in the dark about her understanding of these concepts. Especially the close connection between intertextuality and genre, fundamental to Genette's theory of the *architext*, would have helped both the author and the reader to conceptualise the layered interactions between texts.

In conclusion, Miocevic's study of Clas Livijn's novels will most likely be a standard reference in future mandatory reading for anyone interested in Livijn's work. This beautiful book is as well-researched as they come, and the empirical foundation is rock solid. Still, the lack of theoretical considerations fetters the line of thought, which rarely reaches beyond empirical evidence.

Mattias Pirholt
Södertörn University, Sweden

About the Authors

D. Gareth Walters is Professor Emeritus of Hispanic Studies at Swansea University, having previously occupied Chairs at the universities of Glasgow and Exeter. He is the author of *The Cambridge Introduction to Spanish Poetry: Spain and Spanish America*, and of *Canciones and the Early Poetry of Lorca*. He has published widely on the literature of the Iberian Peninsula, Spanish music and translation studies.

College of Arts and Humanities, Keir Hardie Building, Swansea University
Singleton Park, Swansea SA12 8PP, United Kingdom
d.g.walters@swansea.ac.uk

Kang-Po Chen is a PhD candidate in English literature at the University of Edinburgh. He obtained his Master's degree in English at National Chengchi University, Taiwan, and is currently completing his doctoral thesis, titled *Rethinking the Concept of Obscenity: The Erotic Subject and Self-Annihilation in the Works of Blake, Shelley, and Keats*, under the supervision of Dr Tim Milnes. His publications so far reflect his primary research interests, which lie in English Romanticism with a particular focus on eroticism, sexual perversions, violence and suffering, and religiosity/sacredness. He is also keenly interested in the modern theorisation of eroticism and its relation to art and religion, especially the philosophy of Georges Bataille.

The University of Edinburgh, School of Literatures, Languages and Cultures
50 George Square, Edinburgh, UK
Kangpo.chen@ed.ac.uk

Andreas Hjort Møller has studied German and Classical Studies at Aarhus University and Eberhard Karls Universität Tübingen, and was a visiting PhD student at Freie Universität Berlin in 2011. In 2014 he published his doctoral thesis *Der Lebensphilosophische Frühromantiker. Zur Rekonstruktion der frühromantischen Ethik Friedrich Schlegels (Schlegel-Studien 9)*. He has, since 2018, been a postdoc at the Department of Comparative Literature and Rhetoric at Aarhus University, and has also worked as a high school teacher since 2012. His current research is conducted within the frame of the project Medievalism in Danish Romantic Literature (Danmarks Frie Forskningsfond).

School of Communication and Culture – Comparative Literature, Aarhus University
Langelandsgade 139, building 1580, 124, 8000 Aarhus C, Denmark
andreashm@cc.au.dk

Dr. Natalya Khokholova, is an Associate Professor at North-Eastern Federal University in Yakutsk, Russia, at the Department of Translation and Regional Studies. She also manages and creates the Russian content for the UArctic website, as a member of the UArctic team in the department in Yakutsk, RF. Natalya received her Ph.D. from University of Illinois at Urbana-Champaign in 2015. Her dissertation, *Imagined Wealth and the Real Misfortune,* represents a study of the digressive interplay of money and gossip in the nineteenth-century Russian prose. Dr. Khokholova's research interests encompass the socio-economic aspects in the late nineteenth-century Russian prose fiction writing, Russian Colonial Politics and Orientalism, as well the subject of sustainable communities for survival in the cultural discourses on the lost and found children in the Arctic wilderness. She also teaches a variety of courses, such as Reading Short Stories of Chekhov, Echo of the Past- Sci-Fi on the grounds of the Cold War, and Russia's Orient. Currently, she conducts research in Yakutia, on taletelling as a cure for addictions and fragmented identities.

North-Eastern Federal University, 58 Belinsky Str, office 804
Yakutsk, RF.
nkhokholova@gmail.com

About the Authors

Marie-Louise Svane is an associate professor emerita of Comparative Literature at the Department of Arts and Cultural Studies, Copenhagen University. She has published within the fields of literary and cultural history and historiography, and nineteenth-century European literature and aesthetic debates. Her recent research is focused on nineteenth-century European orientalism, as well as on modern Turkish literature. Together with Anne Fastrup, Peter Madsen, and Pia Schwarz Lausten, she is currently in the process of editing a literary history in five volumes entitled *Islamic Culture in European Literature*.

Copenhagen University, Department of Arts and Cultural Studies
Karen Blixensvej 1, 3, DK-2300 Copenhagen S, Denmark
mlsvane@hum.ku.dk

Troy Wellington Smith is a PhD candidate in the Department of Scandinavian at the University of California, Berkeley. He received his BA in English literature and history from Swarthmore College, and went on to receive an MS in library science from Clarion University of Pennsylvania. He also has an MA in English literature from the University of Mississippi, where he focused on the intertextuality of Kierkegaard and Anglophone literature, writing a thesis entitled *Kierkegaard and Byron: Disability, Irony, and the Undead*. His articles have appeared in The Byron Journal, The Søren Kierkegaard Newsletter, Kierkegaard in Process, Acta Kierkegaardiana, Scandinavian Studies, The Kierkegaard Studies Yearbook, The Literary Encyclopedia, Anderseniana, and Libraries: Culture, History, and Society. He has been a guest researcher at the Søren Kierkegaard Centre of the University of Copenhagen, and a Summer Fellow at the Hong Kierkegaard Library of St. Olaf College in Northfield, Minnesota. Currently, he is working on a dissertation tentatively entitled *Kierkegaard and the History of the Book and Reading*.

University of California, Berkeley, Department of Scandinavian
6303 Dwinelle Hall, Berkeley, CA 94720-2690, USA
twsmith@berkeley.edu